PURSUIT OF A PREDATOR

Susan waited about ten minutes, facing south, expecting Victor Thomas to arrive by car. Instead, he appeared "from nowhere" at her side. Rather than the casual attire she had seen at the mall, he now dressed in a business suit. He carried a folded portfolio of papers in one hand, along with a pen.

It startled Susan to see annoyance on Victor's face. He growled, "That isn't what I told you to wear. I'm going to take you somewhere to change." Softening his voice a little, he continued, "Let's go somewhere to have a drink and talk about the roles. It will help you get very prepared." One of Victor's arms thrust forward and he laid a hand on her upper arm, near the shoulder, as if to guide her.

With combined fear and doubt rising in her gut, Susan replied, "I'm not going anywhere with you until I see some identification."

Victor frowned and mumbled something about leaving his wallet and identification at the studio, or at "the lot." When Susan insisted, he warned, "You're giving up the opportunity of a lifetime."

"We need to go," he insisted.

Glancing toward the spot where Mark Wilson had parked, Susan saw him move the Jeep Cherokee forward, stop again, leap out of the driver's side, and sprint toward her and Victor. Susan turned and hurried to meet him. Apparently unnerved by Mark's sudden appearance, Victor dashed toward a wrought-iron security gate blocking a driveway, tried unsuccessfully to open it, then vanished around a corner.

The telephone number proved to be bogus. But the claim of carrying no identification had been true, so Susan and Mark still only knew the fleeing man as Victor Thomas.

Also by Don Lasseter:

Die for Me

If I Can't Have You, No One Can

Body Double

Killer Kids

Cold Storage

Going Postal

Savage Vengeance

Property of Folsom Wolf

MEET ME FOR MURDER

DON LASSETER
WITH
RONALD E. BOWERS

PINNACLE BOOKS
Kensington Publishing Corp.

http://www.kensingtonbooks.com

Some names have been changed to protect the privacy of individuals connected to this story.

PINNACLE BOOKS are published by

Kensington Publishing Corp.
850 Third Avenue
New York, NY 10022

All Kensington Titles, Imprints, and Distributed Lines are available at special quantity discounts for bulk purchases for sales promotions, premiums, fund-raising, and educational or institutional use. Special book excerpts or customized printings can also be created to fit specific needs. For details, write or phone the office of the Kensington special sales manager: Kensington Publishing Corp., 850 Third Avenue, New York, NY 10022, attn: Special Sales Department, Phone: 1-800-221-2647.

Pinnacle and the P logo Reg. U.S. Pat. & TM Off.

ISBN-13: 978-0-7860-1927-4
ISBN-10: 0-7860-1927-1

First Printing: April 2008

10 9 8 7 6 5 4 3 2 1

Printed in the United States of America

FOREWORD

The idea for this book took form in December 2006 over lunch with Ron Bowers. We had considered collaborating on a project earlier, and he mentioned the case of Kristi Johnson's murder in the Hollywood Hills. In his long experience with the Los Angeles County District Attorney's Office, a span of forty years, he had seen numerous cases in which predators lured young women with the use of cameras, often promising to make them models or movie stars. Ron mentioned a few of them and said it would be interesting to show the eerie similarities between those crimes and Kristi's death. The book could conclude by offering tips to other young women for avoiding these killers. We agreed to explore the possibility.

Before the month ended, Ron took me for an all-day field trip in his SUV to the actual sites where several of these slayings had taken place, concentrating mostly on places related to the Kristi Johnson case. We drove into the Hollywood Hills and stopped on Skyline Drive to ponder the sharp contrast between breathtaking views and the horror of what occurred up there.

When I arrived home that night, tired and hungry, I flipped on the TV, and my jaw dropped. A documentary had just begun on MSNBC titled "Death in the Hollywood Hills: The Murder of Kristi Johnson." I watched in stunned fascination as the program visited the same spots I had seen that day. Usually, I'm fairly well informed of true-crime coverage on television, but had never heard of this show being filmed and originally airing on NBC earlier that month.

Right then, I knew that this book must be written.

True-crime reporting is sometimes controversial. I attended a seminar in Hollywood at which about forty news media representatives, filmmakers, authors, and other interested parties discussed the issue of sensitivity in dealing with murder victims' families and loved ones. It's not an easy thing to handle. I've often said that the most difficult part of writing true-crime books is dragging these survivors through the trauma again by interviewing them. Yet, if the reporter maintains integrity and veracity, it is a necessary step, for two purposes. First, to help commemorate the victims by presenting facts about their hopes, dreams, goals, values, accomplishments, happy or sad moments, and funny events in their lives. An author cannot hope to accomplish this without cooperation from people who knew and loved the individual. Second, to tell the story with the best possible accuracy. Personally, I hate reading nonfiction books in which the facts are embellished or made up.

I've heard criticism, too, about turning murders into entertainment. I absolutely agree with these critics. I do not write true-crime books to entertain. I do it to inform.

An Internet Web site, www.pomc.org, an acronym for Parents of Murdered Children, addresses this problem. Its statement of purpose is "to provide support and assistance to all survivors of homicide victims while working to create a world free of murder." By launching a program called MINE,

Murder Is Not Entertainment, the site wishes to alert society about insensitivity toward murder and its aftermath, which is "inflamed by a myriad of sources including TV, toys, games, and other means of entertainment." A list of objectionable factors in products, promotion, film, or print media is itemized.

I believe it is an admirable organization, with noble objectives, and I encourage visitation to the Web site. It's been my honor to know and count as friends several members of POMC.

While I entirely agree with criticism leveled at the production of toys, games, trading cards, videos, cartoons, or other insensitive portrayals of murder, especially when children are the marketing target, I believe that the public still needs to be informed of lurking dangers. We cannot hide our heads in the sand and pretend that monsters don't live among us. Should we censor or eliminate informative documentaries on television about crimes, including *Dateline, America's Most Wanted, American Justice,* Court TV, and other serious presentations of the facts? Don't hardworking law enforcement agencies across the nation deserve recognition for dedicating their lives to stopping these killers? Shouldn't we know of their heroic efforts, some of which cost investigators their very existence?

Educational film, television, and books do serve a social purpose.

I don't believe that Parents of Murdered Children are advocating Draconian censorship, or complete elimination of informative attempts to increase awareness among potential victims and possibly help save their lives.

It is our earnest hope that this book might aid in serving that purpose.

—Don Lasseter, 2007

CHAPTER 1

AUDITION TO DIE

With a pounding heart and soaring spirits, Kristi Johnson wondered if it could really be happening. The moment seemed right, and the magical surroundings couldn't have been more perfect. She stood in Century City's outdoor shopping mall, built on the former back lot of 20th Century Fox Studios. One block away, Avenue of the Stars intersected with Constellation Boulevard, signaling confluence of astrological destiny with the world of entertainment. Adjacent MGM Drive added yet another golden name, telling Kristi that something very special must have brought her to this spot at this moment. Just a couple of miles away was the legendary site where an editor of *Hollywood Reporter* allegedly discovered Lana Turner at the soda fountain in Schwab's Drug Store. Maybe Kristine Louise Johnson's film or modeling career, which she passionately desired, had also arrived, just twelve days before her twenty-second birthday.

The man who stopped her near a Victoria's Secret store and admired her beauty wasn't like those other clumsy jerks telling her that she should be a model. That line had worn out long ago. Kristi understood the blessing of her attractive features and the resulting double takes by randy men. Her wide-set luminous blue eyes, middle-parted long blond hair, shapely five-nine figure, and especially her coquettish lips when parted into dazzling smiles drew frequent attention, both pleasant and annoying. Most scam artists hitting on her or playing the role of model seekers used trite, threadbare pitches that were sure strikeouts. The few who tried to be creative still sounded phony.

But this guy obviously knew his business. Dressed in casual clothing appropriate for a cool Saturday in February, he stood a little over six feet and moved gracefully. Perhaps in his late thirties, his distinctive face radiated power, with full lips, an aquiline nose, large blue eyes turned down at the outer corners, noticeably arched brows, dimpled chin, and dark hair thinning a bit above the high forehead. What set him apart from phony "agents" was his calm demeanor and professional certitude. After remarking on her attractiveness, in a cultivated, pleasant voice, he had explained his involvement in producing promotional material for a new James Bond film and that he needed some fresh faces. Hers was perfect, he said, and she possessed other physical attributes to match. He hadn't launched into a windy sales pitch preceded by, "You should be a model and I can help you." Rather, he had simply stated what would be required of her. If she wished to audition, he told Kristi, she needed a black miniskirt, panty hose, black stiletto heels, and a white dress shirt.

Other "photographers" in search of models had never been so specific. This man appeared to be more interested in business than in carnal needs. The amateurs had been pushy and nervous. But this James Bond fellow delivered simple statements that made sense. And he had even mentioned rather offhandedly that if selected for the job, Kristi could be paid about $100,000!

After giving her directions to an address on Skyline Drive high atop a ridge in the Hollywood Hills, where she could audition that same evening, he told Kristi to be there by five-thirty, thanked her, and left. She knew that secluded homes situated up there, mostly in the million-dollar-plus price range, housed all levels of Hollywood's glitterati. The prestige location added even more credence to this once-in-a-lifetime opportunity.

Now Kristi ramped up her shopping trip. Her mother had called from Northern California that same morning, Saturday, February 15, 2003, as she did nearly every day, and offered to reimburse Kristi if she would go to the Century City mall and purchase something she liked. It could be for her pending birthday or for the Valentine's Day that had just passed. Perhaps Kristi could buy a set of candles she had recently seen and admired. Or maybe she could find something to wear that night at a rave concert near downtown Los Angeles. Kristi had made reservations, earning her a place on the VIP list to avoid standing in a long line.

The James Bond encounter, though, erased any thought of candles or concerts, and changed Kristi's thoughts about selecting inexpensive casual clothing. Instead, she rushed across the walkway into Bloomingdale's to first pick out two pairs of Sheer Hosiery brand panty hose, then rode the escalator to the second floor to examine white dress shirts. One Styleset Collection blouse stood out from all the others. The price tag of $185 didn't even slow her down. At the checkout counter, Kristi charged a total of $226.24 to her Bank of America debit card at 1:33 P.M.

Still bursting with the thrill of anticipation, Kristi hurried into the adjacent Guess store, and immediately found the per-

fect black miniskirt for $73.61. She completed the purchase
at 1:36 P.M.

The black stiletto heels proved more difficult to find at
affordable cost. Kristi hadn't minded the clothing price tags,
but didn't want to pay between $500 and $1,000 for Jimmy
Choo or Manolo Blahnik footwear available in these upscale
stores. Undeterred, she left the mall in her 1996 white Mazda
Miata convertible and sped three miles into West Hollywood.
She glanced at her watch and realized the need to hurry. On
La Cienega Boulevard, she pulled to the curb in front of a
corner stucco building painted in blinding pink. A sign told
her that the store dealt in TRASHY LINGERIE. Across the street,
flashing neon on the facade of a bar advertised LIVE NUDE
GIRLS. The gaudy ambience contrasted sharply with the ele-
gant mall she had just left, but Kristi didn't care. She needed
those stiletto heels.

Entering the lingerie store, Kristi stopped at a barrier and
paid the unusual two-dollar membership fee, which allowed
her access to the interior. The management apparently didn't
want curious browsers or street "pervs" shopping for nothing
but a lascivious thrill. She found the shoes she sought, black
ankle-strap Ellie brand, size 9, with six-inch heels, and paid
$54.13 for them. So far, she had invested almost $354 for the
apparel required to achieve success at the audition up on Skyline Drive. At nearly two-thirty, with about three hours left
before the audition, she still needed to return to her Santa
Monica residence, shower, do her hair, and apply makeup.
Everything had to be perfect.

Satisfied with her purchases, Kristi headed west along Pico
Boulevard in unusually heavy and frustrating traffic. Thousands of antiwar marchers had gathered for a demonstration
on Hollywood Boulevard earlier that afternoon, near the foot-
printed forecourt of iconic Grauman's Chinese Theatre, to
protest the threat of a U.S. war with Iraq. Kristi threaded her

way through the homeward-bound vehicles, past a parking lot close to Elm Street, where the body of a young model had been dumped a few years earlier after being lured into the desert and savagely slaughtered by a "photographer." That happened long before Kristi moved to the entertainment capital of the world. She zipped past the entry to 20th Century Fox Studios, driving along the greenbelt of Hillcrest Country Club and the Rancho Park Golf Course. Eight miles later, she pulled into a gated underground garage at the apartment building where she shared living quarters with two women. Excitement bubbled inside her like champagne and she couldn't wait to reveal the thrilling events.

Near the walkway entrance, Kristi spotted a neighbor, a young man she had described to her mother as quite attractive. He greeted her and Kristi told him of her exciting encounter at the mall.

Inside her residence, Kristi found only one roommate at home, and rapped on Carrie Barrish's bedroom door. Barrish had just finished showering when she stepped out and saw the flush of joy on Kristi's face. "I am so excited," Kristi gushed, "I even have hives." A reddening rash on her neck verified the self-diagnosis. In breathless bursts, Kristi rattled off the details of her encounter at Century City. She vanished into her bedroom and reappeared in moments. Twirling around, Kristi modeled the black miniskirt, white shirt, and stiletto heels, struggling to keep her balance in the towering shoes. An empty Guess bag on a chair told Barrish where some of the clothing had been purchased. The white blouse, said Kristi, had to be suitable for use with a necktie, which someone would provide at the audition.

The man she had met must be for real, Kristi said while describing the connection to a new James Bond film. Barrish, in her mid-forties, had been around long enough to realize that "discoveries" of young women in shopping malls, or drugstores, were, as Humphrey Bogart once uttered in a classic film, "the stuff dreams are made of." But if Barrish felt any skepticism or suspicion, she kept it to herself. It did sound awfully good. Kristi's enthusiasm was contagious, and Barrish even felt light-headed from all the excitement.

The filming, Kristi said, would take place out of the country, requiring a passport, and would begin within a week's time. The audition was to be held that same evening, at five-thirty, so she needed to hurry.

After her bath, hairstyling, and meticulous application of makeup, Kristi slipped into the new panty hose, but chose to carry the stiletto heels under one arm, and the short black skirt and white long-sleeved blouse on a hanger. She wore corduroy pants and a light-colored blouse, along with tennis shoes. To ward off the anticipated evening chill, she folded a gray hooded sweatshirt over an arm. With a quick hug for Barrish, Kristi flashed a glowing smile and left shortly before five. The daylight now cast longer shadows and began its quickening fade into rosy dusk.

Once again, Kristi accelerated her Miata across town and turned north on Crescent Heights Boulevard, toward the hills and a region known as Mount Olympus. She passed the intersection of Sunset Boulevard where the old Schwab's drugstore had once stood, and crossed Hollywood Boulevard at which point Crescent Heights changed its name to Laurel Canyon. The road morphed from arrow-straight into a winding, ascending gauntlet heavily wooded on each shoulder. On both sides, residential structures gripped tenaciously to the steep slopes. Kristi followed red taillights of drivers climbing the torturous four-mile passage over the hills from West Hollywood to the San Fernando Valley.

The James Bond man had instructed her to turn left on Lookout Mountain Avenue. In the darkening canyon with endless twists and bends, it was difficult to see the street signs, but somehow Kristi made the sharp left turn. Next, she was supposed to veer left at a "Y" intersection and proceed on Wonderland Avenue. After a few hundred feet, she would come to another "Y," at which she needed to turn right on Wonderland Park. With less than one block to go, she should turn right on Green Valley Road, then finally right again on Skyline Drive. That last intersection, she had been advised, would be easy to recognize because a house on one corner looked like a castle.

All of these snaking lanes, no wider than most alleys, would confuse anyone who didn't traverse them daily. Parked cars along the curbless edges made it nearly impossible for oncoming vehicles to squeeze by each other.

Kristi negotiated the first few turns, but soon came to a dead-end cul-de-sac and realized she was lost. The clock had already ticked past five-thirty, blowing her intention to be punctual. Unable to think of any other solution, growing more desperate with each passing second, she snatched her cell phone from the purse on the passenger seat and called information twice. Of course, the effort was futile, and she ended the second call at 5:37 P.M., simultaneously with the red-ball sun disappearing behind the hills.

A ray of hope came to Kristi when she spotted a middle-aged man standing in a driveway. She jammed on her brakes and rolled down her window.

"Where's the 'Castle House'?" she blurted, obviously distressed.

The stranger, with salt-and-pepper hair, startled at the brusque question, looked up and replied, "What do you want?"

Realizing that she had sounded rude in her panicky state, Kristi softened her tone, told the man that she had been driving "all over" trying to find a particular place, and asked in polite terms if he knew of a castlelike house in the neighborhood.

The local resident, recognizing the girl's desperation, relaxed and thought about her question for a few moments before telling her there was no such thing as a castle around the area.

Kristi's face saddened as she explained that she was supposed to turn right at a corner where there was a house that looked like a castle.

A woman standing in shadows up the driveway spoke softly to the man, and like a light going on in a dark room, his expression brightened as if he had solved a perplexing riddle. "You mean the old gray house that looks like a castle on the corner of Skyline Drive. That must be the place you're looking for." He gave her directions to find it.

A beaming grin replaced Kristi's frown and her voice purred. "Thank you so much. You have just saved my life." She gunned the Miata's engine and shot away, not realizing how wrong she was.

The Samaritan shook his head and stared at the vanishing red taillights. He felt good about helping a young lady in distress. Besides that, she was so pretty, attractive enough to be a model or even act in movies. He allowed himself a satisfied smile as he turned, joined the woman, and walked up the driveway to their home.

Following the instructions, Kristi headed downhill and turned on Green Valley. Had she gone in the other direction, to Wonderland Avenue again, she would likely have passed an unremarkable light yellow house, two stories atop a ground-level two-car garage. In July 1981, four people, two men and two women, had been bludgeoned to death inside the home as the result of drug-connected crimes. Unique transactions had been made there by lowering a basket on a rope down from the balconies to pick up money from a buyer inside a waiting car, and then delivering cocaine by the same means. One of Liberace's boyfriends reportedly stopped there frequently. Notorious porn star John Holmes was suspected of participation in the killings, but almost a year later, a jury found him not guilty. Two of the homicide cops on the case would eventually investigate a scandalous double murder about ten miles away, in which a suspect named O.J. Simpson also found a sympathetic jury.

The slayings in the light yellow house, dubbed the "Wonderland Murders," spawned books, television documentaries, and two movies based on the gruesome events—*Boogie Nights,* in 1997, and *Wonderland,* in 2003.

The latter film hadn't yet been released when Kristi Johnson drove close to the murder scene, on February 15. She had no idea that the bucolic hills and eclectic homes might attract drug-dealing killers. More pleasant prospects swirled in her mind as she found the "castle house." A gray Norman-style structure on three levels, it resembled a small French village complete with a towering turret capped by a conical blue tile roof. Because Kristi now approached it from the opposite direction of her original route, she turned left on Skyline Drive, looped around a long hairpin turn, and climbed to the top of a narrow house-lined ridge.

A spectacular panorama came into view down below, in several directions. Off to her right, a steep brush-and-tree-covered slope plunged hundreds of feet to the bottom of a canyon, beyond which early lights twinkled in the vast, receding sprawl of the San Fernando Valley. Behind her, on a distant hillside, the venerable giant letters spelling out HOLLYWOOD seemed small in the dimming dusk. From a high lot on the dead end ahead, the silhouette of downtown Los Angeles could be seen. No wonder these home sites were so treasured by enormously wealthy residents.

Kristi Johnson slowed in the 8500 block and sighed with

relief when she spotted a fenced-in stucco house to her left. Just ahead, the pavement came to a dead end. She could barely make out the street address numbers given to her by the man she had met earlier on that incredible day of destiny. On a magic Saturday evening, she thought her fondest dreams would soon be realized.

CHAPTER 2

DESPERATE SEARCH

Under a heavy, gray overcast of threatening clouds, Los Angeles County yawned and woke up on Sunday morning. From the mansions of Malibu to the cardboard hovels of Main Street, where homeless denizens of skid row huddled for warmth, the population shook off effects of sleep and faced the probability of a frigid, rainy day. Over coffee and juice, or bagels, or eggs and bacon, or tortillas and frijoles, residents opened the *Los Angeles Times* and read of international unrest, murder, mayhem, and a basketball defeat for a favorite local college team. Not much good news for this wet day of rest and worship.

Page-one headlines screamed of antiwar rallies involving millions of angry protesters around the world disapproving of a probable attack on Iraq by the United States as a result of President George W. Bush's confrontation with Saddam Hussein. (The attack occurred on March 20, just five weeks away.) Other articles took readers into the gruesome underworld of crime. One told of a federal appeals court judge who had visited a convict on death row, perhaps mitigating the jurist's ability to hear capital punishment cases. Local news described homicide investigators' inability to identify a woman whose nude torso, arms, and legs had been found the previous July in separate alleys. The head, hands, and knees were still missing and police sought help from the public.

Basketball fans turned to the sports section and, accustomed to championships won by the UCLA Bruins, cringed at news of their tenth conference loss.

The only upbeat news offering any hope was found in a story of a mother and daughter being reunited after twenty-three years of painful separation.

In Santa Monica, Kristi Johnson's two female roommates were puzzled, but not deeply concerned when they discovered that she hadn't returned home from the "James Bond" audition, or from the rave concert. Maybe she had met someone at the crowded dance and spent a romantic night with him. Kristi had recently tapered off a relationship and would certainly feel free to have fun with someone new. She could be enjoying a nice breakfast with some special guy. The two women had known Kristi only a short time, just two months since she had moved into the three-bedroom apartment on December 9, 2002. All three tenants had been compatible, but hadn't really found enough time to learn intimate details of their respective lives, romances, or social activities. Each of the trio worked in separate places, and Kristi attended Santa Monica City College two nights a week. Frequently, on weekends, she drove two hours up to Santa Maria to visit her paternal grandmother, so her absence on Sunday morning raised no particular worries with her fellow tenants.

More than three hundred miles to the north, Kristi's mother tried to ward off a growing anxiety. In Los Gatos, halfway between the lower tip of San Francisco Bay and the coastal resort city of Santa Cruz, Terry Johnson had given birth to Kristi on February 27, 1981. Nestled at the base of the Sierra Azule Mountains, Los Gatos was given the Spanish name for cats in the 1880s, inspired by the screams of mountain lions roaming in the adjacent wooded hills. Despite being a part of the "Silicon Valley" boom, the quiet community of twenty-nine thousand retained its small-town ambience. Kristi's mother and her father, Kirk Johnson, with their young son, Derek, and their baby daughter had left in the early 1980s and moved to Michigan. After her parents' marriage ended, Kristi traveled back to California in 2000 to stay with her grandmother in Santa Maria. Her mother soon followed and made her home once again in Northern California.

Now going by the name Terry Hall, she had last talked to her daughter on Saturday at noon, prior to Kristi's departure for the Century City mall shopping trip. Hall had tried several times to phone Kristi again later that afternoon without success.

All of the daily calls from Hall were through cellular service, or occasionally to her daughter's number at her workplace. The mother had purchased Kristi's cell phone, and regularly paid the monthly bill, to assure that they could communicate at any time.

Several attempts by Hall to reach her daughter on Sunday failed. Perhaps Kristi had let her cell phone battery die, or maybe she was just busy with friends. By that evening, Kristi still hadn't called.

On Monday morning, observation of Presidents' Day gave some Los Angeles commuters a break from work—mostly, employees of banks, schools, and the government. Not so at the cellular network communications company where Kristi worked in Marina del Rey, about three miles from her apartment. When she didn't show up, it perplexed the operations manager. In the three months of Kristi's tenure as a data entry operator for the firm, working nine to six, she had never been absent, and was late only twice. Both times she had telephoned in advance with explanations. "She's a vibrant person," he said, "always smiling." Her mysterious failure to arrive on this day, with no contact, aroused the curiosity of not only the manager, but of coworkers as well. They thought of her as outgoing, friendly, and quite dependable. One employee, who considered himself a good friend of Kristi's, remembered her mentioning on Friday that she was going to a party on Saturday night. But she hadn't given any details about the location, or if anyone was going with her. He hoped that nothing had gone wrong for Kristi, causing her unexpected and unexplained absence.

Early Monday morning, Terry Hall resumed her efforts to reach Kristi, but calls to her cell phone resulted only in frustration. In one of their earlier conversations, Kristi had said that even though Monday was a holiday for some people, she would still have to work. Just minutes after nine, Hall tried Kristi's number at the firm, and connected only with her recorded message.

Another call, this one to the company's main telephone number, allowed her to speak with a manager. Hall asked, "Is Kristi there? Do you know of any reason why she isn't picking up her phone?"

"No," the supervisor replied. "She didn't come in this morning."

"Do you know where she might be?"

"We don't. She has always been punctual, but we haven't heard from her since Friday."

Turning to the Internet, Hall accessed Kristi's cell phone account and her Bank of America status, both the debit card and small savings account, but found nothing helpful.

At one o'clock, Monday afternoon, she decided to telephone

the Santa Monica Police Department (SMPD). Maybe Kristi
had been in some sort of an accident and they would have a
record of it. But the officer Hall reached said there had been no
reports involving that name, and suggested that the mother
contact hospitals in the area where Kristi lived.

Hall spent the next hour following that advice, only to hear
repeated negative answers. She also telephoned her former
husband, Kirk Johnson, in Holland, Michigan. He hadn't
heard from their daughter, either. Johnson voiced his deep
concern, and said that if she didn't show up right away, he
would come to California as soon as possible. Hall made yet
another call to Kristi's older brother, Derek, a member of the
U.S. Air Force in North Carolina, to ask if he had heard from
his sister, and then informed him of the alarming situation.

At last, Hall contacted the Santa Monica Police Department again to state that Kristi was unequivocally missing, and
to request official help in finding her.

Most police departments across the nation prefer not to
accept missing persons reports until the individual has been
absent at least forty-eight hours. In the great majority of such
cases, especially with teenagers, the missing person is often
an angry runaway, a love-struck young person off on a romantic rendezvous, or someone who just needs some private
space for a while. Most of them soon return home. Frequently
the whole thing turns out to be a simple misunderstanding.

In 2003, according to the California Department of Justice (DOJ), 40,780 residents of the state (17,885 females)
were declared missing for a variety of reasons. A great majority, almost 83 percent, were classified as voluntarily
missing (any adult who has left of his/her free will). Nearly
all of these reunited with their families. Those counted as
missing under "suspicious circumstances," indicating abduction by a stranger, numbered 585, fewer than two people
out of every one hundred reported. These statistics give

foundation to some police decisions not to consider missing persons seriously within the first two or three days.

Officer Mark Holland, Santa Monica Police Department, took Terry Hall's call. He listened only a few minutes before deciding this report needed immediate attention. It had suspicious circumstances painted all over it in flaming red letters. He rapidly filled out the department's form 3.16.1., entering names, addresses, and telephone numbers of Kristine Louise Johnson and her mother, along with any information that might offer clues to solve the mystery. Under *Possible Cause of Absence,* Holland printed *Unknown.* Asking Hall the necessary questions, he noted that Kristi's vehicle, also missing, was a 1996 Mazda Miata convertible, white with black top, California license plates. In a space for description of the missing person, Holland printed: *Tattoo of a hibiscus flower (geometrical) on small of lower back.* He also listed contact information of Kristi's roommates and her workplace. Terry Hall mentioned that Kristi had an ex-boyfriend by the name of Dick Sawyer (pseudonym) who had lived in West Hollywood and had since moved to the Santa Maria area where Kristi had lived with her grandmother. Holland noted this in his report. Santa Maria is a little more than one hundred miles northwest of Santa Monica.

Only thirteen minutes after the conversation with Terry Hall, Holland spoke by telephone to Carrie Barrish, the last known person to see Kristi on Saturday, before she vanished. Alarmed by the police involvement, Barrish nervously told Holland of Saturday's events. Kristi, she said, had met a man at the Century City mall who told her he was looking for a fresh face for film work. The man had asked her to come to an address somewhere in Beverly Hills or the Hollywood Hills to try out for the role. Kristi had been very excited, Barrish recalled, and said that if she got the part, she would be gone in a week to start the project.

"Did Ms. Johnson tell you the address where the tryout was to be held?" Holland inquired.

"No, she didn't." Barrish mentioned that Kristi had planned to attend a party that Saturday night. "I think it was somewhere in Hollywood."

Trying to fill in as many blanks as possible before escalating the case to detectives, Holland telephoned Kristi's workplace in Marina del Rey and learned that she hadn't reported for work that morning, nor had she called her supervisor to explain why. A manager told the officer of Kristi's reliability and said she would normally call in before being late or absent. Her failure to do so was most unusual.

By two o'clock on Monday afternoon, Officer Holland had completed the collection of preliminary information along with his hand-printed report. He rushed up a flight of stairs to the detective bureau and found only one investigator in the office. By her lone presence, Detective Virginia Obenchain inherited one of the most challenging cases of her career.

A nineteen-year veteran of the SMPD, Virginia Obenchain had started as a patrol officer. After more than a decade of uniformed duty in black-and-white vehicles, chasing everything from speeders to serial rapists, she was selected to become an investigator. Her meticulous work habits and dedication during a span of four years caught the attention of superiors who decided that she belonged in the Robbery/Homicide Unit. This led to specialized training at the Rio Hondo Police Academy, and seven weeks, spread out over a few years, at the prestigious Robert Presley Institute of Criminal Investigation (ICI). With branches in six California cities, including Los Angeles, the Presley organization provides experience-based techniques of learning through the use of realistic and practical applications. Obenchain's curriculum included basic investigation, homicide, domestic violence, sexual assault, and techniques of interview and interrogation.

Born in Los Angeles, Obenchain knew from early childhood that she wanted a career in law enforcement. Asked why, she said, "I don't know. That's what I always wanted to do from the time I was a little girl. I had no relatives in the business nor any acquaintances." The goal remained with her all the way through high school and college. She spent four years at the all-girls Immaculate Heart High School, a time-honored institution built in 1906 in the foothills overlooking Hollywood. Her Bachelor of Arts degree came from Loyola Marymount University, near Marina del Rey, founded in 1911. She signed on with the Santa Monica Police Department in August 1984.

Obenchain isn't boasting when she says, "During my tenure as a police officer, I have investigated hundreds of violent crimes, including numerous assaults, robberies, and several murders." The daily routine of dealing with the dregs of society, though, hadn't dented Obenchain's positive outlook and wicked sense of humor. Her light blue eyes still lit up when exchanging jibes with fellow officers or inquisitive journalists.

As soon as Mark Holland told Obenchain of the circumstances of Kristi Johnson's disappearance, the detective sensed the enormity of this case. "The hair on the back of my neck started to rise," she later said. And she immediately thought, *Oh my God, do we have another Linda Sobek on our hands?* Obenchain prayed that this disappearance wouldn't turn out like the notorious murder in 1996. It had been splashed across newspaper headlines and television reports for months. A photographer named Charles Rathbun had been convicted of killing an ex-cheerleader for the NFL Raiders named Linda Sobek. He had lured her to a remote dry lake bed in the desert near Palmdale, forty miles north of Los Angeles, to pose for an automobile magazine layout. Something went wrong and her lifeless body was later discovered in a shallow, sandy grave along a branch road from the twisting Angeles Forest Highway in the mountains between Pasadena and the Mojave Desert.

Obenchain forced that image from her mind and mentally began the process of planning future moves to find Kristi Johnson. The first step was to enter information about her and the Mazda Miata into an automated missing persons data bank.

Missing persons cases designated as "suspicious circumstances" are like ticking time bombs to police investigators. The urgency is palpable, with the top priority screaming for quick action and implementation of every possible measure to save a life. The pressure is on to hurry, but not at the expense of overlooking subtle bits of information that might help. It's a contest of speed, wits, and endurance.

She next telephoned Terry Hall to ask a few more questions. A possible avenue of pursuit, Obenchain thought, could be through cell phone calls made by Kristi and purchases with her debit card. Hall verified that she had paid for the cell phone and all of the monthly bills, with the account in her name. She also revealed that the debit card was a joint account, mother and daughter, through Bank of America/Visa.

Just to make certain of the facts, the detective asked Hall to repeat a description of her daughter. Hall said that Kristi was five feet nine inches tall, blond, weighed approximately 140 pounds, and had blue eyes. The tattoo, she said, was a colored hibiscus flower in a "scrolly" geometric form that spanned across the small of Kristi's back, about two inches high and four inches long. She had it applied during spring break a few years earlier at an unknown parlor in Florida. The colors, Hall thought, might be "muted" by now.

Hall's next comments suggested a possibility to Obenchain. Kristi, the mother revealed, had shown "interest" in a man who lived in her apartment building. The only name Hall had heard was "Lucas," and she recalled that Lucas said that he would be moving out soon and wanted to take Kristi to Hawaii with him. Could this man be involved in her disappearance? It would certainly require some investigative follow-up.

Another man's name came up in the conversation. Hall said she had telephoned Kristi's ex-boyfriend Dick Sawyer to ask if he knew where she might be. Sawyer told her of speaking to Kristi on Friday morning. Obenchain asked the mother if she knew how well the couple got along. Hall hesitated for a moment, then stated that she thought the relationship might have been "physically abusive" at times. Dick, she added, had been quite possessive and behaved in a bizarre manner when angry. He had once locked Kristi out of her apartment and out of her own car. At the detective's request, Hall provided Sawyer's telephone number.

Hall's voice trembled as the conversation wound down, saying, "I was hoping she would call me and tell me everything was fine. I was hoping it was reckless abandonment of youth, and I was hoping she would just turn up."

At least a few slim leads had emerged for additional investigation. Before the day ended, Obenchain contacted a Bank of America security office, but they were closed in observance of Presidents' Day. She left a message for the law enforcement liaison officer to call her.

Just to satisfy her own curiosity, Obenchain called Kristi's cell phone number. Maybe someone would answer and provide a clue, no matter how small. But the connection landed on nothing more than a voice mail recording.

One final effort on the late afternoon of Monday, February 17, gave Obenchain a tiny ray of hope. "I contacted the Los Angeles County Coroner's Office and inquired if there were any Jane Does that matched the description of the missing person. I was told they had not had any Jane Does since January 6, 2003."

CHAPTER 3

A GROWING MYSTERY

Obenchain attacked the puzzle again early Tuesday morning. She refused to allow negative thoughts to obscure any promise of finding Kristi alive and well. Most homicide detectives in Southern California cope daily with an overwhelming backlog of murder investigations, finding it necessary to prioritize the work. The search for Kristi Johnson was still a missing persons case, but Obenchain felt it needed her best efforts, on the double. Piece by piece, she would probe every possible lead, intent on finding Kristi before anything tragic could happen. All avenues offering promise, no matter how minor, would be explored.

After making a call to the Bank of America security office and leaving a message, Obenchain keyed in the license number of Kristi's Mazda on the Department of Motor Vehicles data bank. Only one citation popped up. Exactly one year earlier, on February 17, 2002, a parking ticket had been issued on Palm Avenue in West Hollywood, across the street from the apartment building where Kristi lived at the time.

(The site is only about one mile from a shocking-pink lingerie store on La Cienega Boulevard.) Through a mix-up, her car had been impounded. Obenchain noted the citation address, on the remote possibility that it might provide some kind of a link to the growing mystery, but nothing would ever surface from it.

A better chance to track Kristi's movements, Obenchain hoped, lay with the use of the missing woman's cell phone. A quick check with the service provider revealed that it had last been used on February 15 at 5:34 P.M. The call to information lasted three minutes. Numerous attempts by callers to reach Kristi had been made, but none were completed. Also, the company agent said, the call to information had connected through a "cell site," or relay tower, located at Ventura Boulevard. Cell sites, she explained, typically receive signals from phones within a three-mile radius. These facts established only that Kristi was probably within three miles of that address the last time she used her phone.

The next step for Obenchain is one commonly used by police organizations—an effort that sometimes produced powerful results, but more often created a chain of futile blind alleys. Appealing to the general population for help through the news media might lead observers to believe that it is a last-ditch measure of desperation. Actually, it's a common tool for investigators, especially in missing persons cases. Most news watchers have seen countless appeals from police agencies asking for information from the public, and wonder if they really work. Now and then they do; often they don't. Yet, even though hundreds of tips from well-meaning callers turn out to be of little value, sometimes a gold nugget is found among mountains of pebbles. It is a step that cannot be disregarded.

Before lunchtime, Obenchain helped prepare posters, bulletins, and a press release. Featuring a photograph of Kristi, they simply told of a missing young woman and gave her name, age, and description, along with information about her vehicle. Following the mention that she "may have been en route to an appointment with a possible photographer in the area of Beverly Hills," the bulletin and facts for a pending press release requested that anyone with knowledge contact the Santa Monica Police Department. It listed a "tip line" telephone number at the bottom.

That afternoon, Obenchain visited Kristi's apartment to collect items that might produce DNA samples if needed, including her toothbrush, hairbrush, used tissues, razors, and drinking glasses, which would also yield her fingerprints. Among Kristi's personal possessions, the detective found a card from a lingerie store on La Cienega Boulevard. She observed a date of "2/15/03" and a notation reading, "Total: $54.13." The card corroborated information obtained via fax from the Bank of America when an agent returned earlier calls. Kristi had used her debit/credit card five times on February 15:

11:45 A.M.	*Starbucks on Santa Monica Boulevard*
11:58 A.M.	*Unocal 76 (gas station) on Santa Monica Boulevard*
1:33 P.M.	*Bloomingdale's, Century City mall*
1.36 P.M.	*Guess, Century City mall*
2:15 P.M.	*The lingerie store on La Cienega*

To speed up the search, and maximize efficiency, four detectives and several uniformed officers joined Obenchain in the investigation, fanning out to search for and examine various possibilities. Detectives Michael Cabrera and Gregg Kapp took a stack of the bulletins to the Century City mall and posted them. Detectives John Henry and Maury Sumlin drove to Kristi's workplace in Marina del Rey, where they interviewed the manager and requested permission to take Kristi's work computer for examination. He readily complied. Back at headquarters, Detective Shane Talbot analyzed the computer's contents, but found nothing useful.

Detective John Henry had been Obenchain's partner on several previous assignments. About six feet tall, slim and trim, he could disarm bad guys with a quick, dimpled grin and flashing dark eyes, or assume a menacing expression when taking the heavy role in good cop/bad cop encounters. Considering his youthful appearance, crisp white long-sleeved shirts with classy neckties, and wiry physical stamina, no one could believe he had been on the force thirty years—unless he had started at age five. Obenchain had learned long ago that she could rely on Henry in any circumstance, and often did.

One of Henry's next duties in the search for Kristi took him for a recheck with Carrie Barrish. He telephoned her to see if she might remember anything else Kristi could have said or done. Sometimes the most innocuous information provides a key to unlock everything.

According to Barrish, when Kristi left the apartment late Saturday morning, she said she was going to the Century City mall to window shop and just "kick around." Upon her return, between two and three that afternoon, she was obviously very excited. Kristi told Barrish that she had "met a guy who said he was in the filmmaking business," and that he was about to start a project related to a new James Bond action-type movie. For this, he needed someone with a fresh new face and "non-waif figure." He had told her that she was exactly what he was looking for. His company, he claimed, had conducted a search through talent agencies and casting agents, all to no avail. They were supposed to start shooting the movie in a week and needed to quickly make a decision on who would be given the female starring role. The stranger asked Kristi if she had a passport since part of the filming would take place out of the country and she would have to leave right away.

Kristi had seemed especially thrilled by the amount of money she could potentially be paid: $100,000. The man wanted her to interview and audition for the role that same evening at five-thirty. She needed "to dress sexy and sultry and show a lot of leg," and must have a white shirt with a collar, a super miniskirt, and stiletto heels. Someone at the audition would give her a necktie to wear.

Henry asked for details about the required clothing, and Barrish gave quick, specific answers. Stating that Kristi had purchased all of it that afternoon, the roommate itemized it:

- A white long-sleeved shirt made of very nice, soft cotton with a pointed collar, darts in the back, and designed so it could not be buttoned at the neck. (Barrish thought Kristi had bought it at Macy's, but she had actually made the purchase at Bloomingdale's.)
- A black miniskirt made of polyester or Lycra-type fabric. She found it at a Guess store.
- A pair of Ellie brand patent leather black pumps with six-inch stiletto heels, purchased at a lingerie store.
- A pair of sheer panty hose.

Barrish said that when Kristi modeled the ensemble, "she had a hard time walking because of the stiletto heels."

Pausing periodically to recall the details, Barrish said that Kristi was supposed to meet the man in "a really nice area of Beverly Hills." Other girls would be there to interview for the role, but the man had told Kristi that he really wanted her to get the part.

Curious, Henry asked if Kristi had been at all skeptical about the man's veracity. Yes, Barrish said, Kristi did express

some concern about the legitimacy of the man's offer, but also
felt a slim chance that he was telling the truth and that she
would win the part.

"Do you know anything about a party Ms. Johnson
planned to attend?"

Yes, Kristi had talked about the Saturday-night reservations, Barrish thought. "There was supposed to be a house-
type party and people would be all dressed up." A slight
problem popped up, though. Kristi had mentioned that she
didn't particularly want to go by herself, but couldn't think of
anyone she could find to go with her. She had already purchased admission.

The next words from Barrish rang an alarm in Henry's
mind. "Kristi said she was supposed to meet with a man on
Sunday morning at ten-thirty." She had met him on Venice
Beach approximately one year ago, and he said something
about being "an energetic healer or acupuncturist." Barrish
thought he lived in a Venice bungalow. Another avenue of investigation would have to be explored.

"Did Ms. Johnson have any boyfriends or other men in
her life?"

Barrish recalled that Kristi's ex-boyfriend was named Dick,
but she couldn't remember the last name. "They often fought
verbally." Kristi had driven north to Santa Maria to visit him
the previous weekend of February 7. Barrish added that neither she nor Kristi's family really approved of the guy.

"Can you tell me what Ms. Johnson was wearing when you
last saw her Saturday afternoon?"

Women can usually recall in considerable detail what other
women wear, and Barrish lived up to the reputation. She described the clothing: "Powder blue corduroy pants that hang
off the hips and have a three-to-four-inch slit at the fringed
bottoms and a white collarless, sleeveless cotton top with
powder blue piping that matched the fringe at the bottom of

the pants." Kristi had purchased the clothing just one week earlier while visiting her grandmother in Santa Maria.

Detective Henry expressed his gratitude for Barrish's cooperation.

Sergeant Robert Almada spent much of that Tuesday afternoon contacting area hospitals, as Terry Hall had done earlier, but none of them had treated a Kristi Johnson or any unknown persons fitting her description. The sergeant then tried another avenue. He typed a message to Kristi's e-mail address, on the slim chance that she might try to access her messages. Like the other efforts, this one also petered out in a dead end.

The police investigators next looked into Kristi's e-mail regarding the party, and entered a peculiar world of entertainment. They learned all about a growing phenomenon in the culture of youth while unearthing details about the rave party for which Kristi had reservations on the night she vanished.

Raves, or rave parties, is a term used by youthful hipsters to describe gatherings, often secretly organized, at which uninhibited, all-night dancing to loud subculture music is the main theme. The name came from wild fests conducted in London four decades earlier, usually initiated and attended by Caribbean natives. They often involved illegal drug usage. New York revelers adopted the sobriquet and it spread across the nation. A few communities have tried to outlaw raves to curtail the noise and drugs, but these efforts only sent them underground and made the activities more attractive to young adventure seekers.

For the February 15 party Kristi planned to attend, a rave organizer had rented a club in the eastern sector of downtown Los Angeles. The two-story building, once an industrial warehouse, had been converted for various events, dances, and

even an art gallery. Its interior boasted a theater stage, cement
dance floor, a makeshift bar, and spectacular light and sound
equipment. Online information listed the artists who would
perform that night. In the "Main Room," Juan Atkins, Terence
Dixon, DJ Bone, Acid Circus LIVE, and Subversive. In the
"House Room," James Todd, Ruh-son, DJ Gruven, Kazell,
and Zack Hill. Kristi had evidently discovered the event on an
Internet chat line and e-mailed the organizer.

On Thursday morning, February 13, Kristi typed the note.
She began with a friendly comment about not having gone
out in a long time, and confirmed that she definitely planned
to attend this event. The lineup of musicians, she stated, reminded her of the "Plurkids days." This evidently referred to
a production company called PLURkids, based in Detroit,
Michigan, which specialized in entertainment events including rave parties. Kristi asked that she be placed on a list of attendees who would pay an admission fee of fifteen dollars,
and expressed her appreciation.

The Los Angeles organizer replied by e-mail that same afternoon. It informed Kristi that her name had been added to
a special VIP list, but advised her that being on the list did not
guarantee admission. Since nearly all of the tickets had already been sold, the letter added, no other names would be
added after capacity attendance for the venue had been
reached.

Later events would indicate that the note may have been a
pitch to purchase tickets through an online seller, thus assuring the money would be paid in advance.

Information about the rave party and its location came as
a welcome piece of news for Obenchain. She telephoned the
promoter and arranged to send a detective the next day to see
if information about Kristi's attendance, or absence, could be
produced.

Still working at six-fifteen that evening, Obenchain answered yet another phone call. Radio broadcasts only a short time earlier had already produced a response. A man named Lee Randall (pseudonym) told the detective that he had seen Kristi on Valentine's Day, and had some information about her.

"What time did you see her and how did you know Johnson?" Obenchain asked. Randall responded that he had met Kristi at a rave party about one year ago and that he also knew her ex-boyfriend Dick Sawyer. The caller admitted that he befriended Kristi, and sometimes visited her at a Hollywood apartment and then later after she relocated in Santa Monica. On February 14, at about ten o'clock at night, he had gone to Kristi's apartment. They watched a movie together on television, and he was embarrassed that the noise had awakened one of the roommates. Randall said he left at two the next morning.

Her trip to the mall took place less than ten hours later.

Curious about Kristi's participation at the rave events, Obenchain asked, "Do you know if she took drugs at these parties?"

"I don't think so," Randall replied. "I have no knowledge of her indulging in any type of drugs. She would dance and enjoy herself, but wouldn't get intoxicated or high."

Obenchain thanked Randall for his voluntary call. She stayed in her office another hour to enter the day's events into a logbook and a detailed police report, and tried to think of anything she could do. Any delay—each hour and each minute—could make a life-or-death difference.

Early Wednesday morning, Obenchain called Kristi's father, Kirk Johnson, in Holland, Michigan. The two-hour time difference gave the detective comfort that she wouldn't be waking him before dawn.

Sorely troubled by his daughter's disappearance, Kirk Johnson readily answered questions. He said that he and Kristi talked by telephone at least monthly, and that he had last spoken to her on February 9 while she visited her grand-mother in Santa Maria. Describing his relationship with Kristi as "loving and positive," Johnson said he had been planning to send her airline tickets so she could visit some-time during the coming summer. Now and then, when she needed it, he would wire money to her. Johnson also men-tioned that Kristi maintained regular contact, via e-mail, with her brother, Derek, at his various posts with the U.S. Air Force. Derek had told him of receiving an e-email from her on Valentine's Day.

Johnson told Obenchain that he planned to fly to Califor-nia on Friday to join in the search for his daughter. He would be perfectly willing to meet with the detective and help in any way he could.

As the investigation escalated, Santa Monica police chief James T. Butts Jr. decided to hold a press conference regard-ing the case. Obenchain later recalled the process of prepar-ing facts to feed the news media. "We knew that we could give only limited information regarding Kristi's disappear-ance and the last words she had said to her roommate. We wanted to inform the public about our search for Kristi, and that she had vanished under suspicious circumstances, along with a general indication of where she might have been going. But we needed to limit the specifics to avoid compro-mising the case and to prevent a flood of useless calls by every nutcase in L.A."

Standing side by side, Chief Butts and Lieutenant Frank Fabrega, the public information officer, held the conference at ten o'clock on Wednesday morning. Fabrega faced re-porters and delivered the terse statement:

> *On February 17, 2003, the Santa Monica Police De-partment began a missing persons investigation regard-ing the disappearance of Kristine Louise Johnson. The*

*preliminary investigation disclosed that Ms. Johnson was
last seen leaving her residence in Santa Monica on Saturday afternoon, February 15. . . . Family and friends
have not heard from her since Saturday and are concerned about her safety. She may have been en route to an
appointment with a possible photographer in the area of
Beverly Hills. Ms. Johnson was last seen driving her 1996
Mazda Miata convertible. . . . Anyone with information is
encouraged to call the Office of Criminal Investigations
tip line.*

He gave reporters the telephone number and said it would
be manned around the clock. By early afternoon, the commu-
niqué was distributed to newspapers, radio, and television
broadcasters. Several stations carried it in their five o'clock
reports.

Detective Obenchain didn't attend the conference, preferring to use every hour in the intense search. Huddled with
Detectives Henry, Sumlin, Cabrera, and Jon Murphy to divide
up the growing list of facts and people still to be investigated
that day, Obenchain coordinated the multiple activities. She
prepared search warrants and fed necessary information into
the California Department of Justice Missing and Unidentified Persons (MUPS) Unit. The data would then be dissemi-
nated through DOJ's system, resulting in a Tracking and
Recovery of Abducted Kids (TRAK) statewide bulletin being
issued.

Henry, meanwhile, drove to the Century City mall to pick
up videotapes recorded by a security camera. It would take
endless hours of watching grainy images to see if Kristi
showed up on any of them, and if so, if she could be seen talking to a man. From there, he drove to the lingerie shop on La
Cienega to interview store employees and to borrow a pair of

stiletto heels, duplicates of the ones Kristi purchased, to be photographed.

Sumlin tracked down the Venice Beach person Kristi had mentioned to her roommate, the one who might be an "energetic healer." He turned out to be a faith healer. When Sumlin questioned him, the cooperative individual recalled that Kristi had said she would drop by his place on Sunday, February 16, but she hadn't kept the appointment or called to cancel it. He provided an account of his time and activities that satisfied Sumlin, absolving the healer of any suspicion.

One of Terry Hall's comments to Obenchain needed follow-up. Kristi had recently said she was "interested" in a man named Lucas who lived in her apartment building, and he wanted to take her to Hawaii. Detective Murphy took on the assignment, found Lucas Rose, and spoke to him. Rose said he had seen Kristi on the afternoon of February 15 when she returned home from a shopping trip, and that she appeared to be very excited. Kristi had told him that she was going to an audition, but gave no details. The investigators lost interest in Rose when he could unequivocally account for his time, also eliminating him as a possible suspect.

More important information came from Detective Murphy's drive to the eastern environs of downtown Los Angeles to check out the rave party connection. He questioned the promoter, a woman named Ahnne Araza. Without hesitation, she recalled the e-mail from Kristi, which arrived several days before the event. It had indicated that the entertainment might remind her of "the Plurkids [sic] days" in Michigan.

"Do you know if Kristi Johnson showed up that night?" Murphy asked.

"She definitely did not," the promoter replied with surprising certainty. Araza explained that several people, including herself, her mother, a brother, and four friends, had carefully checked each arrival. They had divided up the alphabetical guest list, requested identification from each of the 135 people who entered, and used yellow felt pens to highlight the names. Five people with the surname "Johnson" were on the list, but only two showed up, and their names were highlighted on the guest list. Kristi was not one of the two. Araza said that when someone from the Santa Monica Police Department had called, she immediately checked the list. Kristi Johnson's name was not highlighted; therefore she had not attended the rave party.

Murphy understood the crucial importance of this information. If true, it would eliminate numerous possibilities, and curtail the need to investigate the rave connection any further. Process of elimination is a major ingredient of good detective work. Sir Arthur Conan Doyle's Sherlock Holmes, the greatest sleuth of all, said it best: "Whenever you have eliminated the impossible, whatever remains, however improbable, must be the truth."

The name Dick Sawyer, Kristi's former boyfriend, had popped up twice with hints of abuse and fights. Boyfriends and husbands are frequently "persons of interest" in missing persons or murder cases, since 32 percent of female murder victims are killed by mates or lovers. Could Sawyer be somehow responsible for Kristi's disappearance? The possibility certainly needed exploration, so Obenchain called Dick and asked him if he would come from his residence in Santa Maria for an interview at the Santa Monica Police Department. Sawyer readily agreed and promptly made the hundred-mile drive.

In his statements to the detective, Sawyer said he had met Kristi three years earlier at a "smokeout" session in San Bernardino, about seventy miles east of Santa Monica. They developed a friendship over the next month, which turned intimate on Halloween night, 2000. Over the next nine months, the relationship continued until his move to Texas in August. They didn't have any contact for several weeks, but then began exchanging letters and phone calls. In February 2002, she flew to Texas to see him.

The detective asked what kind of problems came up in the relationship. Sawyer said the biggest "downfalls" were distrust, jealousy, and Kristi's unemployment.

Again, in April 2002, she visited him in Texas. At that time, he said, they discussed their situation and consumed a moderate amount of alcohol. They kept in contact after she went home, and a month later, she convinced him to return to California. He moved in with her at a West Hollywood apartment. Strain developed between them, and in late November it erupted into an argument and physical confrontation. According to Sawyer, the dispute was about money, and Kristi "began to strike him." He admitted that he locked her keys in her car and that he slapped her. Two days after Thanksgiving, he moved out.

Obenchain listened carefully to Sawyer's story, making regular notes. Then she asked him, pointblank, if he could account for his whereabouts on February 15, the day Kristi vanished.

Yes, he could, said Sawyer. He had spent the day with a buddy near Vandenberg Air Force Base, on the coast just south of Santa Maria. He provided the name and telephone number of his pal, and while Obenchain continued the interview, Detective Cabrera made a call. The friend convincingly corroborated what Sawyer had said. Any suspicion about Dick Sawyer evaporated like early-morning fog on Santa Monica bay.

Obenchain thanked him for his courteous cooperation.

On the third day of investigation, Thursday, February 20, the search for Kristi Johnson seemed to resemble L.A.'s freeway traffic—stalled, frustrating, and endless.

It wasn't from a lack of effort. Detective Obenchain and her investigative team struggled against the odds with searches, probes, and telephone calls that morning, hoping for a solid lead in the case. Friends of the missing girl and other concerned people pitched in to help. Her fellow employees at the Marina del Rey firm distributed flyers in various Santa Monica neighborhoods.

The first major break came that afternoon. A beautiful young woman in Hollywood, Susan Jennifer Murphy, read a short article on page B-4 of the *Los Angeles Times,* and sensed something terribly wrong. "My heart dropped," she later said.

CHAPTER 4

THE JAMES BOND CONNECTION

The *Los Angeles Times* ran a short, six-column-inch article in the local news section, part B, tucked back on the fourth page. Under a smiling portrait of Kristi Johnson, the headline read: SEARCH IS UNDERWAY FOR WOMAN. The article reflected exactly what Lieutenant Fabrega had said in Wednesday's press conference. "A 21-year-old Santa Monica woman who may have been on her way to Beverly Hills to meet a photographer has not been seen for five days, police said Wednesday." A description of Kristi and her vehicle followed. Friends, the article said, "told police that Johnson . . . was supposed to meet a photographer, possibly to pose for pictures, on Saturday. . . . Anyone with information about Johnson's whereabouts is asked to call police." It concluded with the tip line phone number.

The reference to a "photographer" probably jarred more than one reader who recalled other articles, over a period of years, about rapes and murders in which men pretending to be photographers had lured attractive young women into remote locations and assaulted them. One of the most prominent had been the murder of Linda Sobek.

Whether or not Susan Murphy knew of these incidents when she read about Kristi Johnson, she still felt a deep intuition that she had possibly escaped fatal circumstances herself, just three weeks earlier. She scanned through the article again. Could Kristi have met the same man Susan had encountered? Or was this merely an unimportant, unrelated coincidence?

Like Kristi, Susan Murphy's radiant face and figure attracted stares, whistles, and countless clever pickup lines. Her brown eyes gave off sparks of secret amusement under quizzically arched eyebrows, while her perfect bow lips naturally turned up at the corners in effervescent mirth. She literally glowed when she talked. With looks like hers, she had learned a hundred ways to ignore drooling men. But when a fellow calling himself "Victor Thomas" had spoken to her at the mall, his approach had just enough panache to catch her interest.

Susan struggled with feelings aroused by the *Times* article. Her experience probably had nothing to do with Kristi's situation. Or did it? The only similarities she could find between her encounter and Kristi's situation was the mention of photography and Beverly Hills. It didn't even say how Kristi knew the person she was supposed to meet. Yet, Susan's instincts wouldn't let go.

Well, certainly it wouldn't hurt to call the tip line number and let the police know of her experience on January 24.

At half past twelve, on Friday afternoon, Susan keyed in the number and spoke to a tip line operator. The woman listened as Susan spoke of her experience, and asked the informant to hold on for a minute. She immediately transferred the call to Detective Obenchain. Susan repeated what she had told the operator, about a guy at the Century City mall who said he wanted her to be a James Bond girl for which she had to wear certain clothing and shoes. She readily answered a few questions the detective asked.

Listening with growing excitement, Obenchain realized that the investigation had taken a powerful, galvanizing turn. She asked Susan, "Can you get down here to the Santa Monica police station right away?"

Susan arrived at Obenchain's office in the early afternoon and sat with her in an interview room. She told the detective that when she read the *Times* article, it brought back a memory of something that happened to her three weeks ago. In clear, articulate detail, Susan said that she worked as an accountant for a business management firm in Century City, and after completing her shift at 5:30 P.M., on Friday, January 24, she changed clothes before leaving. Wanting to look fresh for a planned dinner meeting with someone at a restaurant in the mall, she put on a gray miniskirt with front buttons, a very tight long-sleeved black crew-neck sweater, dark nylons, with black knee-high boots, and walked to the mall, only a few minutes from her office. She arrived about fifteen minutes later and used the Constellation Boulevard entrance to Macy's department store. With plenty of time to spare before the seven o'clock date, Susan rode the escalator to the second floor and stopped to look at a table of sweaters in the Charter Club/Ralph Lauren area of the women's clothing section.

A man appeared at the table and stood beside her. He seemed a couple of inches over six feet, thin, had blue eyes, a long oval face, was clean shaven, had short, curly brown hair, and was maybe in his mid-thirties. Dressed casually in khaki pants and a tan coat, he wore an Eddie Bauer–type, well-fitted baseball cap. Yes, she said, she would definitely recognize him again.

Susan recalled that the stranger complimented her with the simple statement, "I think you are very attractive."

She thanked him and replied, "That's very nice of you to say that."

The stranger turned as if to walk away, took a few steps, apparently reconsidered, and returned to her side. He said that he worked for Silver Screen Partners, an affiliate of the Walt Disney Company, and introduced himself as Victor Thomas, director of photography. They were working on a new James Bond film, still hush-hush. And even though he was not part of the casting crew, he thought that she would be perfect for some promotional photography they were working on.

"We've been casting all day," he said, "and you're the look we want. You are perfect." He even told her that he preferred heavier legs and smaller busts than most models possess.

While relating the encounter to Obenchain, Susan's voice broke with bell-like humor, admitting that both of those characteristics matched her perfectly.

Continuing her narrative, Susan told the detective that she felt somewhat skeptical, but the guy sounded authentic. His comments flattered her and the proposition held a certain intrigue. She accepted his offer to have coffee together and walked with him to the mall's food court. "I don't drink coffee," Susan told Obenchain, "so he bought me a Snapple drink." They sat at a table and continued to talk.

"You'll be on a billboard for the new James Bond film that is top-secret and will be uniting Sean Connery with Pierce Brosnan," said Victor Thomas. "If you are selected, you will make about one hundred thousand dollars."

The offer took Susan's breath away. While it seemed too good to be true, she admitted hoping that it would turn out to be valid. Certainly, she had enough experience to recognize a come-on. Yet she thought, *What if it is true? Wouldn't that*

*be great? How fun would that be—to be a Bond girl? It's
every woman's dream.*

The next comment from Victor pretty much sealed it for
Susan. "Pierce Brosnan and Sean Connery are going to be at
the studio tomorrow. I would like very much for you to come
in and meet them. You can do an informal casting, even
though it's not an official casting day. Are you interested?"

Susan said yes, she was.

Okay, Victor told her. She needed to wear certain clothing
at the meeting tomorrow. He was very specific, Susan told
Obenchain.

"He wanted me to wear a black miniskirt, as short and tight
as possible, a white button-up shirt, man's style, sheer black
panty hose, and 1940s-style black pump stilettos." Her dark
hair should be "slicked back in a very tight ponytail." She
also needed a Hugo Boss necktie, but he would bring one
for her. Victor told her to show up the following day, Saturday afternoon, five-thirty, at an intersection on La Cienega,
one block south of Santa Monica Boulevard. Victor jotted the
address on a slip of paper, gave it to Susan, and said he would
meet her there on the northeast corner.

Susan agreed to the rendezvous and glanced at her watch.
She told Victor of her intention to meet someone at seven
for dinner on the other end of the mall. He replied that he,
too, planned to eat there, so they walked in that direction together. Suddenly he announced, "I'm too excited. You go
ahead. I'm going home. You go on and go out to dinner." They
parted company.

Obenchain asked if Susan had seen him go to a vehicle.
No, said Susan, she hadn't.

That evening, Susan said, she told her fiancé, Mark
Wilson, about the encounter with Victor Thomas and the opportunity to be in a James Bond production. To Wilson, a
former London, England, police officer, or bobby, the whole

thing sounded like a scam. Susan also expressed doubts, but wanted to show up at the meeting site just in case the offer turned out to be legitimate. To Obenchain, she explained, "I told him that I didn't want to go alone, and even though I was intrigued, I was suspicious, too. I asked him if he would please come with me because I was too afraid to go alone."

Together they worked out a plan. Wilson would drive Susan to the address on La Cienega and wait in his Jeep Grand Cherokee, parked about twenty yards away. From the driver's seat, he could observe when Victor showed up. This way, Wilson wouldn't interfere unless something went wrong. Susan agreed not to get into any other car or leave the area without Wilson.

They arrived punctually the next afternoon. Instead of wearing the prescribed miniskirt and stilettos, Susan chose to dress in cargo pants, the recommended white shirt, and tennis shoes, but carried the other clothing with her. She explained to Obenchain, with a laugh, "I thought that wearing stilettos and a miniskirt while standing on a street corner would probably put me in a very vulnerable position."

Mark parked east of the intersection as planned, under the canopy of a blossoming schefflera, or umbrella tree. The thick growth of fingerlike leaves and red elongated flowers, giving the tree its nickname of "octopus plant," provided him and his three-year-old daughter with a shadowy observation point. Susan walked twenty yards to the intersection and stood near the corner of a building with curved stucco walls painted dark gray.

She waited about ten minutes, facing south, expecting Victor Thomas to arrive by car. Instead, he appeared "from nowhere" at her side. Rather than the casual attire she had seen at the mall, he now dressed in a business suit. He carried a folded portfolio of papers in one hand, along with a pen.

It startled Susan to see annoyance on Victor's face. He

growled, "That isn't what I told you to wear. I'm going to take you somewhere to change." Softening his voice a little, he continued, "Let's go somewhere to have a drink and talk about the roles. It will help you get very prepared." One of Victor's arms thrust forward and he laid a hand on her upper arm, near the shoulder, as if to guide her.

With combined fear and doubt rising in her gut, Susan replied, "I'm not going anywhere with you until I see some identification."

Victor frowned and mumbled something about leaving his wallet and identification at the studio, or at "the lot." When Susan insisted, he warned, "You're giving up the opportunity of a lifetime."

No smile on her face now, she snapped, "You know, actually my safety is much more important."

"We need to go," he insisted. Gesturing in the direction across La Cienega, he said, "We should go and meet my friend Natasha and talk about the role." The reference to "Natasha" made no sense to Susan, since he hadn't previously mentioned the name. She stepped back to break any physical contact. Victor snapped, "Okay, just forget it. I don't think you are right for the part anyway. Forget it."

Glancing toward the spot where Mark Wilson had parked, Susan saw him move the Jeep Cherokee forward, stop again, leap out of the driver's side, and sprint toward her and Victor. Susan turned and hurried to meet him. Apparently unnerved by Mark's sudden appearance, Victor dashed toward a wrought-iron security gate blocking a driveway, tried unsuccessfully to open it, then vanished around a corner.

Inside his car again, Susan and Mark drove around the block and through an angular alley between the buildings. They caught sight of Victor cowering in a cluster of shrubbery, but he vaulted out and ran. After another circuit in the Jeep, through the alley once more, they again spotted him emerging from a courtyard, dusting his clothes off. Mark braked to a halt, slid out of his driver's seat, and confronted Victor. Using experience from his service with the London constabulary, he began "patting down" Victor for any weapons, and said, "I don't know if I'm going to kill you or drag you to the police station." His preference, he said, was to kill him. "Do you have any ID?" Victor shook his head in the negative. "Who do you work for?" asked Mark.

Victor's panache had crumbled away as tears welled in his eyes and spilled out. Trembling, he said that he was an employee of the Disney Company. He added something to the effect that he would never do anything like this again.

Still using the tone of an arresting officer, Mark demanded a telephone number where Victor could be reached. The trembling reply was almost inaudible, but Mark jotted down the ten-digits coming from the blubbering mouth of Victor. He probed his own pocket for a cell phone, intending to verify the number, but realized he'd left it in the car. "If this isn't correct," he threatened, "I'm going to hunt you down." Ordering Victor to remain standing in place, Mark stepped over to his Cherokee to make the test call. As he tapped away at the keys, Victor broke loose like a frightened dog, loped away, and dodged through heavy traffic on La Cienega. Mark thought momentarily about another pursuit, but decided against it, mostly in consideration for the safety of his young daughter.

The telephone number proved to be bogus. But the claim of carrying no identification had been true, so Susan and Mark still only knew the fleeing man as Victor Thomas.

Later that evening, Susan said to Obenchain, she had tried to call the police and report the incident. She was put on hold, and while waiting, she decided that no crime had really been committed, so she hung up. Previously, Susan revealed, she had made another interesting call. It was to the Screen Actors

Guild (SAG), in which she held membership. The only role
Susan had ever landed, she laughed, came in a film where her
hands had doubled for the star's hands. Susan asked the Guild
if a new James Bond film was in production. No, they told
her, there was no current project on that subject.

The whole spiel by Victor Thomas had, indeed, been a scam.

The incredible narrative from Susan Murphy left Detective
Virginia Obenchain reeling. It matched the accounts related
to Kristi Johnson in amazing detail. No doubt existed in Obenchain's mind that the two women had met the same man.
Susan, though, had taken the precaution of asking her fiancé to
be there with her, while Kristi had gone to the "audition" alone.

Five days had passed since Kristi vanished, and Obenchain
wanted more than anything to find her alive. With this new information from Susan, the chances of success appeared to have
improved. But it would still be a perilous race against time.

The detective figured that the name Victor Thomas was
probably an alias. She made a mental note to check it against
computerized data of known criminals, but really didn't expect
to find anything helpful. And that hunch proved correct.

Taking a detailed description of Victor from Susan, Obenchain gave it to Detectives John Henry and Jon Murphy. She
dispatched them to Macy's at the Century City mall to view
security videotapes from January 24, as well as February 15,
and see if they could pick out a man matching the clothing
and features Susan had described.

Next, on that same Thursday afternoon, Obenchain telephoned Sandra "Sandy" Enslow, a sketch artist from the L.A.
County Sheriff's Department (LASD). Sandy happened to be
at a substation on L.A.'s west side, and after obtaining permission from her supervisor, she agreed to make the short
drive over to Santa Monica.

In the interview room, it took nearly two hours to develop
a composite drawing of Victor Thomas, with Sandy patiently

guiding Susan through the task. Susan later described it: "There is a procedure. First she showed me a bunch of pictures of face shapes." Examining each one, Susan selected the configuration that, in her memory, best fit Victor. "Then she would show me noses, so I would pick out the one that best matched him." All the other features followed: mouth, eyes, eyebrows, ears, and hair, with Susan pointing to the ones that seemed to match her recollection of Victor's features. She felt the final result was close, if not a perfect representation of the shyster.

After the session with Enslow, Obenchain drove Susan to the mall and asked her to retrace every step she had made on the day she met Victor. They covered it together while the detective took notes. As they reached the food court where the suspect had bought Susan a Snapple drink, Obenchain's cell phone buzzed. On the other end, Detective Henry, sounding excited, asked if she and Susan could join him at the Macy's security office.

In the cubicle, they stopped in front of a video monitor. Obenchain later said, "There was an image frozen on the monitor screen of a male wearing a baseball hat. Susan Murphy looked at it and shrieked, 'That's him! Absolutely, without a doubt.' We viewed the videotape a short time and saw Susan enter the store via the southeast door. Several moments later, we saw the suspect enter using the same door." The soft-focus images didn't provide much facial detail, but every little bit of new information helped.

Events for tired investigators on that long, productive Thursday raised new hopes, inspiring even more work that took them well beyond the ends of their shifts. Obenchain drove Susan to the La Cienega location where she and Mark had confronted Victor Thomas, and asked her to point out exactly where everything had happened. Two other detectives, Michael Cabrera and Larry Nicols, accompanied by artist

Enslow, traveled to Burbank. They met Mark Wilson at his job and asked him to examine the composite sketch of Victor. He suggested a few minor alterations, including slightly lowering the hairline by adding more growth to the upper forehead and narrowing the nostrils. Cabrera took a detailed statement from Wilson about the entire confrontation with the suspect on January 24. It dovetailed perfectly with the narrative from Susan Murphy.

Kirk Johnson, Kristi's father, arrived in Santa Monica on Friday and met Detective Obenchain at her office. The detective later said, "He was very, very concerned, almost frantic, and nearly in tears." He told Obenchain that he had tried to talk his daughter into moving back to Michigan in 2002, and now sorely regretted her decisions to remain in California. It might have saved her from whatever had happened. But he was proud of her enrollment at Santa Maria Community College that year with the goal of transferring to Cal Poly (California Polytechnic State University, San Luis Obispo) to become an engineer. Unfortunately, those plans had been deferred when she moved to West Hollywood, and then to Santa Monica, where she attended the local community college.

A strangely foreshadowing event had taken place just eight days before Kristi vanished, Johnson said. She had visited her grandmother in Santa Maria, and on Friday, February 7, a man had approached her in one of that city's malls and said that she would be perfect for acting or modeling. Kristi had laughingly mentioned it to her grandmother that evening and even noted that "the man was good-looking."

Sometimes, the worried father said, people took advantage of Kristi's good nature. She had been involved in a minor accident with her Mazda Miata, and had been overcharged at a repair shop by "dishonest" people. When her car had been impounded one year earlier, the tow truck driver had been "gruff" and mistreated her.

Expressing his ardent hope that Kristi would be found, Johnson said he would assist in any way he could. He left the police station to help distribute posters and flyers asking for anyone with information to call the tip line.

A dedicated community effort resulted in a team of more than forty people, including employees of the Marina del Rey firm where Kristi worked, fanning out in various neighborhoods to search for any clue that might help. They not only posted requests for help, but scoured the hills adjacent to Santa Monica just in case she might be lying injured somewhere. No one wanted to acknowledge it, but they also looked in the Topanga Canyon ravine, along a roadway slicing through the Santa Monica Mountains from the beach to the San Fernando Valley. The route had been used by more than one killer to dump bodies of victims.

The team of officers working with Obenchain had no qualms about sacrificing their time off to stay with the investigation, and their shifts stretched into twelve hours, then fourteen, and some even stayed on the job up to eighteen hours.

Intensive efforts to find Kristi continued in full force over the weekend, with Obenchain and several members of the investigative team working the entire time. They spent most of Saturday patrolling the area around La Cienega where Susan Murphy had encountered Victor Thomas, hoping to spot either Kristi's car or someone fitting the suspect's description. On Sunday, two tipsters called in to report that a white Mazda Miata convertible had been parked at an intersection in Tarzana, twelve miles from Santa Monica. (The community is named after the famous fictional "ape man." Tarzan's creator, Edgar Rice Burroughs, lived there in the 1920s and subdivided his land for development that eventually became the town.) Detectives Almada and Cabrera met there with K-9 handler Anne Anderson and let her dog sniff clothing borrowed from Kristi's closet. The dog searched with tail-wagging enthusiasm, but could find no trail, nor was the white Mazda seen.

Another telephone tip came in suggesting that Kristi was being held captive in Mexico City. Nearly every possibility, in Obenchain's view, merited checking out. She contacted a State Department foreign service officer who looked into it. It proved to be one more futile effort.

The hard work that weekend yielded nothing important. But on a cloudy, drizzly Monday morning, the second welcome break in the case gave investigators another shot of adrenaline.

Within a few minutes of Obenchain's arrival at work on the ninth day of Kristi's absence, Sergeant Almada rushed into her office with good news. The Mazda Miata had been found.

Security personnel for a parking garage shared by two upscale Century City hotels, the Century Plaza and the St. Regis, had performed a routine check of vehicles left in place too long and noticed the white Mazda. For more than a week, it had been in a stall reserved for valet use. They called the Los Angeles Police Department (LAPD). Officers arrived, recognized the license number from the Be on the Lookout (BOLO) bulletins, surrounded it with yellow crime scene tape, and kept it secure pending arrival of detectives.

Before driving to Century City, Obenchain called the LASD crime lab to request assistance in processing the Mazda for fingerprints and other trace evidence. Fifteen minutes later, she braked to a halt under a massive half-circle overhang in front of the St. Regis.

Scanning the scene, she noticed that the Century Plaza hotel, on the corner of Avenue of the Stars and Constellation Avenue, was a stone's throw from the south entrance to the

Century City mall, where Kristi had shopped nine days earlier. The seventeen-story hotel formed a graceful curve about three football fields in length. Directly adjacent, on the southwest side, the equally luxurious St. Regis towered thirty stories above the circular driveway entrance where valets picked up and delivered patrons' Mercedes, Rolls-Royces, and other premium vehicles, along with those of lesser grandeur.

Kristi's Mazda, mantled in a thin layer of dust, appeared undamaged. Two LASD criminalists arrived and went to work, meticulously examining every inch of the vehicle, inside and out. Along with an Arrowhead water bottle and a commercial videotape movie, they found a cell phone on the seat. After the technicians had completed their work at the scene, a tow truck transported the Mazda to a police impound site and secured it in a protected garage.

Since hotel officials had found the car in a slot reserved for valet parking, Obenchain and Detective Cabrera asked a manager at the St. Regis Hotel if it could be linked directly to any of their valet parking attendants. Within a few minutes, the name Roberto Marquez (pseudonym) came up. Fortunately, Marquez happened to be on duty that very Monday morning. Summoned to an office where Obenchain and Cabrera waited, Marquez told them he had been parking and retrieving cars for the St. Regis and the neighboring Century Plaza since 1986, when the St. Regis was called "the Tower." After it changed names, he worked there exclusively five days a week.

The nervous attendant said that he remembered parking the Mazda very early on Sunday morning, February 16. He had been working the graveyard shift, from 11:00 P.M. to 7:00 A.M. From his chair in the valet office, Marquez said, he saw the white sports car enter the hotel driveway at about five forty-five in the morning. The driver parked in the northernmost spot of the valet circle, got out, locked the vehicle, and started to walk away. Marquez had hustled out, caught the driver, and said that he couldn't park there because it was for valet parking only.

The man seemed to shake himself out of deep thought, tossed the keys to Marquez, and said, "Well, valet it then." He walked away in the direction of the Century Plaza hotel. Marquez wondered if the guy might be an employee of the Plaza, maybe a waiter, arriving late to work and needed to hurry over there. Asked to describe the driver, Marquez characterized him as an "average American," white, and "fortyish." He had short brown hair, almost blond, with a little gray at the temples. Wrinkling his face into a contemplative look, Marquez scratched his chin, eyed Cabrera, and said that the man was built very much like the detective, who stood six feet tall and weighed 220 pounds. The valet's next words created a much better mental picture: the driver, he said, seemed like a "Rambo" type.

Obenchain showed Marquez the composite sketch that had been in the news over the weekend, and asked if it resembled the driver. It looked "more or less" like the driver, Marquez said, but he thought the guy was a little "heavier, or thicker," and his face wasn't quite that long.

After arranging for Marquez to come to police headquarters on Wednesday to look at photo layouts, Obenchain arranged for K-9 officers to bring scent dogs to the hotels and search for any trace of Kristi Johnson. She found ready and willing teams from the L.A. sheriff's office, Ventura County Sheriff's Department (VCSD), and Torrance Police Department (TPD), in L.A.'s South Bay area, all eager to help. They explored both hotels, the parking building, and surrounding areas, but found nothing.

Crime scene investigation (CSI) team criminalists and technicians checked the entire Mazda for latent prints, especially glass surfaces. One particular place often yields good results—people tend to automatically adjust the rearview mirror without thinking about it, and leave prints. But the exhaustive effort turned up only Kristi's fingerprints and a few unidentifiable partials. Another potentially strong opportunity led nowhere.

The cell phone found in the car proved to be Kristi's.

Recovery of Kristi's car dampened Obenchain's optimism for finding the missing woman alive. It had been parked by an unidentified man at the St. Regis only fifteen hours after she had last been seen leaving her apartment. The discovery raised a myriad of new questions and offered little encouragement. Of course, the possibility remained of her being held captive somewhere, so the search would continue at a high intensity level.

Obenchain telephoned Kristi's parents, Kirk Johnson and Terry Hall, to inform them of the vehicle discovery. They both expressed a mix of sorrow and hope. Hall mentioned that Kristi's birthday loomed only three days away, and she had arranged for a candlelight vigil to be held on that evening, Thursday, February 27. It would take place at St. Augustine by-the-Sea Episcopal Church, on Fourth Street in downtown Santa Monica, only four blocks from the city's landmark Palisades Park.

The scene resonates with colorful history. Atop a high cliff, the long stretch of palm trees and lawn, seen in countless movies, overlooks the wide beach below, where William Randolph Hearst, Marion Davies, Peter Lawford, and other screen luminaries over the decades had built mansions. Beyond lay endless blue Pacific breakers in the wide, curving bay. To the left could be seen the municipal pier with its time-honored carousel and Ferris wheel, the terminus of old Route 66, the nation's "mother road." The modern Episcopal church, first constructed in the late 1880s, had suffered a disastrous arson fire in 1966. Rebuilt the next year, it featured colorful contemporary stained-glass windows and a spectacular east-facing great window. Both Kristi and her mother loved the serene place of worship.

While rain soaked all of Southern California on that Tuesday afternoon, February 25, Santa Monica police chief James T. Butts Jr. called a second press conference. He told assembled reporters that a "concerned woman" had called the hotline. After describing the experience of Susan Murphy, without naming her, the chief distributed copies of the composite sketch. He also announced the discovery of Kristi Johnson's Mazda in a Century City parking garage. Butts commented that investigators had no reason to suspect foul play, but the passage of eleven days in the case worried them. "It's our hope we'll be able to return her safely to her family. But that is tempered by the fact that the longer it takes to find her, the less likely the chances for that are."

Butts also provided the press with a statement from Terry Hall, made in Los Gatos: *I was elated that they found the car and that this would be a clue to Kristi's whereabouts. But Kristi was not found and I was of course disappointed. We are making progress and I know the Santa Monica Police Department is working around the clock on this effort and they have continued to reassure me that they have all the resources to find Kristi. I have absolute faith in them. . . . It is very disturbing and horrific to know that there is a man that has captured my daughter, and for me to think about what type of situation she may be in, is absolutely overpowering. I can't think about it. We will find her. No matter what is happening to her, we will find her.* She concluded her statement by begging whoever had taken Kristi to *please release her gently.*

On that same Tuesday, Obenchain received news that the man who had left Kristi's car at the St. Regis may have been lurking in the adjacent Century Plaza Hotel and watching all of the police activities. A tipster called to say that he had seen a man who looked exactly like the composite sketch leave the hotel about an hour after the officers departed.

If this was, indeed, a near miss, it was nothing compared to a powerful hit that took place the very next day.

CHAPTER 5

RAP SHEET OF DEPRAVITY

State parole officer Maryanne Larios paid little attention to television or newspaper reports on Wednesday, February 26, until she saw a familiar face. It wasn't a photograph or a film clip—nothing more than an artist's composite sketch. But it snapped Larios instantly out of her lethargy as she realized who it depicted. The news included a tip line telephone number, but Larios really didn't need it. She had spoken many times to various investigative agencies, and knew whom to call.

At two o'clock that afternoon, Detective Shane Talbot in Santa Monica answered the phone and listened as Larios explained that she had seen the composite and thought she recognized the man as one of her parolees.

"If this is the right guy," she said, "his name is Victor Paleologus." This man, Larios added, had been paroled from state prison, California Men's Colony (CMC), at San Luis

Obispo, on January 20, just thirty-seven days ago. While they spoke, Talbot accessed computer records and saw that Victor Paleologus, age forty, was currently in custody at the Los Angeles County Jail, charged with "grand theft auto." Larios confirmed it, saying that he had been arrested on February 17 by the Beverly Hills Police Department (BHPD).

Based on those time frames, it didn't appear very likely that Paleologus could be the man sought in connection with the Susan Murphy incident and with Kristi Johnson's disappearance. The composite had been drawn based on descriptions from Susan and Mark Wilson after their encounter on February 3 and 4. That was only two weeks after Paleologus had been released from prison. Could he have developed such a sophisticated scam and started carrying it out so soon? Certainly possible, but ex-cons usually wait a little longer before committing new offenses. The mysterious James Bond guy seemed smooth and polished, so confident. His game didn't sound much like a nervous convict trying to avoid recidivistic trouble.

Kristi Johnson had vanished on the evening of February 15, only two days before Paleologus had been arrested. Maybe he had something to do with it, but the possibility appeared remote.

Still, the computer told Detective Talbot something that sent suspicion skyrocketing again. In addition to having the same first name as the wanted suspect, the most recent residential address for Victor Paleologus was amazing. He had been living in a building, containing a former restaurant, on La Cienega, one block south of Santa Monica Boulevard. That is exactly where Victor Thomas had suddenly appeared out of nowhere to meet Susan Murphy, while her fiancé observed from a comfortable distance.

Detective Talbot couldn't wait to inform Obenchain. Both of them felt that familiar tingle, the one that comes with solid intuition of being on the right trail. Obenchain joined the phone conversation with Larios, who said, "You know, the composite really looks like someone I know, one of my parolees. Can you send me a clearer copy of it?" Within minutes, Obenchain sent a high-resolution fax of the sketch. Larios said, "Yes, that looks very much like Victor Paleologus. He was just released from prison. He's a 290, and he's in custody."

The mention of a "290" sent chills through the detectives. It referred to California Penal Code 290, which states that any person who has been convicted of a sex crime is required to register with the police department of the city where he or she resides.

Larios said she had visited Paleologus at the La Cienega address three days after his parole, and asked him about crimes in 1989 and 1998, including attempted rape, for which he had been convicted and imprisoned. He had denied the rape, but admitted pulling a scam on a female victim by pretending involvement in the motion picture business.

Now Obenchain's heart raced—Paleologus had told Larios that his pretense sometimes involved a claim of working on a James Bond film.

Grateful for Larios's welcome contribution, Obenchain enlisted the help of a criminal analyst, D. Anderson, who ran a complete history of Paleologus and gave the detective a hard copy of it. Devouring every word, she saw detailed confirmation of the parole agent's mention that Paleologus had once been arrested for rape and, nine years later, was convicted of a sexual assault.

Using the criminal history summary, combined with reports from various police precincts, Obenchain viewed a chronicle of evil behavior by one of the most diabolical con men she had ever encountered. No screenwriter could have imagined a performance like that of Victor Paleologus's.

It began nearly fourteen years earlier, 1989, in Manhattan Beach.

Down the coast a few miles from Santa Monica and Marina del Rey, Manhattan Beach is a magnet for young singles. Its broad swath of sand hosts legions of sunbathers along with surfers, volleyball tournament players, and filmmakers. A concrete path borders the beach for the entire length of the city, and on summer days, joggers, skaters, and pedestrians flow back and forth like freeway traffic. Rustic beach cottages once lined the strand's inland side, but they have been largely replaced by modern, multistory apartment buildings and condos. Near the city's pier, crowds swarm at night to restaurants and nightclubs.

In the autumn of 1989, at one of these hot spots featuring jazz entertainment, Carol Newman (pseudonym), twenty-one, met a man calling himself "John Maroni." He complimented her dark hazel eyes, the shiny brown hair cascading around her graceful neck, her overall attractiveness, and the way she moved like an experienced model. She told him that she did have some experience as an actress, and listened while Maroni spoke of his involvement in the business. He said he was a music executive with Columbia Records. Asking her for a dinner date, he promised that he'd pick her up in a limousine. They would attend a movie industry party at a luxury hotel in downtown Los Angeles, where she could meet the top people in his world. Madonna would probably be there. Dazzled with the wonderful opportunity, Carol agreed to go.

On October 24, Maroni picked Newman up in a sedan, not a limo, and first took her to a nightclub in the Century City mall. After a few drinks, she asked when the big party would start. He smiled, escorted her back to the car, and headed toward the thirty-five-story Bonaventure Hotel in the heart of downtown L.A., with its distinctive five glass towers.

A short trip up an outside elevator, providing a spectacular view of the city lights, took them to a room Maroni had booked in advance. When Carol stepped inside, she wondered where the party was. No one else was there. Maroni at first tried to assure her that the movie people would be arriving shortly. Then his mood changed.

With no warning, Maroni turned into an octopus. He groped her with what seemed like more than two arms, puckered his lips, and tried to force a kiss. Her attempts to push him away were defeated by his superior strength. According to her subsequent account of events that night, he threw her on the bed and pulled at her clothing, attempting to strip off her panty hose and underwear while growling, "I just wanted you for sex." As she tried to get her breath and fight back, he paused momentarily and pulled something from behind the bed. It horrified Carol to see ropes in his hands. Still, she fought, to prevent him from tying her up, broke free, and ran into the bathroom. Before she could lock the door, he forced it open and dragged her back to the bed. Twice more, she struggled free, only to be subdued again. Locking her in a stranglehold, Maroni said that if she would let him tie her up, he would be nice and then set her free. Carol resisted. He tore the belt from her dress and tried to tie her hands with it. That failed, and he made another attempt with his necktie, holding her facedown to lash her wrists behind her back.

Using every bit of her remaining strength, Carol wriggled from his grasp and vaulted out into the hallway. The occupant of a neighboring room heard her scream and opened his door to see what was wrong. Carol rushed over to him, trembling, and crying hysterically. Gasping for breath, she screamed that a man was trying to rape her. Seeing her torn clothing and shredded panty hose, he realized she was telling the truth and offered shelter in his room. At the same moment, a hotel security officer, having been notified of screams echoing down the hallway, arrived.

A call to the LAPD soon brought several officers, who began a search for John Maroni. Within a few days, they discovered his true identity: Victor Paleologus. They tracked him to his workplace and made the arrest. The district attorney (DA) charged him with felonious attempted forcible rape, assault with intent to commit rape, and false imprisonment by violence.

In trial, Paleologus argued that Newman had willingly gone with him to the hotel suite and consented to his advances. A minor struggle followed, but he insisted that it wasn't anything like she had described.

A jury weighed the evidence against Paleologus, and despite proof of rope burns on Carol's wrists and bruises on her body, they couldn't unanimously arrive at a verdict. Rather than face another trial, the defendant worked out a bargain to plead guilty to only one of the charges.

Under California Penal Code 236, false imprisonment is the unlawful violation of the personal liberty of another. Part of the law's definition states that it includes *substantial and sustained restriction of another's liberty accomplished through fraud, deceit, coercion, violence, duress, menace, or threat of unlawful injury to the victim or to another person, under circumstances where the person receiving or apprehending the threat reasonably believes that it is likely that the person making the threat would carry it out.*

Conviction for this crime is punishable by imprisonment for not more than one year and/or a fine not exceeding a thousand dollars. If the false imprisonment is effected by violence, menace, fraud, or deceit, it is punishable by incarceration in a state prison.

While waiting for sentencing, Paleologus presented the court with a letter apparently signed by the vice president of a financial firm where the defendant worked. It stated that although Paleologus had been an exemplary employee with the highest test scores in the country, the company could not license anyone who had more than a misdemeanor conviction on their record. If the judge could reduce the current felony charge to a misdemeanor, it would be greatly appreciated.

On November 23, 1993, the judge complied with the request, reduced the conviction to a misdemeanor, and sentenced Paleologus to three years' probation.

It later turned out that the letter was a forgery. In reality, Paleologus had been fired by the company. The vice president who had supposedly signed the letter revealed that the company had endured a series of thefts during Paleologus's employment, all of which stopped after his termination.

Still on probation for assaulting Carol Newman, Paleologus left the West Hollywood area and moved to an apartment on Ketch Street in Marina del Rey. The narrow lane, no more than a block long and flanked with colorful apartment buildings, ends at Ocean Front Walk, along the sand of Venice City Beach. Not far away, a variety of restaurants line the expansive marina's waterfront, offering every imaginable menu, along with panoramic views of floating vessels, from yawls to yachts, tied up along mooring basins. Paleologus found work managing one of the Italian food cafés.

In late 1994, an auburn-haired beauty who lived nearby attracted Paleologus's attention. At first, they only exchanged casual greetings, but within a few weeks, a friendship developed.

Annie Olson (pseudonym) lived with a man, but the relationship had turned rocky, so when Paleologus asked her for a date, she accepted. They went out, enjoyed it, and did it again, repeatedly over the next six months. Victor Paleologus, though, didn't fare much better with Annie than her live-in boyfriend had. Midway through 1995, she decided to stop dating him. But ending it turned out to be more difficult than she anticipated.

Soon after Annie told Victor that she didn't want to continue the romance, he began calling her incessantly. She later spoke of his behavior: "He cried and said that he was dying and that he was alone and he had a terminal illness and didn't have long to live." At first, he complained of a blood clot in his brain. Later he elevated it to a brain tumor. He might die at any time, he groaned to Annie, so he needed to store his valuables with someone he could trust. Could he put them in her safe-deposit box?

Hesitant, but feeling sorry for Victor, Annie agreed to his request. Out of pity, she continued seeing him, but only on a friendship basis with no more dating. Nearly every day, she stopped by his apartment to make certain that he wouldn't die alone. In this manner, the relationship extended into the beginning of 1996.

Late in January, Paleologus telephoned Annie and asked if she could come and meet him at a restaurant. She first thought he meant the place where he worked, but he corrected her and gave directions to a different spot, a seven-mile drive north of the marina, where Paleologus planned to acquire a vacant restaurant and open it. He explained that he had misplaced his key to the safe-deposit box they shared and needed to borrow hers as soon as possible. She reluctantly acquiesced and drove over to meet him. With some difficulty, she found the place on San Vincente Boulevard, in Brentwood. It wasn't far from the notorious crime scene where O.J. Simpson's ex-wife and her friend Ron Goldman died.

Victor invited her to sit at a table to talk. After a few minutes, Annie decided to leave, fished the key from her purse, handed it over to Victor, and rose. He sprang up at the same moment and stepped forward as if to give her a quick hug. Without warning, she felt her feet go out from under her. He hoisted her up like a life-size rag doll. While she kicked, struggled, and screamed, he carried her into a restroom. Pinning her against a wall with one hand on her throat, he used the other to rip away her clothing and sexually assault her. At last, Annie broke his grasp and dashed out into the vacant restaurant, with Victor in hot pursuit. Fortunately for her, a maintenance worker entered at that moment.

To the new arrival, Victor yelled, "No, not now. Don't come in now." In the confusion, Annie dashed past the worker and made it to her car. Victor caught up with her. Annie later recalled, "He followed me to the car and cried and said that he'd never hurt me. That he was sorry." She felt nothing but contempt as she jammed the accelerator and sped away. She decided not to call the police.

As far as Annie was concerned, the assault ended any shred of remaining friendship. Paleologus called to beg for reconciliation. He played the pity card again by saying that he was moving to Hawaii to live out his last days on earth. Annie hoped that he meant it.

Late one night in the first week of February, while relaxing and watching television in her apartment, Annie heard a noise that sent her heart racing. It seemed to come from her guest bedroom. To be certain it wasn't from the TV program, she pushed the mute button on her remote and listened. Twice more, from the same direction, the odd muffled thuds broke the silence. Working up her courage, she grabbed a canister of pepper spray, eased into the hallway, and opened the guest room door. Tiptoeing in, she looked across the bed toward a mirrored wall. In the reflection, Annie saw something that made her want to scream, but she suppressed it. On the floor, hidden from her direct view by the bed, a man lay on his back in the shadows.

Evidently aware that he'd been seen, Victor Paleologus sprang up and lunged over the bed toward Annie. He carried a two-foot length of white cord, or perhaps electrical wire, and he stretched it toward her neck.

In retreat, Annie gave full throat to a piercing scream, raised the canister, and showered the intruder with a heavy dose of pepper spray. It stopped him long enough for her to scramble out of the apartment to a neighbor's place and call 911. A pair of officers arrived within five minutes. Paleologus escaped, but not before snatching some jewelry and a 9mm Beretta handgun.

Annie told the police every detail of her problems with Victor Paleologus, including the sexual assault ten days earlier. A warrant for his arrest was issued, kicking off a major manhunt by several law enforcement agencies.

Paleologus eluded capture for more than a month, until an SUV he had stolen was spotted in the parking lot of a Cape Cod–style bed-and-breakfast north of Malibu Beach. Sheriff's deputies arrived, found the room he occupied, and knocked on the door. The fugitive locked himself in the bathroom and shouted to the officers, "I have a gun and I'm going to kill myself." He demanded that they leave him alone.

Reluctant to ignite a dangerous gun battle, the deputies chose to wait for the arrival of a SWAT team.

In the bathroom, Paleologus looked around for a possible escape route. He found it in the ceiling. He managed to lift himself up, opened a hinged skylight, and scrambled to the exterior roof. After crawling the length of the building, Paleologus jumped eight feet to the ground and made a dash for the neighboring mobile-home park.

Bending low to avoid being seen, he sprinted from unit to unit until he found an unlocked door. Pulling it open, he vaulted into the living room. A startled young boy sat in front of him, staring in frozen silence. Paleologus ignored the child and hurriedly stacked furniture against the door as a barricade.

The deputies at the inn, discovering that Paleologus had

fled, tracked him into the mobile-home park. A door-to-door search revealed the fugitive's hiding place. Ordered to come out with his hands up, Paleologus refused. He grabbed a broom and poked the handle repeatedly into the ceiling, attempting to break out through the roof, but failed. It took nearly three hours to convince him to surrender.

Later speaking of the chase and standoff, Paleologus denied most of it. He said, "I did not barge into anybody's house. . . . When I went to the door, I asked [the boy] if it was possible to use the phone. . . . I paid him twenty dollars to use it and called my attorney in Century City. . . . The young man was watching the news at the time and he saw everything coming together and realized what was happening. And he knew the sheriffs were outside, so he left and told one of the sheriffs that I was inside. Nobody tried to stop him. I didn't try to stop him or anything else like that." He insinuated that he planned to turn himself in, but everything went wrong.

Facing a battery of charges, including first-degree residential burglary, grand theft, stalking, and false imprisonment by violence, Paleologus posted bail.

If the incredibly slow American court system sponsored a vehicle in a NASCAR race, it would probably be a Model T. The crawling, languid pace finally brought Paleologus to trial in July 1998. A judge listened to arguments by both sides and examined the defendant's bulky file of background information. It contained several previous infractions of the law, including the 1989 false imprisonment of Carol Newman, resulting in thirty-six months of probation. Earlier that same year, he had been convicted of making a false financial statement in a credit card application for "Victor Paleo" and using someone else's Social Security number. For this, he again served no jail time. In 1994, Paleologus had used forged documents in a scheme to defraud a business out of $80,000. Caught, he wheedled the system into a lesser charge and accepted conviction for making a false financial statement, for which he would receive nothing more than additional probation.

One year later, Paleologus went to an automobile sales agency in Culver City and drove out in a Saab, paid for with a bad check and lies on the credit application about his finances. Incredibly, he was convicted once again only on the charge of making a false financial statement and served no time.

In January 1996, his landlord sought to recover massive overdue rent payments through court action, complaining that Paleologus had paid with a check that bounced. Yet again, he escaped incarceration by admitting guilt for "making and uttering fictitious instruments." Under California Penal Code 476, every person who makes, passes, utters, or publishes—with intent to defraud any other person—any fictitious or altered bill, note, or check for the payment of money or property of any real or fictitious financial institution is guilty of forgery. His long string of avoiding time behind bars was uncanny.

Paleologus had already shown his crafty ability to manipulate women. Now he emerged as an equally clever manipulator of the law, using the tool of plea bargaining. Somehow, in the new case involving the assault on Annie Olson, despite stealing the gun and her jewelry, and invading the mobile home where a young boy cowered in fear, Paleologus managed another miraculous escape. He and his attorney won the skirmish to have the charges of stalking, grand theft, and false imprisonment dismissed "in the furtherance of justice." Confessing guilt only in the charge of first-degree burglary, he appeared contrite while the judge sentenced him to six years in prison, all *suspended*! No prison time. The defendant would, however, be subjected to probation for 104 months.

The threat of going to prison for violating probation apparently didn't worry Paleologus very much. Just a few weeks after the court hearing, he targeted another beautiful woman.

In a trendy Hollywood bar, Dawn Cooper (pseudonym) and her friend Karen Miles (pseudonym) finished their drinks close to midnight on Friday, August 28, 1998. As they left and walked up Sunset Boulevard, Paleologus, dressed in a tailored business suit and tie, caught up from behind, complimented them, and opened his well-practiced spiel. He introduced himself as a producer from the Disney studios and said he was searching for a specific type of model to use in promotional media for a new James Bond film. Would they be interested in trying out?

Dawn later described it. "He was basically talking to me. Karen was standing there. I said I wanted to know more about it, so he described different aspects of it. It was more of a poster thing than acting. And I said I might be interested in talking about it." The "producer," Dawn said, "was very professional, dressed in a suit, and didn't seem to have been drinking at all. He was very soft-spoken, really nice." The whole approach, she recalled, appeared legitimate. "Just the way he was talking about the movie, aspects of the industry, he seemed like he knew all about it."

Victor set the hook by mentioning that Dawn would be well paid if selected. She would probably have to take a couple of months off from her regular job. If she was seriously interested, he proposed, they could meet on Sunday morning at the Ritz-Carlton in Marina del Rey. Oh, and by the way, Dawn should wear a black miniskirt, nude-colored panty hose, and black high heels. The audition would be "closed," so she should come alone.

Intrigued and excited, Dawn kept the appointment at eight-thirty Sunday morning, wearing the required clothing, plus a jacket as protection against the ocean chill. She met Paleologus in the hotel lobby. "It was a huge room with windows overlooking the harbor, a bunch of tables, chairs, and couches in there." They sat on one of the couches and Paleologus handed her a portfolio of papers describing the opportunity. She glanced through the convincingly realistic material that included "the pay, what the movie was about, and who was in it." He spent several minutes describing the various poses in which she would be photographed. Whatever doubts Dawn might have felt evaporated.

The next step, Paleologus told her, would be to meet his colleague, an important woman in the motion picture business, at an office on San Vincente Boulevard, about seven miles north, in Brentwood.

Paleologus offered to take Dawn there in his vehicle, but she declined, preferring to drive her own car and meet him. She had no way of knowing that the address was an empty restaurant where he had sexually assaulted a woman two years ago.

Dawn arrived in about twenty minutes and saw Victor standing near the entrance. He pushed the door open and escorted her inside. The audible click when he closed the door made her wonder if he had locked it, and why. The interior puzzled Dawn. "It was dark. There was one light, three chairs, no tables, nothing in there at all except some stacked chairs in one corner." Feeling a little nervous, she accepted his invitation to sit. The woman who would conduct the audition, he said, should arrive shortly. Dawn asked to use the restroom while they waited. He pointed it out. "It was a little bit strange," she recalled. "Really dark. There were no lights in the bathroom. And there was a little window into another room that looked like a kitchen."

When she returned to the dusty, vacant room, Paleologus suggested they review some of the poses that would be required, since his colleague would want to see her try them. Okay, Dawn nodded, and took off her jacket. In her recollection, she said, "one pose was sitting with my legs crossed. He was kind of positioning my legs so the ankles were close together. He was making a real big deal about them being close together. Then he described another pose where I would be sitting on the floor with my legs crossed and my ankles close together again. I sat down on the floor the way he told me to. At that point, he pulled something out of his pocket and tied it around my ankles." She described it as either a thick black cord or a nylon strap with a buckle, which enabled him to cinch it up tight.

Appalled by the sudden aggressive move, Dawn protested that the binding was uncomfortable and reached to remove it. Paleologus, saying nothing, grabbed her shoulders and pushed her backward so that she lay flat on the floor. "He looked crazy, really scary, and angry. His eyes were huge and they looked almost bloodshot."

He broke his silence by ordering her to calm down, not to struggle or even move. But Dawn had no intention of passively surrendering. "I was struggling a lot, trying to fight him off, but I couldn't move my legs very well. He was trying to keep me down. He took off his necktie and tied it around one of my wrists and was trying to get it on my other wrist. I kept struggling, and he brought the tie close to my neck." Breathing heavily, Paleologus pulled one end of the necktie around her throat. Dawn forced her free hand under the ligature to prevent being choked.

"Then he rolled me over onto my stomach. I tried to scream a few times and he put his hand over my mouth. He yelled at me not to scream and to stop fighting, and told me I wasn't going to get away. He seemed very angry at that point."

With his left hand over Dawn's mouth, Paleologus slipped his right arm under her stomach and pulled her upward against his own body. Wedging her in that position, he withdrew the left hand and used it to lift her short skirt. "He pulled down my panty hose to my knees and went for my underwear. He was trying to get his hands between my legs, but I kept struggling."

Lowering his voice, Paleologus hissed words repugnant to Dawn. Telling her how beautiful she was, he said, "The first time I saw you, I knew I couldn't control myself."

Unable to see her attacker, Dawn heard something else that raised her fear to panic. The light clank of metal and the rustle of cloth gave her a mental vision of his belt being removed, and the distinctive sound of a zipper left no doubt what he was doing. "I kept trying to move my legs, kicking back and forth, trying to loosen the cord, and trying to pull away. He kept pulling me up against him, and I would go back down, back and forth."

Her adrenaline-driven motions finally worked when she felt the restraint on her ankles release. She lunged forward, gained her footing, and bolted toward the door. But her assailant reacted with equal speed and blocked her path. It turned into a thrust-and-parry contest of lunging, sidestepping, blocking, and retreating. Paleologus kept urging her not to scream and to calm down because he wasn't going to allow her to leave. She recalled him saying, "I know this must be traumatizing to you, but I'm not going to let you get out."

Backing up to catch her breath, Dawn managed to scoop up her shoes, which had fallen off, her jacket, and her purse. She pleaded with him, promising not to scream if he would just let her go home. Determined to avoid another wrestling match, she gripped one of the spiked-heel shoes to use as a weapon. Cautiously she eased toward the door again. "He wouldn't let me near it. We fought again, with me trying to get to the door and him pushing me away. And I finally—he had his arm out a little bit—and I ducked underneath his arm and slipped past him." She sprinted full speed to her car and sped away. Unfamiliar with the area, she was lost, but relieved to be out of there with no major damage inflicted on her body other than a few scrapes and bruises. As soon as she felt safe, she made a call to the police.

Arrested soon afterward, Paleologus made bail. While he waited for trial to be held in July 1999, he fell behind on his car payments. The Marina del Rey dealer repossessed the vehicle, and while cleaning it out, he found a remarkable array of interesting items in the trunk, including black high-heel pumps, panty hose, neckties, a common sexual lubricant, sections of rope, a water bottle, and a penis-shaped dildo. Apparently, Paleologus felt no embarrassment about these possessions, since he showed up the next day to claim them.

For the crimes against Dawn Cooper, the District Attorney lodged three felony charges against Paleologus: (1) assault with intent to commit rape, (2) attempted forcible rape, and (3) false imprisonment by violence. Before the main trial, a judge held hearings regarding the probation previously imposed on Paleologus. Cooper and her friend Karen Miles testified, and the judge found that the defendant had violated terms of his probation. In the subsequent trial, once again in July, it at first appeared that Paleologus, like a snake crawling out of its own skin, would again evade punishment. The attempted rape and false imprisonment counts were dismissed "in the furtherance of justice."

This time, though, his Teflon luck failed. He was convicted of felony assault against Dawn Cooper, and sentenced to serve two years in prison. For violating his long-standing probation, the judge tacked on another six years. Facing a total of eight years, Paleologus was remanded to custody of the California State Prison system at the end of July 1999.

He served nearly 3½ years before being paroled on January 20, 2003. Four days later, he approached Susan Murphy, complimented her beauty, and said she would be perfect to model in a James Bond promotion. And only three more weeks passed before Kristi Johnson went to a "James Bond audition" and vanished.

Paleologus now sat in Los Angeles County Jail, accused of grand theft auto. This charge stemmed from an incredible stunt he pulled in the early evening of Monday, February 17, two days after Kristi disappeared.

At about 6:00 P.M., wearing blue jeans and a hooded light brown overcoat, he walked into a BMW dealership on Wilshire Boulevard, Beverly Hills. After inspecting a few models on the showroom floor, Paleologus spoke to a sales manager about purchasing a new BMW, a metallic blue X5 sports utility vehicle. Giving his name as "Robert Morton," he worked his usual smooth con man routine, spewing false statements with well-practiced ease. He answered the dealer's questions and helped fill out all the necessary forms, but claimed that he had left his driver's license and any other photo identification at home. In the finance manager's office, Paleologus continued his litany of lies, and smiled when he heard a patient explanation that the transaction could not be completed without proper identification. Could Mr. Morton return the next day with those documents, at which time he could drive out with the new luxury vehicle? Paleologus agreed and walked out of the office.

In the interim, a porter had prepared the shiny blue X5 for its new owner, and driven to a gas station to have it filled up. As he turned back into the garage entrance, he spotted the man who called himself Robert Morton standing just inside. The porter stopped and asked, "Are you taking this car tonight?"

Paleologus nodded a congenial yes.

"Please hold on just a couple of minutes," the porter requested, and trotted toward the sales manager's office for approval to release the vehicle. He left the keys in the ignition.

The manager glanced up from his paperwork to answer the coverall-clad employee, and replied, "No, he can't take it yet.

He didn't bring any identification with him." At that moment, both men looked out a window, and Morton seated himself in the X5 and drove away. Instantly, the manager called the Beverly Hills Police Department to report it.

At a few minutes before nine, uniformed officer Eric Drescher, driving a black unmarked car, received a radio call describing a suspected grand theft auto. A full description of the blue X5, with a temporary paper license number in the rear window, followed along with details about the man who had absconded with it. About five minutes after the broadcast ended, the stolen car passed, traveling in the opposite direction on Wilshire Boulevard. Drescher made a quick U-turn, caught up, and followed without lights or siren, waiting for other units to assist him.

The blue SUV turned north on La Cienega with Drescher right behind, then angled left on San Vincente. Two blocks later, it wheeled left into the entry of a multistory parking structure connected to the Beverly Center shopping mall, at the intersection of Third Street and San Vincente Boulevard. The officer followed, along with a newly arrived black-and-white patrol car. When Paleologus caught sight of the police vehicles, he accelerated. After speeding up a curved ramp, he skidded to a halt, leaped from the car, and sprinted away, ignoring shouted orders to stop.

The police set up a perimeter around the mall, and two of them spotted a man wearing blue jeans and a hooded light brown overcoat leaving San Vincente Boulevard and walking westbound on the sidewalk along Third Street. By this time in his checkered career, Paleologus probably should have known to stay away from San Vincente Boulevard, the street on which the vacant restaurant was located, where he had sexually assaulted two women.

One of the cops yelled a command at Paleologus to stop, but instead he dashed across Third Street, barely avoiding traffic rushing in both directions. With uniformed officers in close pursuit, he bolted into a sushi restaurant, ran all the way through, and reached for the back-door knob. One of the cops grabbed the flapping overcoat tail and ordered him to hit the floor, facedown.

Paleologus wilted, turned around as if surrendering, hesitated, and opened his mouth to protest. In the police report, the arresting officer noted: *We assisted the suspect to the ground.* After a moment or two of "passive resistance," in which Paleologus refused to put his hands behind his back as directed, the officers gave him a little more help: *We pulled the suspect's hands one by one behind his back and handcuffed him without further incident or injuries.*

After employees of the BMW dealership arrived and confirmed Paleologus as the man who drove away in the blue SUV, the officers placed him under arrest. A "pat down" to search for weapons revealed that he hadn't forgotten his wallet after all, as he had claimed at the agency. An officer pulled it from his left inside coat pocket and found a California driver's license, in the name of Victor Paleologus, with a photo of him, and a residential address on La Cienega Boulevard. It also contained driver's licenses, checks, credit cards, and other documents owned by several other people, including Robert Morton, the name he had used in credit applications at the BMW agency. One driver's license and credit card belonged to a man who lived on Warbler Way in the Hollywood Hills, and a few blank checks bore a resident's name from Hancock Avenue, just a few blocks from Paleologus's residence. Both places had been shown to Paleologus by a real estate agent. A third driver's license and credit card in his wallet had been reported stolen by a guest of the Century Plaza Hotel, taken while he used the spa inside.

The officers "assisted" Paleologus to a seat in the back

of a patrol car and transported him to the Beverly Hills police station.

Detective Obenchain completed reading the computer printouts reflecting the criminal history of Victor Paleologus. Certainly, she realized, it appeared that he could be the guy who lured Kristi at the Century City mall. Yet, she couldn't rule out the possibility that someone else had done it. Anyone could have adopted the same phony scam, perhaps another ex-convict who had heard Paleologus bragging in prison about its effectiveness.

Two victims, Dawn Cooper and Susan Murphy, had accused Paleologus of offering them duplicitous opportunities to be James Bond girls. Obenchain wondered how many other starstruck young women he had approached. With any luck, some of them might see the media coverage and come forward.

For the moment, though, she wanted nothing more than to find Kristi Johnson alive and well.

CHAPTER 6

THE FACE OF
A CON MAN

Kristi Johnson hadn't always wanted to be a part of the magical, glamor world of Hollywood. To the contrary, at one point she announced that she wanted to be an engineer, and enrolled in college to pursue that ambition.

After her parents moved from Los Gatos, California, to Saugatuck, Michigan, while she still wore diapers, Kristi and her family lived far from urban crises, crowds, and crime. In the tiny community situated on the southwestern shore of Lake Michigan, she developed happily in a comfortable, upper-middle-class environment. While rocking her to sleep, Kristi's mother would sing a special song, "You Are So Beautiful to Me," a tune they both would always treasure. Kristi later adopted another melody as her favorite—"Hero" by Enrique Iglesias, a number one Top 40 hit in 2001.

A self-confident, bubbly child, she played with her older brother, Derek, in a safe, secure world. Her sky blue eyes and

straw blond hair attracted compliments even then. Raised in
the religious faith of her parents, the Episcopal Church,
Kristi, according to her father, "was a true believer and shared
God's spirit."

Kirk Johnson proudly observed that his little girl, by the
time she reached the age of twelve, started finding part-time
jobs. He later commented that she had a "little trouble" holding on to them, though.

Her idyllic life changed directions when her parents di-
vorced. She loved both of them, and would divide time living
with each one. She cried when her brother, Derek, left to join
the U.S. Air Force.

In high school, Kristi discovered athletic skills, particularly
in water sports. During summer visits to her grandmother in
Santa Maria, California, she often found her way to the broad
sand dunes and surf at Pismo Beach, and the picturesque curl-
ing waves at Santa Barbara. "She loved the beach," said her
mother, "and told me how beautiful it was and how much she
enjoyed being in California."

Following her 1999 graduation from Saugatuck High
School, in a class of only sixty-two seniors, Kristi enrolled at
Western Michigan University, the state's fourth-largest higher-
education institution. She attended the school in Kalamazoo,
forty miles southeast of Saugatuck, no more than two semes-
ters. Campus life was okay, and she enjoyed social activities,
such as attending dances and a rave party produced by
PLURkids. During spring break, she went to Florida with girlfriends, and visited a tattoo parlor, where she had a geometri-
cally designed hibiscus flower inked on her lower back.

Dividing time between her parents, Kristi worked as an administrative assistant for a drilling contractor in Holland,
Michigan, and in management for two different retail outlets
in Saugatuck.

Upon returning to the college, Kristi found the bone-

chilling winds from Lake Michigan and the icy winter un-
bearable, causing her to think often of the warm, sunny days
on the West Coast. Her mother said, "She always wanted to
go back to California where there is more opportunity and
better weather."

After one year at Kalamazoo, Kristi made the decision to
migrate west. In 2000, she moved to Santa Maria and lived
with her paternal grandmother. She quickly found work as
a systems administrator with an electric supply company,
and enrolled at the city's community college. The classes
she took were aimed at transferring to California Polytechnic University, San Luis Obispo. She planned to become
an engineer.

While visiting that campus one day, about twenty-five
miles north of Santa Maria, Kristi stumbled upon a part-time
job that would make a big impact on her life. She landed
work as a security guard on the set of a motion picture production starring Sandra Bullock, Ben Chaplin, and Michael
Pitt. Her duties included exercising crowd control procedures,
assuring the protection of expensive equipment, and in her
words, "implementing security standards for Sandra Bullock
and Michael Pitt." The whole ambience of moviemaking
thrilled and fascinated Kristi, and she wondered if her future
might be in that industry.

The film *Murder by Numbers* had an eerie plot, according
to media publicity releases: *The body of a young woman is
found in a ditch in the woods of the small California coastal
town of San Benito. Cassie Mayweather, the seasoned homicide detective and tenacious crime scene specialist, is assigned to the case. . . . The detectives make their way through
microscopic hints of evidence, which seem to indicate a
random act of violence, but Cassie has a gut feeling that there
is more to this murder than meets the eye.*

It hit theaters in April 2002, ten months before Kristi would vanish.

While she worked among movie stars in San Luis Obispo, Kristi had no way of knowing that a man named Victor Paleologus resided behind bars, just one mile north of the city limits, on State Highway 1, waiting for a parole that would finally come in January 2003.

Influenced by the movie experience, and wishing to expand her opportunities, Kristi moved to West Hollywood, close to the world of motion picture production. She enrolled at the Make-up Designory, in Burbank, to study film industry techniques used in making actors' appearances fit their movie roles. The specialized school, known as MUD, founded in 1997, had relocated from its original roots in North Hollywood to a larger facility in Burbank, and publicized its proximity to well-known studios, including Warner Brothers, Walt Disney, NBC, ABC, as well as its propinquity to Universal and Dreamworks.

While attending MUD, logging more than four hundred hours in classes, Kristi used her training on jobs with a half-dozen small film production companies and several fashion model firms. In an e-mail to her father, July 2002, she wrote, *I was so nervous when I got down here, but I knew this is what I wanted . . . so I stuck with it. And now I'm on my way.*

Her mother recalled Kristi's experience during that period. "She was working as a makeup artist living in West Hollywood, but it was a tough life and it was hard finding work. About that time, she decided a four-year degree was something she wanted."

Searching for more substantial employment, Kristi found work at the cellular communications company in Marina del Rey. With her mother's help, she located the pleasant apartment in Santa Monica and moved in with two female roommates. To continue her education, Kristi began taking night classes at Santa Monica College. Originally planning a transfer to Cal Poly, she now set her goal to attend UCLA for a bachelor's degree.

But on Saturday, February 15, 2003, while shopping at the Century City mall, her old dreams of working in the make-believe world of movies came alive again when a stranger admired her beauty and offered her the opportunity to audition for a part in a James Bond film promotional project.

The next step for Detective Obenchain required a current photo of Victor Paleologus. She easily obtained one from the state prison system, which takes pictures of all parolees just before they are released. The shot of Paleologus brought to mind a comment made by Roberto Marquez, the parking valet at the St. Regis Hotel, when he described the man who left Kristi's Miata as a "Rambo" type. The features and especially the hairstyle vaguely resembled that of actor Sylvester Stallone.

Selecting five other color mug shots of men who bore similar characteristics to Paleologus, Obenchain prepared a "six-pack," by attaching the 2½-inch by 1¾-inch pictures to a sheet of paper, equally spaced, with bold numerals from 1 to 6 under each one. Paleologus occupied the third position.

By telephone, she contacted Susan Murphy, who agreed to come down to the police station, view the six-pack, and see if she could identify any of the men in connection with the one who called himself Victor Thomas. Susan readily agreed and arrived at five-forty that afternoon. According to procedure, the detective read aloud a witness admonishment, which was printed on the back of the six-pack sheet:

I am going to show you a group of photographs. The fact that the photographs are shown to you should not influence your judgement. You should neither conclude nor guess that

*the photographs contain a picture of the person who committed
the crime. You do not have to identify anyone. It is just as important to free innocent persons from suspicion as it is to identify
those who are guilty. Please keep in mind that hair styles,
beards, and moustaches are easily changed. Photographs do
not always depict the true complexion of a subject, i.e. they may
be lighter or darker. Please do not discuss the case with other
witnesses or indicate in any way to other witnesses, whether you
have identified someone.*

Susan stated that she understood, and Obenchain placed
the six-pack on a table in front of her. The room heated up
with Susan's instant surge of tension. She trembled, pointed
her finger to number three, and snapped, "That's him! I'm
one hundred percent sure."

"What makes you so certain?" Obenchain asked.

"It's that square look on his forehead, and the nose, and the
dimple in his chin. I had forgotten about that." When she had
helped forensic artist Sandy Enslow prepare a composite
sketch, there had been no mention of a chin dimple. With a
blue-ink pen, she drew a circle around the picture of Victor
Paleologus, scribbled her initials next to it, and noted,
2/26/03,100% sure this is the man!

Both Obenchain and Murphy signed the admonishment on
the reverse side. Before leaving, Susan handed Obenchain a
slip of paper she had brought with her. Paleologus had used
it to write down directions for their meeting place on La
Cienega last January.

Needing another photo identification of the suspect, this
one from Mark Wilson, the man who had gone with Susan
to meet Victor on La Cienega, Detective Michael Cabrera
drove over to Burbank to meet him. Wilson had no trouble
picking out number three, but noted that Paleologus looked
"more tired" than he had when they met on that street corner.
He, too, signed the six-pack with unequivocal confidence.

A third showing of the lineup didn't work out quite as well. Detective Cabrera found the valet parking attendant at seven o'clock that same evening and read him the admonishment, both in English and in Spanish. After establishing that Marquez understood, Cabrera handed him the sheet containing six numbered photographs, with Paleologus's image in the upper right corner.

The witness wrinkled his forehead, studied each face, and drew a circle around number six in the lower right corner. The wrong man. Certainly, Marquez couldn't be faulted for his error. The individual who tossed him the Miata keys and barked, "Well, valet it then" had been in the attendant's sight no more than a few seconds, ten long days ago. Marquez had helped scores of customers since then, and couldn't keep a mental inventory of all their faces. Trying to be helpful to the police, he simply did his best and made an honest mistake.

If Marquez's error was a setback, the welcome emergence of another volunteer witness counterbalanced it. Real estate agent Charlie Simon (pseudonym), a pale, slim man in his mid-thirties, with thick black hair, dark eyes, and a gold ring dangling from his left earlobe, telephoned the Santa Monica police on that busy Wednesday, and spoke to Detective Larry Nicols. Simon had seen news reports featuring the composite sketch, and thought it resembled a potential client to whom he had shown numerous empty homes around the Hollywood area.

"His name is Victor Paleologus."

The soft-spoken agent said that Victor had walked into his office, located on Santa Monica Boulevard, about a block from La Cienega, on Friday, February 7, close to seven o'clock that evening. The events, according to Simon in subsequent interviews with Detective John Henry, revealed another amazing, prolonged con by Paleologus.

* * *

On that Friday, Paleologus told Simon that he had recently arrived from New York, where he owned a business, the "Logus Corporation," and planned to expand into the Los Angeles area. He wanted to buy a home in the price range of $500,000 to $750,000, and preferred empty places, since he wished to move in right away. A little puzzled by the request, since a purchase would still have to clear escrow whether the residence was empty or not, Simon nodded concurrence. Eager for the chance to pick up a nice commission, Simon said he'd be pleased to help, but since it was too late that day to view any properties, it would be great if Victor could come back on Saturday. Victor agreed, chatted amiably while filling out a "New Client Information Sheet," and made an appointment for eleven o'clock the next morning.

He arrived promptly and climbed into Simon's Mercedes-Benz for a tour of available homes. As many real estate agents tend to do, he selected places in a higher price range than his new client had described.

They drove up Laurel Canyon Boulevard through the hills and turned left on Lookout Mountain Avenue. At a "Y" intersection, Simon steered left onto Wonderland Avenue. After a few hundred feet, he came to another "Y," at which he twisted the wheel into a right turn, right on Wonderland Park. In the 8700 block, he braked to a halt in front of an attractive, modern structure with a FOR SALE sign posted in front. Even though it was not really empty, they went inside to look around. Simon mentioned that the owner was eager to sell and might be willing to negotiate the asking price.

They left the Wonderland Park home, drove onto Green Valley Road, and turned right on Skyline Drive, near an interesting structure resembling a castle. At the top of a narrow ridge with spectacular views, they pulled up in front of another home for sale in the 8500 block. A sign outside told them that it was an OPEN HOUSE. They entered and found another real estate agent taking his prospective buyers on a tour of the two-story villa-style home. The house had reportedly been rented to actor Laurence Fishburne until a few months ago. After their walk-through, Victor told Simon that he often jogged for exercise. This place would be perfect, said Simon, and pointed uphill to where the road dead-ended. Past that, a trail just above a steep, heavily wooded drop-off to the right made an ideal place for hiking or jogging.

Simon and his new client visited two other houses that afternoon before heading back to his office. Paleologus shook hands with Simon and said he would like to see more properties on Sunday. They set another appointment for early afternoon, allowing Simon to attend church in the morning. Victor left on foot, explaining that he planned to buy a new car in the near future. For now, he said, he could walk to his own office just a short distance away on La Cienega, a block south of Santa Monica Boulevard.

Another extensive tour of homes in the hills, examining eight different properties, took most of the day Sunday. They repeated the routine on Monday, seeing four more homes, even though looming black clouds had dumped a heavy downpour of rain, soaking the southland. This time, Simon drove several miles west to pick up Paleologus at the Century Plaza Hotel, on the corner of Constellation Boulevard and Avenue of the Stars. He understood that his client probably attended important business convention meetings there, so Simon would meet him out front in the valet parking area. The clothing Victor wore each day—jeans, tennis shoes, and a light brown hooded overcoat, with a red-and-white Swiss Army knife logo on the breast, didn't seem quite right for business, but it mattered little to the agent. Hollywood denizens seldom wore traditional business apparel.

On Tuesday, again after meeting at the Century Plaza, Simon and Paleologus looked at a half-dozen homes, including one on Warbler Way, also in the Hollywood Hills. Simon apologized because it wasn't empty, but Victor didn't seem concerned. Instead, he explained that his work would require a completely quiet environment, and asked Simon to step into the bedroom with another agent who happened to drop by. He wanted them to converse in normal voices to see if the sound traveled throughout the house. He seemed satisfied. Not long afterward, the homeowner reported the theft of his driver's license and Visa credit card.

Wednesday's expedition had to be shortened so Simon could attend church choir rehearsal, but they still visited three houses for sale. They didn't venture far on Thursday, examining one place on Hancock Avenue, only a few blocks from Paleologus's "office" on La Cienega. The owner of that house later discovered that some blank checks and documents were missing from his desk.

Another short trip on Friday, Valentine's Day, February 14, rounded out the week of house hunting.

In reporting these events to the police, Simon at first confused a couple of the dates, but later clarified it, and insisted that they did not meet on Saturday, February 15. "I was at home waiting for someone to come over to the house for voice lessons, but they didn't show up. Two of my friends came over and we were all together at the house until noon or so. When they left, I walked over to a nearby restaurant to have lunch. When I returned home, I forwarded some e-mails to my office computer, about a cruise I was planning to take." He confided that he was trying to keep the cruise a secret from his roommate. "At the office, after retrieving the e-mail,

I surfed the Internet, trying to find information about the Logus Corporation, but I wasn't very successful."

That Saturday evening, said Simon, he had plans to meet a friend at eight o'clock, so he went home to get ready. Asked again if he saw Paleologus that day, he adamantly denied it.

They did, however, resume the search for homes on Sunday evening. After driving past a few of them, the two men stopped at an electronics store, where Paleologus wanted to shop for a new television set. Simon left Victor at the store, close to 8:40 P.M., and returned home.

They spent a final day together on Monday. Simon again picked Victor up at the Century Plaza Hotel, and drove to the real estate office to prepare an offer on one of the houses. Sitting at a desk, Paleologus commented, "I'm tired of taking cabs. I think I'll buy a car. Is there a BMW or Mercedes dealership anywhere around here?"

"Sure," said Simon, "there's a BMW store right over on Wilshire. If you want, I'll give you a ride over there."

At about six o'clock that evening, Simon dropped his client off at the curb of the BMW agency and drove back to his office. A couple of hours later, Simon received a call from Victor, who said he needed a ride home because he'd forgotten to bring a photo ID and couldn't take the new car without it. But, just as Simon started to leave, his phone rang again. Victor announced that he had been able to take the car after all, so he no longer needed a ride.

On that long, extraordinary Wednesday, jammed with amazing developments in the search for Kristi Johnson, Virginia Obenchain remained at her desk long after her shift should have ended. She wanted to finish writing a search warrant and affidavit spelling out all of the supporting information. Not a simple process, it required a detailed statement of every known fact about the case and the ensuing investigation. She typed six single-spaced pages summarizing the events up to that evening, and requested authority from a judge to perform two searches. First, she wrote, she wanted to seek and seize *Paleologus's clothing from L.A. County Jail because it may contain evidence related to this crime. . . .* Second, she asked to search all of the homes visited by Paleologus with real estate agent Charlie Simon, *because the suspect in this case may have used one of these locations to commit a crime against Ms. Johnson.* She added, *I also believe that based upon the above stated facts that Paleologus is involved in the abduction, sexual assault and/or murder of Kristine Johnson.*

In her heart, Obenchain prayed that the last dreaded part of that assertion would turn out to be untrue.

CHAPTER 7

VIGIL

Thursday, February 27, dawned in abject gloom for Terry Hall, Kirk Johnson, and other people who loved Kristi Johnson. They had hoped and prayed that she would be with them to celebrate her twenty-second birthday. Instead, her absence remained a painful mystery for the twelfth interminable day.

Hall arrived in Santa Monica that morning in preparation for conducting a candlelight vigil to honor Kristi. The worried mother had planned every detail, and scheduled it for seven o'clock that evening at St. Augustine by-the-Sea Episcopal Church on Fourth Street in Santa Monica.

For Virginia Obenchain, the investigative process consumed most of the day. She accompanied Detectives Henry, Almada, Cabrera, and Murphy to serve the search warrant at the building on La Cienega where Paleologus had been living since his parole from prison. A pair of Los Angles Sheriff's Department criminalists, Dale Falicon and Alex Strauser, joined them for the probe.

At the building's entry, near a large empty room that had

once been a restaurant, Cabrera knocked and announced their presence, but heard no answer. Two more attempts raised no one, so they forced the door and entered. The interior appeared to be unused office space rather than residential. The officers climbed one flight of stairs and fanned out through several rooms, including a tiny cubicle Paleologus had been occupying. Someone had recently restuccoed the walls and painted them. Could it be to remove or cover bloodstains? The absence of any electric lighting in the rooms made the search even more difficult.

The officers collected a variety of items most people would regard as rubbish, but to detectives, it might well be crucial evidence. It included a magazine, cigarette butts, threads, and hairs. In a basement containing Paleologus's stored luggage, Cabrera gathered clothing belonging to the suspect, while Almada found several empty shopping bags from Bloomingdale's, Guess, and Macy's. They would be processed for fingerprints. A few envelopes and the magazine bore addresses and labels of the Century Plaza Hotel and Spa. Increasingly, it became apparent that the suspect liked to hang out there among affluent patrons. Some of the stolen ID documents found in his wallet had been reported missing in the spa.

Before any of the seized items were touched, or bagged and tagged, one of the officers photographed each one in its original position. All of it would be examined in a lab for trace evidence.

The building owner had known Paleologus for several years. The owner's son showed up on the premises during the police search, and spoke to Detectives Cabrera and Murphy. He said that he knew Paleologus, and confirmed that he had been living there in recent weeks.

Information from this man filled in several pieces of the puzzle about Paleologus's past. He had been part owner of a restaurant on San Vincente Boulevard, where he had sexually assaulted two women. The building was owned by the individual's father. After it closed, Paleologus, with a partner, had opened a replacement restaurant in the La Cienega building. When Paleologus left, en route to prison, the business closed. Paleologus claimed that he had been sentenced for credit card fraud, actually committed by a partner, but Paleologus had taken the blame for it. "When he was released," said the owner's son, "he came back here and asked my father if he could stay for a while. My father let him move in, but it agitated him when the guy started hanging around in our office, using the telephone, the computer, and snooping around. I even tried to help him build a Web page for a business he wanted to start called Logus Corporation."

Detective Cabrera wondered aloud if they had seen any women Paleologus might have brought around.

"No," he said, "I haven't seen him with any woman since he had the restaurant in operation, a few years ago. Maybe my father would know more because he had more contact with him than I did." He gave Cabrera a number to call his father, Art Vartanian (pseudonym).

As soon as the senior Vartanian answered, he grew angry and belligerent, yelling, cursing, and denying that he knew Paleologus very well. "He used to be a tenant of mine in Brentwood (the restaurant on San Vincente) and again in West Hollywood (the restaurant on La Cienega). He got out of prison recently and came by to see me. He bought me lunch, and that was it." Asked if Victor had been living in any properties owned by him, Vartanian growled an adamant no.

Cabrera had seen evidence that Paleologus certainly did live on the second floor, and rephrased his question. The vitriolic reply, again laced with "cussing," stiffened his denial. Asking the man to calm down, Cabrera told him the son had already confirmed that Paleologus lived there. Faced with that news, Vartanian admitted it, explaining that when Paleologus came to see him, fresh out of prison and asking for a job, he'd felt pity. "I couldn't offer him a job, but when he asked to stay on the premises until he could get on his feet, I felt sorry for him. He had been a prior tenant, so I decided to let him stay for a while. Recently, though, I noticed he was spending a lot of time in my office, and I didn't like it. I told him that he would have to find another place to stay, soon. And I haven't seen him for a few days."

"Have you ever seen him with any women?" Cabrera asked.

"Yes," Vartanian replied. He described an incident that occurred "several years ago," when Paleologus had brought a beautiful woman to the empty restaurant on San Vincente after telling her he was working for a movie producer and wanted to introduce them to each other. Later, according to Vartanian, Paleologus had talked to him about it and said, "I really fucked up. I lied to that girl and she got pissed off. But I did not rape that girl." Vartanian couldn't remember the woman's name. But Cabrera realized that it was probably either Annie Olson, who reported Paleologus for sexually assaulting her in 1996, or Dawn Cooper, who made the same charge in 1998.

While Obenchain and her team searched the building on La Cienega, two other detectives focused their efforts on the possibility that Kristi Johnson might be imprisoned somewhere, or even worse, that she had been murdered and her body stuffed into a hiding place. Everything so far, all circumstantial evidence, suggested that she was on her way to meet Paleologus before she vanished. Could he have taken her to one of the two dozen homes he had visited with real estate agent Charlie Simon?

On the chance that one of these locations could be a crime scene, or a place of imprisonment for Kristi, the investigators

asked Simon to help by leading them to each site. They drove
the winding, narrow Hollywood Hills roads all day long and
stopped repeatedly to execute the search warrant granted by
a judge. Included in the houses they examined was one
perched on a high ridge called Skyline Drive. The officers,
though, had no way of knowing that it was the one for which
Kristi had so desperately searched, and found, shortly after
sunset twelve days earlier.

In the county jail, Detective John Henry executed a warrant for "seizure and search of any property" held in storage
under the booking of Victor Paleologus. He collected the
clothing that Paleologus had been wearing during his arrest,
and found the cell phone he'd carried with him. Examining
the phone, Henry saw that its memory held a record of calling a certain number at 11:49 P.M., February 15, the night
Kristi disappeared.

Henry called the number and spoke with a man who identified himself as Willie Craven (pseudonym). Answering the
detective's questions, Craven said that he worked at a drugstore near the corner of Santa Monica Boulevard and La
Cienega. Henry recognized the address as being only one
block from the building where Paleologus had been living,
visited by Obenchain's team that same day, within just a few
steps of the site where Susan Murphy had met with Victor.

Wondering what connection Paleologus had with Craven,
Henry asked when they could meet to discuss it in more
detail. The detective particularly wanted to find out why
Victor had called him so late on the night Kristi disappeared.
In a hesitant, quaking voice, Craven said an interview would
have to wait for a few days, until March 3, since he was going
out of town that night. Henry made it clear that he would
follow up on that date.

* * *

While detectives worked overtime on the evening of February 27, Police Chief Butts and Terry Hall stood outside the Episcopal church in Santa Monica and spoke to reporters before the vigil started. Regarding the ongoing investigation of Victor Paleologus, Butts announced, "We have a strong focus and a viable lead, but we have less than probable cause to make an arrest at this time." He did not name the "person of interest."

The information officer, Lieutenant Frank Fabrega, filled in a little more information, stating that the tip line had been productive. Manned by cadets of the LAPD Police Academy, it had brought in an average of twenty to twenty-five calls every hour, from as far away as Connecticut. He also revealed that search warrants had been served in the case, but gave no details.

Hall spoke of her missing daughter. "She is so beautiful, inside and out. When she comes into a room, it just lights the place up. She's a wonderful spirit. I love and adore Kristi so much, I just want to hear that she is all right." Hall struggled to keep her voice from faltering. "The minute she was born, she was a special, special child. She is strong. . . ." Momentarily pausing again to compose herself, Hall delivered a message directly to Kristi. "We are working so hard to bring you back. . . . What is happening to you won't last forever. Remember that you are strong."

Pleading with whoever took Kristi away, Hall asked that she be returned unharmed. She also encouraged the public to continue calling in with tips. "We need to keep the momentum going. I've always had hope that Kristi will come back safely and I'm hoping that we will soon get that break we need to find her."

Butts, too, addressed the captor. "Find it in your heart and return this beautiful young woman to her family."

The mother and the police chief entered the church together. They sat side by side.

The moving ceremony opened with soft instrumental music. From the pulpit, prayers by Reverend Hartshorn Murphy followed. Guests filled every pew and bowed their heads to the intonation, "O God of peace . . . with hope in our hearts and courage in our breast, we give thanks to you for the birth and life of Kristi Johnson. And we put our trust in you, o God, who can do more than we can ever ask for. . . ."

Following a reading of lessons from the Bible, a vocalist filled the chamber with a lullaby that Hall had so often sang to her infant daughter, "You Are So Beautiful to Me." Chief Butts could be seen consoling Hall as they listened to the familiar lyrics.

After additional reading from the Bible, Terry Hall spoke to the assembly, sharing beloved thoughts about her daughter. On this special day, she said, she had planned to celebrate with Kristi by skating together along a paved path on the beach, and then going out to shop. She prayed for her daughter's safe return and for guidance "through these very difficult moments."

The reverend thanked her, and presented his "homily" in which he recognized Kristi's birthday and wished that it had not been overshadowed by the pain of her mysterious absence. The usual joy of birthday celebrations, he said, always includes the fun of eating and drinking, sometimes too much. But this night, he worried, ". . . we suspect she is not in a place of joy."

Again the vocalist stood to sing, presenting Kristi's favorite piece of music, "Hero." She had often expressed how much she liked the tune by Enrique Iglesias. The next prayer asked God for Kristi's safety and well-being, and "the protection of her heart, mind, body, and soul," along with "guidance for police officers, detectives, and all those searching for Kristi."

The ceremony, nearly an hour long, concluded with a processional. Each person carried a candle and filed through the south door into the courtyard. Encircled around a tree, they lit the candles and joined together in singing "Amazing Grace."

In Holland, Michigan, Kristi's father, Kirk Johnson, attended a similar vigil at which fervent hopes and prayers for her deliverance were offered.

Victor Paleologus, in the Los Angeles County Jail, sat waiting to see if the police could link him to the disappearance of Kristi Johnson. Maybe he wouldn't have to worry about it. For the past few days, he had been searching for a way to escape, and had found it. The time had come to put his plan into action.

CHAPTER 8

EXIGENCY

On the thirteenth day of Kristi Johnson's absence, February 28, Detective Obenchain, with guidance from the district attorney, decided that an "exigency" applied to this case. She observed, "There was still a chance that she could be alive and in dire need of medical assistance." At Obenchain's request, Detective Almada prepared a removal order for Victor Paleologus, to be read immediately by a judge. By noon, it was approved. Almada, with Detective Cabrera, arrived a short time later at the county jail in downtown L.A., planning on driving the suspect back to the Santa Monica police headquarters for questioning.

An hour later, Cabrera called Obenchain with alarming news: Paleologus was missing. A full lockdown of the men's jail section had been ordered and immediately activated. An intensive search for the absent inmate occupied all available staff members. They carefully checked identification wristbands on each man in custody.

Paleologus's great escape lasted only about two hours. A

sheriff's deputy found him hiding in the elevator area of the basement kitchen. A subsequent investigation brought forth three inmates who talked about Paleologus's behavior prior to his attempted breakout.

According to the first informant, who worked in the basement, Paleologus had claimed that he needed to get out of jail because he was facing the gas chamber. He offered $5,000 if the worker would face the other way while Paleologus hid in a large trash bin. No, the inmate had said. It wouldn't work because the sheriff's deputies who guarded the jail used long iron rods to poke into the trash bins. An alternative had been proposed, in which the two men would exchange wristbands, allowing Paleologus freedom to move about in the basement. The informant again refused.

A second inmate also refused the request to exchange wristbands. And a third one, who couldn't speak English, described through an interpreter how Paleologus had gestured the same offer by pointing alternately to their respective wristbands. No, he had said, because *"Yo no quiero ningúna problemas,"* meaning "I don't want any problems."

Caught and returned to his cell, Paleologus faced additional charges. First, though, Detectives Almada and Cabrera took charge of him for transport to Santa Monica.

The investigators knew in advance that Paleologus would probably deny knowing anything about Kristi Johnson's disappearance, and refuse to speak without the presence of an attorney. But if any chance existed of coaxing information from him that might lead to finding her, the officers had to give it a try.

It is commonly believed that when an arrested suspect requests the presence of an attorney, the interview is automatically ended. The widely known 1966 Miranda decision by the

U.S. Supreme Court, and the associated advisory given to suspects before they are questioned, as seen in countless movies and television programs, has turned into an icon of American law enforcement. It stemmed from the 1963 arrest in Arizona of a small-time thief named Ernesto Miranda, who had snatched $8 from the victim. Police officers soon nabbed him. Miranda not only admitted stealing the money, but confessed to kidnapping and raping a young woman just a few days earlier. Tried and convicted, he was sentenced to twenty years in prison. Subsequent appeals, based on the police failure to provide a lawyer for Miranda during questioning, finally landed in the nation's highest court. In a 5–4 decision, the justices overturned Miranda's conviction, and set new constitutional rules from which the well-known Miranda advisory evolved.

A second trial for Miranda, in which his confession did not come forth as evidence, resulted in another guilty verdict, and he served eleven years in prison. Four years after his 1972 parole, he died from stab wounds suffered during a fight. Police soon arrested his assailant, and in a strange twist of fate, the man was reportedly released after refusing to talk to police—under his Miranda rights.

The Supreme Court's decision specified that the person in custody must, prior to investigation, be clearly informed that he (or she) has the right to remain silent, and that anything he says may be used against him in court. The individual must also be clearly informed of the right to consult a lawyer and to have that lawyer present during interrogation. If the suspect is indigent, a lawyer will be appointed free of charge.

The entire court finding has been controversial for decades, and subject to additional legal hearings and decisions. One element has caused endless sticky problems for police investigators. It revolves around the issue of trying to gain information that could conceivably save the life of a kidnap victim being held captive. If the suspect knows where that victim is, should investigators be disallowed from continuing the interrogation, even if a lawyer is requested? Common sense says that saving a life should take top priority.

In the *Miranda* v. *Arizona* written decision, one short paragraph appears to deal with this issue. It states: *If the individual indicates, prior to or during questioning, that he wishes to remain silent, the interrogation must cease. . . . If he states that he wants an attorney, the questioning must cease until an attorney is present.*

It should be remembered that the edict is a constitutional interpretation, not a state or federal code. Basically, the court's decision simply means that information gained in violation of the Miranda guidelines cannot, for the most part, be used in court against the defendant. Yet, an exception to this also exists. If the defendant chooses to testify in trial, the prosecution may, within limits, use that information in cross-examination to impeach the defendant's direct testimony.

In a subsequent 1984 decision, the Supreme Court dealt with continued interrogation, beyond the Miranda requirements. They established a "public safety" exception when "exigent circumstances" require protection of the public. The new interpretation noted: *it will not be difficult for police officers to apply because in each case it will be circumscribed by the exigency which justifies it. . . .*

If a law enforcement officer elects to continue the questioning after a suspect demands legal representation, especially if the purpose is to save a life, it seldom results in any administrative or legal redress, other than excluding from trial the information gained. The great majority of officers who use this "exigency" exception do it with clear, common sense, and reserve it for special cases in which their primary goal is to rescue someone whose life may be in serious danger. A conviction in court is secondary to this purpose.

Obenchain and Henry understood this when they faced Victor Paleologus in an interview room, and read him the standard Miranda advisory. Also, his arrest had been for grand theft auto, and for nothing related to Kristi Johnson. Most of the questions asked of Paleologus came from John Henry.

Dressed in orange-colored jail-issued clothing, Paleologus hadn't shaved recently and wore his usual glum expression as he accepted Henry's invitation to sit in a brown chair. Obenchain wondered if the stubbly beard was intended to change his appearance so he couldn't be identified in a live lineup.

Detective Henry opened the questioning with a congenial, "How you doing, partner?"

"Good, how you doing?"

"I'm all right. I'm going to be doin' better, hopefully, if you tell me something that I'm dyin' to find out. Victor . . ."

"Yes."

"I don't know what you—what all you did in terms of Beverly Hills. Okay? I don't even want to talk to you about them. They've got their thing, I've got mine. I work in missing persons. I'm looking for a missing person." Henry slid a color photograph of Kristi Johnson across the table, and asked, "Have you seen this young lady?"

Barely glancing at the picture, Paleologus uttered a simple no.

"Look," Henry insisted.

In a whining voice, Paleologus replied, "I've seen all the reports on TV, and I haven't seen her." Noticing skepticism in Henry's face, he repeated, "I know—I know what you're looking at. I've seen the reports coming on TV every day. And I don't know her."

With years of practice, Henry had learned and perfected interview techniques, and knew how to control his own reactions, especially his temper. He kept his voice calm. "Victor, listen. Listen to me, okay? This is just a missing person. That's all this is. I need you to help me find her. Listen to me, Victor, before you go any further. Just hear me out, okay? We've been working on this thing around the clock. I've been in contact with a witness—I should say my department's been in contact with a witness who saw you talking to her. So I know you talked with her before she disappeared."

It is not unusual for a police interrogator to stretch the truth a little, if it increases the chances of rescuing a person in danger. Henry continued, "So look at her again. Look at her closely, I mean, 'cause I know you talked to her. I don't know if it was in passing . . . or what the conversation was about, but I know you did talk to her."

The interrogation had lasted less than three minutes before Paleologus invoked Miranda. "I can't say anything to you without my attorney. I'm not going to subject myself to anything that is going to incriminate me in any way."

Henry already knew that the "exigency" of this case took precedence. "Victor, if you haven't done anything, nothing's going to incriminate you. I'm not—I just want to know—"

Paleologus turned his face, stared off into the distance, and crossed his arms in body language of disinterest, saying, "No. I understand that—"

Leaning forward, Henry appealed, "Just listen to me Victor . . . hear me out."

In his characteristic low-key voice, Paleologus remained evasive. "Believe me, I've been—the situations you guys would—you've already identified me in this way. You guys came down—"

A frown stole its way into Henry's forehead. "What do you mean? What do you mean we've already identified you in this way?" Recovering instantly from his hint of impatience, Henry said, "We only know that you talked with her before she came up missing."

Glancing down at his wrist, Paleologus tried another diversion. "I'm telling you right now, this—they changed my wristband over at the jail. The way you guys have, uh, treated me and everything else . . ."

Patiently Henry explained that the wristband had been changed in preparation for sending Paleologus to a different branch of the jail. It had nothing to do with the investigation.

Paleologus interrupted to say, "I'd like to talk to my attorney. I don't—are you the detective?"

"Yeah, Henry. John Henry."

A little more conciliatory, Paleologus said, "John Henry. Okay. Detective, I'm not trying to be arrogant with you. I'm not trying to antagonize you in any way. I'm not trying to thwart your efforts in any way. Okay? I just wanna talk to my attorney."

Henry could see why this guy was able to work con games so successfully. He could shift from defiant apathy to smarmy humility with the ease of a chameleon. It would be easy to see other reptilian comparisons, but Henry resisted the temptation. Remaining pleasant, he said, "Victor, all I want you to do is tell me what the content of the conversation was. I just want to know if she's running away. Is she upset with her boyfriend? Should we be talking to him? That's what I'm interested in."

"Sir, I can't help you. Okay? I would like to talk to my attorney. . . ."

"Victor, what do you need an attorney for? You didn't do anything. All you did is talk to her, as far as we know. That's all we know. . . ."

"I'm a parolee. . . . I'm walking a very fine line on parole. And I can't afford to make any mistakes. I don't want to have any problems."

"What does that have to do with anything? How can you make a mistake if you just tell me the content of the conversation? If she was going to a party, or if she was going to meet her boyfriend, or something. . . ."

Paleologus pressed again for his attorney to be contacted, and spelled out the lawyer's name. But Henry countered that he didn't care about the attorney, only about finding Kristi Johnson. "I know she's out there somewhere. . . . I don't know what the situation is. I just know that you, right now, are the last person . . . that talked with her before she left. . . . What are you going to tell your attorney that you can't tell me? I only want to know what the conversation was about."

Adopting a "woe is me" posture, Paleologus whined, "I have nothing against you. I have nothing against this person. I have nothing against anyone else. Okay? I'm in a bad situation here. I'm in a corner and being interrogated for I-don't-know-what. Okay? And I simply am asking to speak with my attorney. That's all I'm asking to do. Okay? I don't—you know, if you were in my shoes, I think you'd feel the same way."

If any real doubt existed about Paleologus's involvement in Kristi's disappearance, it would be reasonable for an investigator to back off at that point. The ex-convict, who had a record of sexually assaulting women, was certainly within his rights to insist on the presence of an attorney. But Henry couldn't shake the mental image of Kristi Johnson possibly being held captive somewhere, maybe injured, abused, hungry, frightened, and desperate. And the man sitting across from him, who might hold the key to her survival, could only worry about his selfish need for a lawyer.

Calm and logical, Henry replied, "If I hadn't done anything, and I had just talked to somebody, I wouldn't have a problem."

"Well," Paleologus shot back, "that would be great if you weren't a parolee. And if you didn't have a background . . . and anything else."

Kristi Johnson wasn't a parolee, Henry reminded him. "So it's not like you were associating with another parolee." Doing that could send him back to prison. "She's not a criminal, as far as I know, so that doesn't mean you were associating with a criminal. I just want to know what the conversation was about."

"Sir, I've been listening to all the news reports. Okay? And I know what you're after. I don't have the answers for you."

"What do you mean you know what I'm after? What do you—wait, wait. You—there's a misconception going on here somewhere. What do you think I'm after?" Paleologus interrupted to repeat his demand for an attorney. Henry said, "You're gonna be able to talk to your attorney, but just answer this one question for me. What is it you think I'm after?"

Perhaps realizing his misstep, Paleologus stalled by asking for a glass of water. Henry patiently provided one, and repeated his question. "Now tell me, what is it you think I want? Do you know something that I don't know?"

The verbal joust wound down with no real answer from Paleologus. He insisted that he wasn't being uncooperative. Henry rolled his eyes skyward. "When you won't tell me the content of your conversation . . . that's not being uncooperative? Come on, Victor."

Dancing away from the point, Paleologus made rambling comments about his plight—of being in jail accused of grand theft auto, feeling "upset and nervous," and being in a "precarious" spot. He mumbled, "They transport prisoners all the time. They always think somebody's gonna escape from them, so they're paranoid. . . ." Pausing to look at Henry's face, he returned to a disjointed account of his personal worries. "With the type of profile I have, and my background, and the type of media that's out there in the street waiting, and everybody that was waving at them when they walked in— I'm really very nervous about, uh, this conversation. . . . I can understand that. But, you know, you have to keep things in a proper context. Let me ask you a question . . . if you were looking for somebody and you had word that I spoke with them last, do you think that I would be—it would be, um, last that anybody knows about anyway. Do you think that it would be out of the ordinary for me to tell you I don't want to talk to you about it when all I did was had a conversation with 'em and I went on my merry way? And they went on their merry way?"

Such inarticulate muttering certainly couldn't have been evident when this man delivered his smooth recitals to young women, selling them on the opportunity to be in a James Bond promotion. So, could he be playing a game now to avoid coming to grips with personal responsibility? Was he demonstrating what he had learned in prison about evading questions from police? The contrast between this behavior now, and that described by witnesses, suggested that Paleologus was simply dancing to the tune of another con game.

The discussion veered off to the question of arrest. Henry explained again to the inmate that his arrest related only to charges of illegally taking the BMW, and had absolutely nothing to do with Kristi Johnson's disappearance.

"You're not charging me?" Paleologus asked as if astonished. "They said that you were arresting me, that a judge signed a court order to arrest me."

"No, no, no. We couldn't have you brought here without a judge signing a court order. That's all it is, pure and simple. . . . We just want to talk to you." The investigators, he explained, simply needed to know what Kristi might have said about where she was going that evening. To a party? Leaving town? Angry at someone and trying to get away for a while? "I'm at a door

MEET ME FOR MURDER

right now, and the door is closed. I need to find out what happened. What were her plans after she talked with you? That's why I said I need your help."

Ignoring the plea, Paleologus turned it around to his own need for help to summon an attorney, and launched another litany bemoaning his situation.

Henry wondered if a different type of appeal would convince him to cooperate. "I want you to put yourself in this woman's family's shoes, Victor."

"I am sympathetic to them—"

"Obviously, you're not sympathetic enough. I mean, put yourself in their shoes, Victor. If somebody had a conversation with—with your sister or mother or your daughter or somebody that you cared about, and the police were trying to get a simple question answered—what was the content of the conversation? Don't you think it would be a little unreasonable for that person not to tell the police what the conversation was about?"

Paleologus nodded agreement while voicing the caveat that the questions should not be answered without the presence of an attorney. "I have nothing to tell you without him being here."

John Henry could see no sign of compassion or humanity in this consummate liar, only self-pity and reliance on legal machinations.

The interview continued for some time, in the same endless circle. Both Obenchain and Henry realized that this man had compassion only for himself. Not much had been accomplished, except to convince the detectives that Victor Paleologus apparently had something crucial to hide.

Paleologus hadn't said much of any use to Detective Henry, even though his ability to speak, especially to young women, was his hallmark. His very name, derived from the Greek language, bore a relationship to speech: *paleo,* meaning "ancient" or "old," and the suffix *logus,* a derivative of *logos,* meaning "speech." Old speech. Victor's old speech. That must have struck several women as ironic.

Another Paleologus, Manuel II, Byzantium emperor of the Eastern Roman Empire from 1391 to 1425 (sometimes spelled Palaeologus), had used his powers of speech to wrest Constantinople and its throne from an older brother. During that reign, he spoke out about Muhammad, suggesting that the faith was spread by use of the sword. This fueled conflicts related to Muslim beliefs that continue even into the twenty-first century. A speech brought the name into headlines in September 2006, when Pope Benedict XVI delivered a talk at the University of Regensburg. He quoted Manuel II Paleologus's "dialogue with a Muslin" about Muhammad, saying that "Whoever would lead someone to faith needs the ability to speak well and reason properly, without violence and threats. . . ." The Pope's references inflamed leaders and followers of Islam throughout the world.

Whether Victor Paleologus is a descendant of the emperor or not, he apparently inherited the "ability to speak well," even if his motives in doing so were not exactly pure.

Paleologus's early background is unclear, partly due to his well-known tendencies for prevarication and embellishment. He was born on July 16, 1962, in Philadelphia, Pennsylvania. The youngest of five brothers, Paleologus has stated that he grew up in Pennsylvania and New York. His father, an immigrant from Greece, worked as a chef, perhaps leading to Victor's eventual interest in operating and owning restaurants. His mother, he said, was always a homemaker.

In a later interview, Paleologus described his upbringing. "We had a wonderful childhood. My mother was very dedicated." His own wayward tendencies, he noted, were not the reflection of his parents' teaching or love. "The family has always been well formed and well groomed in society." Asked about religious teachings, he said he and his parents belonged to the Catholic Church. He claimed to have graduated from high school in the city of his birth, but the specific one he named does not show up in lists of Philadelphia schools, either public or Catholic institutions.

According to Paleologus, he earned a B.S. degree at the University of New Mexico in 1985, after which he moved to Los Angeles to seek employment. One investigator expressed no doubt that Victor's degree was certainly "bs." He also has spoken of taking an M.B.A. at San Diego State University, awarded in 1993, but no records of it can be found.

Divorce documents on file in Los Angeles indicate that Paleologus was married in 1990, and ended it in 1993. He stated, "I loved my wife very much. We really believed that we could make some changes and correct the issues, you know, pull it together. . . . It didn't work out. You know, it was a very bumpy ride. . . . Divorces are difficult. They're a nasty roller coaster. . . . I used to have a lot of late-night meetings, out-of-town meetings and things like that. It made her uncomfortable."

Repeated attempts to succeed in the restaurant business failed. "I was the owner of one. . . . I ended up losing a lot of money. I tried to go to the banks." But all attempts to find financial help, he complained, ended in futility. And he admitted letting down a friend and other investors. "I'm very disappointed in how things ended up. I take responsibility. [My friend] had some investors that were very eager to make a high-risk investment. I lied to them. I said I could back up the investment with assets. . . . I had a house at the time in the valley, but there was no equity in it. . . . I was desperate, so I lied to them. I was working for a brokerage firm beforehand

[and] made some false documents that supported the fact that I had assets I didn't have. . . ."

His restaurant business career ended in an empty building on San Vincente Boulevard with the sexual assault of two women.

Within a few days, on Monday, Victor Paleologus would be required to stand in a lineup with other men to see if people who accused him of working his James Bond con game could identify him in person.

No one involved in the investigation could predict that Monday would be the longest and most explosive day any of them had yet encountered.

CHAPTER 9

HEARTBREAK

The wettest February in recent memory, and the saddest for Kristi Johnson's loved ones, washed away into history without any breakthrough in the search. On Monday, March 3, investigators forged ahead, still determined to solve the mystery.

Terry Hall had spent the weekend helping coordinate private organizations in searching for her daughter, then had flown home to Los Gatos on Sunday. As the story gained momentum in the media, Hall had also appeared on various radio and television shows. Producers for the cable news channel CNN and ABC's daytime talk show *The View* asked her to guest on both networks. She agreed and boarded a flight headed for New York.

Detective Obenchain, armed with another warrant signed by a judge that same Monday morning, drove to the county jail in downtown Los Angeles. She had arranged for Victor Paleologus to stand with five other men on a raised platform in a live lineup. Susan Murphy and Mark Wilson showed up to sit in a small gallery and try to pick out the one who tried to lure Susan with the James Bond scam. Detective Cabrera brought the parking valet Roberto Marquez to join them. Obenchain also arranged for the presence of a county public defender to assure that no violation of the suspect's rights took place.

Something about Paleologus's appearance had bothered Obenchain during the recent interview. He had let his beard grow, probably to change his appearance with the purpose of confusing witnesses. Detective Cabrera contacted the sheriff's department, who ran the jail, and requested that the inmate be asked to shave off the beard. They complied, but Paleologus refused. Obenchain countered by obtaining a court order demanding removal of the beard, and faxed it over to the jailers. It authorized "reasonable force" to use an electric shaver on him, and to force him into a live lineup if he resisted.

All six men filed into the viewing room. Roughly equal in height, all with dark hair, they wore bright orange long-sleeved jail-issued sweatshirts and tan pants. White placards bearing stenciled numbers, from 1 to 6, hung from each of their necks. Paleologus's new beard had been freshly shaved off. His face was tightened into a combination of woebegone self-pity and suppressed anger.

The six men stood shoulder to shoulder against a light-colored wall. Paleologus occupied the third position from the left.

Susan Murphy instantly identified him as the Victor Thomas who had lured and accosted her. She signed and dated a sheriff's department "Witness Card and Admonition," and hand-printed on it, *100% sure this is the man!!!*

After viewing the lineups separately from Susan, Mark Wilson unequivocally stated that number three was the person he had seen and confronted that day in an alley off La Cienega. A slight change in Paleologus's hairstyle didn't fool Wilson. He noted on the card, *I am completely sure that this is the individual. I have no doubt whatsoever. He did comb his hair forward.*

Roberto Marquez next viewed the lineup. In the photographic six-pack, the previous Wednesday, he had pointed to the wrong individual. Now he studied six men in person and once again picked the wrong one. Marquez simply could not remember any specific features of the man who had tossed him the Miata keys during the early morning of February 16.

By three o'clock on Monday afternoon, as Obenchain walked out of the county jail with Cabrera, her cell phone rang. The caller had been trying to reach her for an hour, but deep in the bowels of the building, the phone had no connection to the outside world. When she answered, her heart dropped and she felt as if she had been kicked in the stomach.

Events spurring the call had started that same afternoon, at about twelve-fifteen.

Four teenage boys, strolling just beyond the end of Skyline Drive, stopped to admire the view. They rested on a grass-covered plateau above the point where the pavement ended and narrowed into a dirt path. A trail curved up the incline, inviting joggers and hikers to the breathtaking sights. From the high ridge they could look westward and see, through a distant gap in adjacent hills, the sprawling San Fernando Valley. Below them, the brush-covered slope dropped precipitously, about three hundred feet, down to a narrow ravine.

While the young men smoked and chatted near a parked gold-colored sedan, one of them edged as close as he could to the rim, scanned the foliage below, and caught sight of an odd, motionless bulk of something, perhaps eighty feet down the slope. It rested adjacent to a rotting plank of wood, partly obscured by thorny vines, and stood out with pale shades of blue, pink, and gray, contrasting against all the various hues of green. He alerted his companions, and they all strained to make out what it might be. "Looks like a mannequin," one conjectured. The boy who had first spotted it volunteered to find out. He eased down a washed-out path, hanging on to shrubbery, and stopped within a few yards. "It ain't no mannequin," he yelled. "I think it's a dead body." After scrambling back up, he and the others wondered what they should do. They decided to find a telephone and call the police.

At one of the homes, about one hundred paces back down Skyline Drive, two of the teens spotted a gardener working and asked if he had a cell phone or could get to one. But he neither had a phone, nor could he get into the house. No one else seemed to be around, so the boys huddled around the parked car again, still unsure about a plan of action. A woman came to their rescue.

Irene Grant (pseudonym) took her three dogs for daily walks from her home on Mariscal Lane, about one mile from the site. She enjoyed the ascending hike up to the ridge, beginning by crossing Wonderland Park, walking up Green Valley Road, turning on Skyline Drive at the intersection where a castlelike house stood, and climbing up past the 8500 block to the plateau. On this Monday afternoon, she reached the dirt road and wondered why four young men, standing around a car and smoking, seemed agitated.

As she circled around the car, one of the youths said to her, "I think there's a body down there." Startled, and horrified, Irene leaned over the cusp to see what he was taking about. To her, it did appear to be a body.

Not one to shy away from an emergency, she tied up her three dogs and worked her way down a rough, washed-out trail, still muddy from the February rains. Arriving at a point just below the body, she knelt for a closer look. The female figure lay on her right side, with the head downhill, the upper back, arms, and head covered by a hooded gray sweatshirt.

Her hands, behind her back, had been lashed together at the wrists with white cord. With her body bent into a sitting position, a blue sleeping bag covered her legs. She apparently wore nothing below the waist except panty hose, leaving her lower back and posterior visible.

Irene could see no blood, and the exposed middle of the girl's back seemed clean. Some of the hair could be seen and Irene made a mental note that it was "dirty blond." She also observed a "hair scrunchy" encircling the right wrist. To her, it appeared that a possible tumble down the slope had been stopped by a tree stump. Irene instantly realized that no life remained in the body.

She climbed back up the incline as rapidly as possible, walked past the boys, and came upon another woman, who agreed to call 911 with her cell phone. Irene waited until the arrival of Los Angeles Fire Department (LAFD) personnel. She later said that no one talked to her, so she untied her dogs and walked home. There, the emotional dam broke. She had been watching the news for two weeks and realized that the dead body was probably Kristi Johnson. Irene wept uncontrollably.

LAFD firefighters and paramedics arrived at the end of Skyline Drive a few minutes before one o'clock. Three of them climbed down to within a few yards of the body, and from their extensive experience, they knew that emergency lifesaving measures would not be needed. Firefighter Glenn Allen, at 1:01 P.M., pronounced the unknown person dead.

A few minutes later, LAPD officers Dawn Gahry and Dean Lewis arrived in response to a radio call of a possible homicide. They spoke to firefighters, and then questioned the four young men who had first seen the body. The uniformed officers cordoned off the area with yellow crime scene tape and secured it pending arrival of homicide detectives and higher-ranking police officials.

One of the officers climbed down the steep slope, about halfway to the body, avoiding the probable route it had taken while "being rolled or dragged down the ravine." Even though it appeared to be the remains of Kristine Johnson, the deceased person would be known only as "Jane Doe 22" until official identification could be made.

The victim had been found in the jurisdiction of the Los Angeles Police Department, but because Santa Monica investigators had been working on the case since it first developed, L.A. officials made a call to the Santa Monica headquarters.

At about 2:20 P.M., Detective John Henry heard from Lieutenant Ray Cooper, of Criminal Investigations. Attempts had been made to contact Detective Obenchain, but in the county jail basement, she couldn't be reached. Henry listened as the lieutenant said that the body of a young female had been discovered in the 8500 block of Skyline Drive, up in the Hollywood Hills. "Can you go up there, make contact with the LAPD officers who are standing by, and see if the body is that of the missing person, Kristine Johnson?"

It's an awful moment for detectives after they have worked their hearts out in the hope of rescuing a missing or kidnapped victim. Henry knew that a real estate agent had shown Paleologus a home for sale in the 8500 block of Skyline. For a female body to be found near there—it was simply too much to hope that it might be coincidental. Still, no one had yet confirmed it as Kristi. Nor had they mentioned a tattoo on the victim's back. Henry hoped that it wouldn't be there.

By the time Henry arrived at the scene, the whole area virtually swarmed with uniformed officers, officials, fire department personnel, and coroner's specialists. He spoke with an LAPD captain from the Hollywood Division, who gave him a briefing on what had been discovered so far. Lieutenant

Cooper also arrived a short time later, conferred with Henry, and suggested that he descend the slope to make a "cursory visual inspection of the body."

Taking the same hazardous muddy trail used earlier by Irene Grant, Henry made his way to the still form. Staying about three feet away in order not to disturb any potential evidence, he made a mental inventory of what he could see. With her head concealed by the sweatshirt hood, except for part of her "dirty-blond shoulder-length hair," he couldn't tell anything about her facial appearance. Even though her legs were covered by a blue sleeping bag, it wasn't zipped up, and the feet protruded out. Henry's heart grew heavier when he saw that she wore black stiletto heels, exactly like the ones he had borrowed from the lingerie store to be photographed.

The hands, he observed, had been tied together behind her back with what appeared to be white shoelaces. The final blow struck Henry when he looked at the exposed lower back. He saw the tattoo of a geometric hibiscus flower.

Official identification would be made by the coroner, but John Henry knew exactly who lay in the mud and brush. After over two weeks of round-the-clock intensive searching, he had found Kristi Johnson.

As soon as Virginia Obenchain received the call on her cell phone outside the county jail in downtown Los Angeles, she and Almada hurried to the Hollywood Hills site. Passing the house near the end of Skyline, they both visualized Kristi arriving there on the evening of February 15, thrilled, eager, and happy.

Obenchain worked her way through the throng, which by now included LAPD chief of police William J. Bratton and SMPD chief James Butts Jr. "The place was loaded with bars and stars," she later said. She found Lieutenant Cooper and Detective Henry, who had just climbed back up after viewing the body. His gloomy expression told Obenchain what she already knew to be true. He described the details, including the stiletto heels and the tattoo.

While they spoke, the LAFD backed a large red truck into position on the plateau and extended the ladder to be used as a boom for bringing the victim up. First, though, they rigged it to provide a means to photograph the scene and the body. Forensic technician K. Kuwahara stood in the basket at the ladder's tip to take wide-angle shots. Then she strapped on a harness at the end of a cable and was lowered to a position within a few feet of the body to take numerous additional pictures.

In old mystery novels and movies, police detectives collected all of the evidence. Now, as known by sophisticated readers of newer books and viewers of television crime scene investigation documentaries or dramas, the intricate work of finding and collecting forensic and trace evidence is performed by highly trained specialists. While other technicians hunted for related evidence at the Skyline Drive site, criminalist Eucen L. Fu assumed the specific task of scrutinizing the body of Jane Doe 22 at the scene, then later in a laboratory. He reported that the fire department lowered him in a harness to within a few feet of the body which lay on a steep incline and was surrounded by thick brush. Fu observed that the decedent wore a zippered gray sweatshirt and that her head was covered by an attached hood. He could also see a beige bra, "skin-tone" panty hose, and black stiletto heels on her feet. The lower limbs were encased in a blue sleeping bag, but since it was unzipped, her left side and buttocks remained visible. A binding lashed her wrists and hands together behind her back. The criminalist later stated that circumstances prevented collection of evidence on the site.

Obenchain needed to see the body, too, before they moved it. The sun had already dropped behind the western hills, converting long shadows into dusk. In later describing the circumstances, Obenchain said, "The LAPD and the L.A. Fire Department were wonderful, setting up floodlights, using the fire truck to give us access to the body, and providing everything we needed." She, too, was belted into the harness, and held her breath. "I don't do heights well," she recalled.

Lowered to the body, she saw for herself what Detective Henry had described. From a woman's viewpoint, though, she hoped to find one other thing a man might not think of—Kristi's purse. But nothing like that turned up. Obenchain also drew a probable conclusion when she saw the panty hose, with "built-in underwear," on the body. This meant to her that Kristi had probably not been raped. No rapist puts panty hose back on a victim before or after killing her.

Obenchain closed her eyes, and held on again with white knuckles while the boom lifted her back up.

A major decision faced the top officials. The Santa Monica team had been investigating every aspect of the missing persons case since February 15. But the body had been found in LAPD's jurisdiction. Which department should take on the homicide investigation?

Lieutenant Cooper had brought Obenchain's "missing persons book" with him—a binder over five inches thick, containing all of the documentation, tips, chronology, and facts related to the case. Chief Butts carried it with him into the mobile command post vehicle for a discussion with Chief Bratton.

Obenchain later spoke of it. "We had thousands of hours already invested in it. I know that when our detective bureau went up there, they took my thick binder. So the brass had discussions about jurisdiction . . . and decided that since we were so deep into it, that it was just better for us to continue. But LAPD was so cooperative and very kind. They even left us their mobile command post and several officers to help out."

After the body and its surroundings had been photographed and technicians completed collecting trace evidence, the remains were carefully placed into a litter and covered. With the same gentle skills that would be used in rescuing a wounded victim, the fire department personnel hoisted the litter up toward the dark sky. With pulley ropes, they eased it toward them, and finally lowered it to the ground. Placed in a coroner's van, Kristi Johnson's body, Jane Doe 22, was taken away by the coroner.

For Obenchain, Henry, and their colleagues, the night's work had just begun. The first order of business was to search the nearby house Victor Paleologus had visited with real estate agent Charlie Simon, the home actor Laurence Fishburne had reportedly rented. In another odd irony, a movie released in 2003 titled *Mystic River* portrayed Fishburne as a detective investigating the murder of a nineteen-year-old woman.

A previously issued warrant had placed limits on the house search, restricting it to hunting for Kristi, or her body. Now the police needed an amendment to look for trace evidence. It would be submitted immediately to a judge for authorization to reenter the home.

Meanwhile, two men approached Detective Michael Cabrera at the crime scene. One of them introduced himself as the husband of the woman who had found the girl's body. His wife, he said, was "extremely upset" by what had happened. He asked Cabrera if he would go to their home, about a mile from there, and speak with Irene. Cabrera said he'd be glad to help, and hopped into a car with the men.

As soon as he met Irene Grant, Cabrera could see her fragile emotional state. She was "visibly shaken," he later reported. "I sat down and asked Irene to tell me what she had seen and done from the time she left her home." The woman, still sobbing, told Cabrera about walking her dogs, sighting the four young men, and climbing down the slope. It had horrified her to realize that she was looking at a dead body.

Cabrera felt sorry for her. "While Irene was telling me what had happened, she continued to weep and at times had to compose herself. I had concerns that she may need some assistance, so I told her I would contact a counseling center." The woman gratefully accepted Cabrera's offer.

Sometimes the general public is shocked by television news clips showing police officers using excessive force on a suspect. It's too bad they never show the deep compassion and personal empathy that is far more prevalent than the rare loss of control found so newsworthy by the media. Cabrera's shining example deserves equal coverage. And so do countless similar incidents so often taken for granted.

Police Chief Butts decided to tell Kristi's parents of the tragic discovery before news media carried it. He called Terry Hall's cell phone several times, but she was on a plane headed for New York and couldn't answer. He did reach Kirk Johnson's cell phone in Michigan and gently asked, "Are you at home?" Johnson said he was, and Butts wanted to know, "Do you have someone with you?" Johnson's heart began to pound when he said that his wife was there.

With compassion in his voice, Butts said, "I'm very sorry. We have found Kristi, and she's no longer with us."

Johnson's world darkened and spun in a dizzying fog. Mental images of Kristi as a child and in young adulthood flashed before him, kissing him and echoing tender thoughts of love. He found his way outside. "I stared up to the heavens. I lifted my eyes and I called out her name and I repeated, 'I love you. I love you. I love you. . . .' And then my whole body just relaxed, and I smiled. I knew she was in heaven with God."

When Terry Hall arrived at the New York airport, Butts finally made contact with her and delivered the sad news. He later said, "They were both very upset and distraught."

That night, at eleven o'clock, a judge signed the amended search warrant. Detectives Cabrera and Nicols, joined by LA sheriff's office criminalists Dale Falicon and Flynn Lamas, examined every room of the unfurnished house on Skyline Drive. They worked until dawn, meticulously scrutinizing, vacuuming, and picking up every odd fiber, hair, fragment of cloth and paper, and looking for anything that might lead to the killer.

Obenchain left the scene at midnight, en route to the Forensic Science Center. She wanted to be present for a comprehensive physical inspection of the body, prior to the full autopsy that would take place later.

Criminalist Fu conducted the examination while Obenchain observed. He used scissors to snip away the shoelace ligatures around the wrists, then pulled away the blue sleeping bag flap covering the legs. Another white shoelace had been used to bind the ankles together. Fu noted that the lace "tightly encircled" each ankle once, then formed two loops around both ankles and was knotted in two places. This, too, he removed with scissors. The tips of both laces bore a small plastic clip with a star cutout, characteristic of Converse brand sports shoes. After more photographs were taken, Fu removed several pieces of jewelry from the victim, including earrings and three rings from her fingers.

Obenchain understood and empathized with the red marks left at the base of the toes when Fu slipped both shoes off the girl's feet. The fit hadn't been perfect, and the high heels would probably have caused blisters if worn very long. Obenchain took a close look at the right shoe and saw scuffing on a section of the patent leather, the type of marking usually associated with someone dragging the victim across a rough surface.

The criminalist collected all of the clothing, hair samples, and fingernail clippings to determine if the victim had scratched flesh from her assailant. He used a sexual assault kit to take swabs from body orifices. Finally he collected maggots from the badly decomposed, blackened face and head.

Obenchain didn't leave the forensic lab until nearly three o'clock in the morning. After nearly twenty straight hours of work, she needed a brief rest before facing the ordeal of observing the autopsy, scheduled for Wednesday morning, March 5. Records had previously been obtained from Kristi's dentist, and they would be used at the autopsy to see if Jane Doe 22's dental characteristics matched. Of course it would, Obenchain knew. But she still dreaded hearing it become official.

From this moment on, the entire investigative focus changed. Every effort turned toward a single goal: to find if any evidence could link Victor Paleologus, or anyone else, to the murder. Was the man in custody really the person who tied Kristi's hands behind her back, lashed her ankles together, murdered her, wrapped her in a sleeping bag, and dumped her down a muddy slope in the Hollywood Hills?

CHAPTER 10

MODEL MURDER

Virginia Obenchain had no doubts about Paleologus being the James Bond guy who lured Kristi into the Hollywood Hills and killed her. The complete absence of hard evidence troubled her, though, and she hoped that something would turn up at the autopsy to physically link him. Nothing had been found in the Mazda, and so far, the tiny scraps collected in the house on Skyline Drive didn't offer much hope.

Flashing back to her first thought when the missing persons report came through, Obenchain mentally replayed it. *Oh my God, do we have another Linda Sobek on our hands?* It brought to her mind one of the most highly publicized murder cases in the recent decade, one that inspired books, movies, and television documentaries.

Seven days before Thanksgiving in 1995, former NFL cheerleader Linda Sobek agreed to meet photographer Charles Rathbun for a suggested modeling job. He had established a

respectable reputation snapping pictures of cars and motor-
cycles, usually in scenic locations, and having them published in
various magazines. Most of his work involved beautiful, scantily
clad models draped over the vehicles or seductively lounging
inside them.

Because Sobek had posed for him three years earlier, she
felt no sense of danger.

Similar to Victor Paleologus's routine, Rathbun asked
Linda to meet him, not in an office or studio, but in a Denny's
restaurant parking lot. And just like Kristi Johnson, Linda
spoke to her mother by telephone before leaving. Elaine
Sobek routinely telephoned her daughter, and called her
before ten-thirty that Thursday morning. She planned a bar-
becue the next weekend, and hoped Linda could attend. In the
brief exchange, Linda said that she wouldn't be able to talk
very long because she wanted to keep an appointment for a
modeling job. She promised to call back later that evening.

Before leaving the Hermosa Beach cottage Linda shared
with three roommates, she recorded an answering machine
message informing callers that she would be unavailable that
day due to being away on a photo shoot. The short drive to
Denny's in Torrance took only a few minutes.

Linda's face and figure had been seen by thousands of
football fans in the Los Angeles Memorial Coliseum. As a
cheerleader for the L.A. Raiders NFL team, twenty-seven-
year-old Sobek had established a niche for herself in the
world of entertainment and modeling. In early 1995, the
Raiders decided to move back to their original home city,
Oakland. Anticipating this a few months earlier, Linda left
the Raiderettes to focus on modeling and a possible film
career. Her hazel eyes, teased shock of wheat-in-sunshine
hair that framed an oval face and cascaded midway down
her back, along with an easy smile, caught the attention of
numerous professional photographers. An abundance of

attractive features, enhanced by a busty, long-legged, sculpted figure, kept her busy posing, mostly in bathing suits and revealing costumes.

Charles Rathbun left early that morning, November 16, from the Hollywood three-bedroom home where he lived with one roommate. He arrived at Denny's in a brand-new dark blue Lexus prototype LX450 sports utility vehicle. The Lexus Corporation of Torrance had loaned it to him for use in the publicity layout he planned to shoot for a well-known weekly magazine. Rathbun told Sobek that some of the shots he planned would feature her driving the vehicle on a dry lake bed in a remote Southern California desert location. She could leave her own car in the restaurant parking lot, ride up there with him on the two-hundred-mile round-trip, and be back later that night.

Even though the bespectacled, blond, blue-eyed, thirty-eight-year-old photographer stood two inches over six feet, with a lanky build, he had a reputation for being rather mild-mannered, even meek at times. If Victor Paleologus bore some resemblance to Sylvester Stallone's Rambo character, Rathbun might be compared to a younger Jon Voight's *Midnight Cowboy* role.

The deal appeared safe enough to Sobek, and the pay would be good. She climbed into the upscale SUV and they headed north toward the mountains and the Mojave Desert.

If Sobek had known what boiled inside Rathbun, she would have refused to be anywhere near him. Two other models would eventually reveal that Rathbun had developed a hatred for Linda when she posed for him in 1993. According to one of them, he spoke of her in denigrating terms. "I'll never work with that woman again," he had reportedly told one of the women. The other one quoted him saying that Linda was "a little bitch and she deserves whatever she gets."

Elaine Sobek marked time that evening hoping for the

phone call Linda had promised, but it never came. The same emotional anxiety that would grip Kristi's mother in February 2003 struck Elaine. Each passing hour fueled her fears. She endured it until Friday morning, then telephoned Linda's roommates to ask if they knew where she was. They had no idea. By midmorning, unable to delay any longer, Elaine contacted the Hermosa Beach Police Department (HBPD).

After preliminary examination of the report, a HBPD detective questioned Linda's roommates, who had already been checking with everyone they knew. It was quite unusual, her friends said, for Linda to be absent without explanation. The investigation turned into a full-blown missing persons case by that weekend.

Initial probes turned up very little information. Sobek had modeled for numerous photographers, but none of them could shed any light on what might have happened to her. Even though she had mentioned to her mother and a few friends that she had an appointment for an assignment on that Thursday, Linda hadn't mentioned the photographer's name or where the shoot would take place. The entire case eerily foreshadowed future events for Kristi Johnson. Sobek's family and friends distributed thousands of flyers with a picture and description, and announced a reward of $20,000 for information leading to her safe return. A press conference in Hermosa Beach, on Monday, November 20, called for the public's help. The HBPD media relations officer provided a photo of Linda Sobek, along with a description of her car and a tip line telephone number.

That evening, a middle-aged unemployed man, Jake Taylor (pseudonym), watched the news on television. Sleepy and disinterested, he reached for his remote, but couldn't find it. When he located the device hiding under couch cushions, as usual, and pointed it toward the screen, something made him hesitate. Right then, the photograph of a beautiful, missing young woman appeared. He thought the face looked vaguely familiar. It took him a little while to remember where he had seen that image.

On the previous Saturday, Taylor, regarding himself as a "hapless schlep," trudged along the Angeles Forest Highway, performing community service as punishment for unpaid traffic tickets. He had been assigned to remove trash from containers chained to posts at turnouts along the dangerous, twisting two-lane road.

Travelers often confuse the Angeles Forest Highway with the similarly named Angeles Crest Highway. Angeles Crest begins at the busy I-210 Freeway in the LaCanada-Flintridge community, north of Pasadena, and winds sixty-six miles through the San Gabriel Mountains at heights of over seven thousand feet. About sixteen miles into the steep grade, at a Y-intersection, Angeles Crest turns east, and Angeles Forest Highway begins, zigzagging over the range for a thrilling forty-five miles before dropping into the flat desert of Antelope Valley, near Palmdale.

The unpleasant duty for Taylor required him to lift overflowing black plastic liner bags from trash barrels and dump them into a truck. The reeking receptacles contained everything from dirty diapers, used condoms, soiled underwear, and rotted food, to soft drink and beer cans or bottles. Taylor saw the opportunity to eke out a few bucks by retrieving the empties and salvaging them for refunds. In doing so, he found something that would turn out to be of crucial value to investigators of the Linda Sobek case. Rummaging through a trash barrel at Call Box Number 309, he spotted some glossy photographs of a beautiful young woman, apparently part of a model's portfolio.

"She's a fine-lookin' woman," Taylor muttered to himself, and selected four of the prints to slip into his backpack. He dumped the remaining pictures, along with loose-leaf pages

from a personal calendar, into the trash truck, and ambled
on to the next stuffed barrel.

The image shown on Monday evening's television news finally connected in Taylor's mind. It looked a lot like the
woman in the photographs he had kept. After a sleepless
night, Taylor realized that if something bad had happened to
the missing woman, his fingerprints were all over those pictures. Still, on Tuesday morning, he called the Hermosa
Beach tip line number. Answering a detective's questions,
Taylor revealed that he had pocketed four photos, but left several more in the trash. Did he know where the garbage might
be now? Yes, he said, it could be in the Dumpster at the Oak
Grove Ranger's Station, if no one had yet hauled it away. At
the officer's request, Taylor agreed to meet investigators at the
Oak Grove station, near the Angeles Crest/210 Freeway intersection, that same day.

As soon as Taylor pointed out light blue Dumpsters, all
packed full of black plastic bags bulging with trash, the detective's hopes soared. If the trash had been taken away to a
landfill, it would have been virtually impossible to retrieve
anything. Now, though, they faced the repugnant duty of digging through mountains of malodorous bundles in search of
the photos and calendar pages.

It took several hours of "Dumpster diving," but the persistent officers miraculously found the soiled pictures and pages.
Twenty minutes later, a truck pulled into the lot to take the
refuse to a landfill. By that narrow margin, the investigation
remained afloat.

A cursory examination of the calendar remnants, including
a page for November 16, confirmed that it belonged to Linda
Sobek. On another page, she had attached three business
cards, one for a hotel in Las Vegas, one for a marketing-
communications firm, and one for CHARLES RATHBUN, PHOTOG-
RAPHER, including an address and phone number. The

searchers also retrieved another interesting piece of paper—a loan agreement indicating that Charles Rathbun had been allowed to borrow a Lexus SUV from a firm in Torrance. The paper contained his telephone number and home address, which matched the business card.

By telephone on Wednesday morning, a detective told Rathbun that they were looking into a missing persons report involving Linda Sobek and that his name had come up on loan agreement documents. Did he know anything about her?

To the detective's surprise, Rathbun didn't hesitate to respond. He admitted meeting Sobek on the day she disappeared, at Denny's in Torrance. He said he had contacted her earlier that day to ask if she was interested in modeling for a photo shoot to be published by *AutoWeek* magazine. According to Rathbun, they had met in the restaurant's parking lot and sat in the borrowed Lexus to discuss it. She had used the opportunity to ask him if he would take a look at her portfolio to make recommendations for improving it. After chatting for a while, he decided not to use her on the new project. He left Sobek in the parking lot, and found another model to pose for the magazine photos.

Thanking him for his time, the detective asked Rathbun if he would come to the station and make a formal statement.

Coincidentally, that same Wednesday morning, a tipster who had seen news coverage about the missing model spotted her white Nissan sports coupe in the Denny's parking lot, and called the police. Another similarity to events eight years later, when Kristi Johnson's white sports convertible would be found in a parking building.

As in the future case of Kristi, two different police agencies worked on the investigation. The Hermosa Beach PD enlisted help from the L.A. Sheriff's Department on that Wednesday. Deputies and forensic specialists rushed out to

Denny's to examine the dust-covered vehicle, but found no helpful leads in it.

Charles Rathbun had already spoken to a pal the previous day, by phone, about news reports of the missing model. The acquaintance would later report that Rathbun made an offbeat joke suggesting that he had killed her and hidden her body. It didn't strike the individual as very funny.

In another odd telephone call by Rathbun, on Wednesday, he spoke to a female friend who happened to be a reserve deputy sheriff. Once again, this time without the joking context, he stated that he was responsible for Linda Sobek's death. In this account, he said that he had taken her to the desert for a photo shoot in which he wanted some action shots of her driving the SUV and doing "spins." When she was unable to create the desired effect, he asked her to watch while he took the wheel and demonstrated. But, he confessed, he had lost control and accidentally struck her with the speeding car. She had died in his arms as he tried to revive her.

With each word to the deputy, who had reportedly dated him at least once, Rathbun grew more emotional. Unsure what to make of it, she would later say that Charles had a well-known reputation for practical jokes, which caused her to shrug it off as one of his pranks. Later that day, she received a fax message from him hinting at thoughts of suicide.

With this alarming new turn, she contacted a mutual acquaintance of theirs, an attorney, and accompanied him over to Rathbun's residence. The lawyer knocked and Rathbun opened the front door. He stood there, silently holding a .45-caliber handgun in his right hand, failing to invite his visitors inside. After only a few words had been exchanged, Rathbun stiffened his arm and fired the weapon. A slug ricocheted off the concrete driveway.

The deputy felt a stinging, hot sensation in her left arm, instinctively clapped her hand over it, and felt the ooze of blood. She immediately called the local police. The wound turned out to be superficial, but her failure to report his "joking" confession was serious. She would face a reprimand and a suspension from duty.

Uniformed officers arrived and placed Rathbun under arrest for illegally discharging a firearm, and seized the handgun. A brief search of his house for other dangerous weapons turned up none. Instead, they found a canvas bag containing an open bottle of tequila, over three grams of marijuana, a length of fuse cord, and a roll of tape with long blond hairs clinging to it. One more item caught their attention. Rathbun had written in a letter, *Please God. Help me. I've killed someone and can not live with myself.*

Now Charles Rathbun could forget the request to come to the sheriff's office voluntarily. Instead, officers led him out in handcuffs for transportation to the LAPD Hollywood Division station. Detectives assigned to the missing person search for Sobek corralled him, but Rathbun refused to answer any questions without the presence of a lawyer.

The same exigency that would eventually fuel the interrogation of Victor Paleologus applied equally to Rathbun. Linda Sobek had been missing for a week, and every investigator on the case wanted to rescue her from harm, if possible. The questioning continued.

Rathbun had originally told the Hermosa Beach police that he rejected Sobek for the photo shoot and used someone else. Face-to-face with determined cops, he changed his story. He admitted driving Sobek to a place in the Mojave Desert known as El Mirage Dry Lake.

Off-highway vehicle (OHV) buffs would recognize the name. Motorcycle riders, all-terrain vehicle (ATV) jockeys, and four-wheel-drive enthusiasts have been visiting the hardpan surface for years, often camping out among creosote bush and Joshua trees. Low, ragged hills, parched brown and tan, and etched with ATV and motorcycle scars, form the wide perimeter. Even though the place is bone-dry most of the year, an actual mirage of blue water can be seen in the distance. It's a place where speed is king, on the ground and in the air. Thirty miles away lies Edwards Air Force Base, where NASA's space shuttle sometimes lands. Chuck Yeager first broke the sound barrier in the blue skies overhead, more than half a century ago, and not long afterward a special track was built for land speed trials. The site is also popular for making automobile commercials and filming movies.

Except for the half-dozen racing events held there annually, it's usually a place of extreme solitude, where the few visitors, spread over hundreds of acres, pay little attention to one another.

According to Rathbun, El Mirage provided a perfect site to take shots of the new Lexus SUV. It offered perfect lighting, especially just before sunset, which would take place a few minutes before 5:00 P.M. in mid-November. Plenty of open space afforded wild maneuvering, abrupt turns, skidding around on the sandy dry lake bed, and doing "doughnuts," all with a beautiful woman in the driver's seat. But Linda didn't do it correctly, so he needed to show her how. As she stood nearby, he accelerated, and might have tried to cut it too close. The car suddenly spun around and struck her. He stopped immediately, leaped out, and rushed to her, but realized that he had killed her.

In his narrative, Rathbun said he didn't know what to do. Fear took over his mind. No one would believe it had happened accidentally; so in a panic, he decided to bury her body in the mountains.

The detectives stared, their expressions incredulous. He had already backtracked on his original story, so why should they believe this version? To corroborate his story, he would have an opportunity to point out the burial site.

It took over two hours to drive over the mountains to El Mirage Dry Lake. Rathbun readily pointed out the exact spot where the "accident" had happened, but again altered the details. In his new recollection, Sobek clung to life after being struck by the SUV, so he loaded her into the backseat. A little while later, he stopped to check on her and could detect no pulse or sign of breathing. Panicky, he drove toward the mountains, stopped in a remote spot, and buried her.

Giving directions to the detectives, Rathbun advised the driver to head up into the Angeles National Forest. For the next two hours, they hunted for the exact site, but Rathbun insisted that he just couldn't recall exactly where he had stopped to dig a shallow grave. Darkness put the futile search to an end.

Back in jail that night, Rathbun sought another way out. Somewhere during that day, he had apparently pocketed a piece of sharp metal or glass, and later used it to lacerate his left wrist. When jailers discovered it the next morning, they rushed him to a medical facility for emergency treatment. Six stitches took care of it. The cell required a major cleanup. Rathbun had used his own blood to print a gory message in four-inch red letters on the wall, next to an aluminum commode: "I'm sorry. I didn't ever mean to hurt anyone." Water in the toilet looked like red wine, and a blood-soaked T-shirt lay on the floor next to it.

Cops guarding Rathbun in the clinic heard several incriminating comments. Obviously depressed, he repeatedly wished that he were dead, and asked the officers if they had ever seen a person die or someone choke to death. He also said, "All photographers play games with models to take their clothes off. . . . That's why I gave Linda liquor to see if she would." He continued a stream of self-condemning statements, admitting that he had covered her burial site with a large rock to prevent coyotes from digging up the remains.

Not long after driving away from El Mirage, Rathbun said, he stopped at a Kmart, and bought a shovel. He later used it, in combination with a flat board, to dig her grave. None of his words would ever be heard in court, since no Miranda advisory had been given before he spoke.

There is a Kmart store in Lancaster, but to stop there, Rathbun would have driven an extra twenty-five miles en route to the Angeles Forest Highway. He may have meant a Circle K convenience store within short driving distance from the dry lake bed.

Perhaps thinking that he had given the police a treasure of evidence, rather than a lot of useless prattle, Rathbun escalated his cooperative behavior. After consulting with an attorney, he agreed to divulge the body's location.

This time, on the day after Thanksgiving, investigators chose to avoid the long, meandering trip in a car. Instead, with Rathbun pointing the way, they used a helicopter to scope out the Angeles Forest Highway and service roads that peeled off to coil over canyons and peaks. Of course, they realized, it might just be another duplicitous ploy by this con man, taking advantage of the opportunity for a free sightseeing helicopter ride. But his behavior did seem different on this expedition. Each time they hovered over a drainage culvert, with concrete pipes under the road, the suspect grew more animated.

Thirty minutes into the flight, Rathbun pointed to an S-shaped curve carved into the side of a steep slope. On one side of the road, a precipitous cliff bore scars from a rock slide that had long ago plummeted earth, shrubbery, and boulders into the canyon hundreds of feet below. On the other, carpeted with scrub pines and firs, a ravine cleaved the mountain where rushing water, in the wet season, cascaded underneath the ribbon of road.

That looks like the place, Rathbun announced.

A radio call from the helicopter pilot sent a crime scene

team to the culvert. After landing a short distance away, and escorting Rathbun into a car, the detectives hurried to rendezvous with them.

Rathbun led the way to a concrete abutment on the upslope side of the road, and stopped to gaze at the dry, sandy streambed. A triangular chunk of cement, surrounded by a few smaller pieces, lay near the bottom of the abutment. It marked the site of Linda Sobek's pitiful grave.

Through inference, deductive skills, and a few comments from Rathbun, the detectives pieced together the probable scenario leading to the model's burial.

Rathbun had changed his story several times about how and when she died. In any event, he found himself in a horrible situation with a dead body in the SUV, and needed to dispose of it. Somewhere along the way back from El Mirage Dry Lake, he stopped to buy a shovel, but hard, rocky soil eliminated most of the potential mountain burial sites. Driving along the Angeles Forest Highway, back toward the Los Angeles Basin, he spotted a side road, drove several miles on a dirt track, and found the culvert with a soft, sandy bottom. The absence of passing motorists on the remote lane, and the onset of night, virtually eliminated the chance of being seen by anyone as he dug just below the low, concrete wall.

Scooping out a pit in the sandy soil frustrated Rathbun, and he needed something to shore the continual caving-in at the sides. From under a floormat in the Lexus, he found a rectangular board, and utilized it along with the new shovel. When he finally reached a depth of about two feet, he pulled Linda's body out of the SUV's backseat and dragged her down the slope. At this point, she wore only a white T-shirt with matching shorts, and was barefoot. Since rigor mortis doesn't usually begin stiffening a body until about three or four hours after death, her limbs remained pliable, as if she had fallen asleep. Rathbun heaved her into the sandy pit, on her left side,

bent at the hips and knees, legs bare, with her left arm across
her chest and her right extended below the abdomen. It took
only a short time to cover her with sand, dirt, and pebbles.
Adrenaline fueled his strength to move a big, triangular
chunk of concrete onto the mound, along with a dozen
smaller stones and fragments. According to Rathbun, he did
it to avoid ravage by animals, but his motive could also have
been to prevent rain from washing away the sand, allowing
for early discovery of her body.

A team of investigators arrived at the scene, and one
jumped down three feet from atop the concrete wall, knelt,
and used his hands to dredge away the sand. Within minutes,
he uncovered a small part of Sobek's arm.

The team erected a blue canopy over the grave site and
began the meticulous excavation process. First they heaved
the heavy concrete piece aside. Little by little, they cleared
away earth, pebbles, and sand, exposing the tangle of blond
hair, the bare, smooth arms and legs, and the white shirt and
shorts. After searching for any forensic evidence, they lifted
her carefully onto a clear plastic sheet, wrapped her, and carried the remains out on a stretcher.

Charles Rathbun returned to the lockup, in a car, and found
himself facing murder charges. He occupied a cell in the
Men's Central Jail, unable to raise the million-dollar bail.

It didn't escape the attention of investigators that Linda
Sobek's body was retrieved less than four miles from the site
where the remains of another female victim had been discovered three years earlier. Kimberly Pandelios, age twenty, had
also sought success as a model, posing in bathing suits and
lingerie. No one had been arrested for the murder.

Before November came to a close, Los Angeles sheriff
Sherman Block held a press conference to announce that
Charles Rathbun was a suspect in the unsolved murder of
Kim Pandelios.

* * *

During the mid-1980s, Rathbun had lived in Lansing, Michigan, about eighty miles east of Saugatuck, where a little girl named Kristi Johnson romped and played in the innocence of childhood. The concept of murder was only something to be seen on television and in movies.

In Lansing, a young woman with modeling ambitions, Rose Marie Lerner, vanished one night after a shopping trip. A little farther east, flight attendant Nancy Jean Ludwig had been sexually assaulted and killed. No one had been apprehended in either slaying, and detectives wanted to know if Charles Rathbun might be a serial killer responsible for both of them.

Ohio investigators also heard about Rathbun and began to dig into his background, wondering if he might be linked to the death of a teenage girl in Fairfield County. After all, he had once been charged with raping a female friend at Ohio State University (OSU) in 1979, but was acquitted.

Born on October 2, 1957, near Columbus, Rathbun lived a comfortable childhood with three older siblings, a brother and two sisters. His interest in photography emerged in his teen years as a member of the high-school newspaper staff. After graduation, he entered OSU and helped pay tuition with a part-time grocery store job. One evening, after accepting a ride home with a young woman who also worked there, he invited her into his apartment, and attacked her. She later told police that he had stripped her and threatened murder if she didn't cooperate. In court, Rathbun stated that the whole incident was consensual, and a judge agreed.

Soon after, Rathbun dropped out of college and found work in Detroit photographing motor vehicles. Even though he had no trouble recruiting women to pose in the cars, he reportedly had few, if any, girlfriends, according to various acquaintances. In 1987, he moved to Southern California and worked steadily with his camera, earning accolades from colleagues and publishers.

A check of his background by detectives revealed no run-ins with the law since the Ohio rape charge. But, similar to future events in the Victor Paleologus case, several women came forward to complain about Rathbun's behavior. In Sheriff Block's press conference, he commented that "a number of women" talked about "sexual overtures" he had made while they modeled or in other social contexts. His Hollywood neighbors characterized him as a quiet loner.

The autopsy of Linda Sobek concluded that she had been sexually assaulted, sodomized, and died of asphyxiation due to neck and shoulder compression. It also revealed that she had a blood alcohol level of .12 percent. The level of legal intoxication in California is .08. On both of her ankles, the coroner observed signs of tight restraints deeply indented into the skin, suggesting that her legs had been separated and bound in a spread-eagle position while she apparently struggled to pull them together.

Criminalists examined the Lexus driven by Rathbun that day, and found blood and saliva stains, but too small for any forensic conclusions.

Anonymous tips in murder investigations vary from consequential to counterproductive. A caller who refused to identify herself told one of the investigators that they should be checking into a man named David Rademaker. She said that he had been involved in burning a car after murdering someone up in the mountains. The officer made notes of the call, filed them, and turned to more promising leads.

One of the most accomplished prosecutors in the Los Angeles County District Attorney's Office (LADA) tackled the duties of trying Rathbun. Steven Kay had first earned his stripes in 1970 by assisting Vincent Bugliosi in the trial of

Charles Manson, and followed with numerous high-profile cases. As head deputy in Torrance, he was a natural for the job of presenting the case against Rathbun.

In another foreshadowing of the future Paleologus investigation, very little physical evidence turned up against Charles Rathbun. Detectives had found enough to support a second-degree murder theory, but proving premeditation and deliberation in Sobek's death could be an insurmountable problem. The defense might logically argue that Rathbun had been motivated by plans to get her intoxicated so that she would consent to a sexual encounter, and that she died as the result of an accident.

If found guilty of second-degree murder, Rathbun would receive a sentence of fifteen years to life, and probably be freed after twelve years.

Steven Kay had earned a solid reputation of understanding criminal law as well as any university professor. In pondering the case against Rathbun, Kay preferred to seek a first-degree conviction by proving felony murder charges. One possible tactic would be to show that Sobek's death occurred during the commission of rape. The law provides that rape is a felony, and if the victim dies during the commission, the crime is elevated to first-degree murder—even if no premeditation or deliberation could be shown. The catch, though, would be to convince a jury that the sex had not been consensual. This could be extremely difficult in view of Sobek's extreme intoxication, and jurors tend to take a skeptical view in such cases.

Another option would be to show that Rathbun had forcibly sodomized Sobek with a foreign object, also a felony. The coroner had found anal injuries, and expressed a willingness to testify that the severity was consistent with insertion by force and violence. Murder during rape, sodomy, or forcible act of sexual penetration constituted a "special circumstance" that, under California law, provides for a death sentence or life in prison without the possibility of parole.

Assessing this possibility, Kay reviewed what detectives had found, along with information available about Rathbun's background. Reasonably good evidence existed in the bag investigators had seized in Rathbun's home, which contained 3.1 grams of marijuana, a partial bottle of tequila, a cord, and tape with strands of Sobek's hair clinging to it. Of course, she had worked with him before, and it couldn't be proved when the hair had stuck to his tape. Rathbun's past history, even though spotted, provided no conclusive indicators. There had been allegations, by several women, of attempted sexual assaults. He had once been formally accused of rape, but acquitted of the charges. Ongoing investigations looked into the possibility that he might be a serial killer, but these were only suspicions, and nothing had been proved. Kay also believed that Rathbun should be considered a prime suspect in the unsolved murder of Kimberly Pandelios, but had no real evidence to support it.

Relying on a rap sheet of criminal conduct, and no felony convictions, Kay faced a formidable task, exacerbated by slim circumstantial evidence that Rathbun had killed Sobek. The defense would claim the whole thing an accident, and that the defendant demonstrated remorse by leading police to the burial site.

Kay and Mary Jean Bowman, his trial assistant, decided that they could not seek the death penalty. But they would go after a conviction for first-degree murder.

A master at trial preparation, Kay sent a team of criminalists to El Mirage in the desert, with a Lexus SUV and a stuffed dummy the size of Linda Sobek, to re-create and film the events described by Rathbun. They wanted to see if his story was at all plausible.

An unexpected development by the defense, shortly before

commencement of trial, sent shock waves into the prosecution's case. In a pretrial hearing, defense attorney Mark Werksman announced that a member of Rathbun's family had discovered five canisters containing rolls of exposed film that might be crucial. According to the relative, Rathbun had whispered about it during a jailhouse visit, confiding that he had disposed of the film in the desert. After retrieving the secret cache, the relative had developed it in his own basement darkroom and realized that it could potentially corroborate Rathbun's claim that sex with Sobek had, indeed, been consensual.

Four of the rolls, mostly containing pictures of Sobek and the SUV at the dry lake bed, revealed nothing of importance, but the fifth one, developed as slides, depicted a woman in the backseat of an SUV, engaged in erotic, masturbatory conduct. Even though the photos appeared to be double-exposed, somewhat out of focus, and the woman's face couldn't be clearly seen, the defense planned to use them. By asserting that the pictures depicted Linda Sobek inside the Lexus at El Mirage, engaging in clearly consensual sex acts, they hoped that jurors might very well see this explosive revelation as exculpatory and find Rathbun not guilty.

Steven Kay sent copies of the slides to a crime lab for analysis. Defender Werksman hadn't spelled out how he planned to use the pictures, so Kay was under no obligation to disclose what the lab found.

The trial finally began in early October 1996.

Kay's opening statements suggested that Rathbun took Linda Sobek to the remote desert site with sex on his mind. There he raped and sodomized Linda, then murdered her to protect himself from being caught. The defendant had brought his "little rape bag" with him, said Kay. It contained tequila, marijuana, binding cord, and tape, which would be introduced into evidence. "She will come out of her grave, figuratively," Kay promised attentive jurors, "and into this courtroom to tell you what happened."

Not true, said defender Werksman. Linda Sobek engaged in consensual sex with the defendant, and died as the result of a tragic accident. She voluntarily drank enough tequila to raise her blood alcohol level to .12, considerably higher than the level of legal intoxication, and willingly posed for provocative sexual photos.

Over the next four weeks, Kay and his colleague Bowman called witnesses to the stand, gradually building the circumstantial case of rape, sodomy, and murder. The senior deputy medical examiner (ME), Dr. James Ribe, told jurors that Sobek had died of strangulation, not of accidental asphyxiation, and that anal injuries inflicted on her had been made by insertion of a foreign object. Sobek had been "grabbed from the rear, restrained by hand and with the use of ligatures on her ankles." She had possibly been struck in the abdomen, and "forcibly penetrated anally with a blunt object." Strangulation caused her death, probably while she struggled to free herself from her assailant.

Most murder defendants comply with the recommendation from their attorneys not to testify in order to avoid withering cross-examination. Rathbun, though, decided he could convince jurors of his claim that Linda had agreed to have sex with him, and had died accidentally.

On the stand, Rathbun modified his story once again, changing details to fit testimony from the coroner. He admitted to stopping en route to the desert to buy tequila, and offering a drink to Linda while they took a break at El Mirage. She accepted, and began sexual overtures by stripping and telling him where she liked to be touched. In his testimony, he acknowledged penetrating her with his fingers, but nothing else. She allowed him to take pictures of her masturbating. Rathbun didn't deny killing Linda, but insisted that it happened accidentally.

The injuries to her body, he said, occurred after the sexual encounter when he accidentally skidded too close to her while demonstrating how he wanted her to drive the Lexus for photographs. He couldn't be certain whether she fell or was struck by the SUV. When he tried to take her for medical treatment, she turned belligerent and "animated." She probably suffocated after he sat on her to keep her from hitting and kicking him. Panic-stricken, he drove up into the mountains and buried her in the sandy culvert.

Observers wondered why Rathbun had driven so far, approximately forty miles, with a dead body in the vehicle, passing an infinite number of isolated sites in the remote desert where he could easily have buried her. And what motivated him to head up into the mountains, then peel off on the narrow, winding dirt road, where he eventually disposed of Linda's body in the sandy culvert? Had he been up there before? Was there any connection to the murder of Kim Pandelios, whose remains were found within a few miles on the Angeles Forest Highway?

To prove Linda's consent to sex, Werksman brought out enlarged prints of the slide photos developed by Rathbun's relative. The victim's family members in the gallery were outraged. They thought it sacrilege to show nude pictures of Linda in open court, especially in this lascivious context. One relative complained to reporters of the shock that came from letting everyone see "photos of her naked."

Stephen Kay also resented the display, but for another reason. He knew the pictures were not of Linda Sobek. Laboratory analysis of the slides proved the woman in the pictures to be someone else, and that the SUV in which she performed was not even a Lexus, but an Oldsmobile, instead.

On cross-examination, Stephen Kay allowed Rathbun to reconfirm that he had photographed Sobek, nude and in overt sexual conduct, on the backseat of the Lexus. The prosecutor also asked Rathbun if he had made anal insertion of any object into Sobek. The defendant unequivocally denied it.

After Rathbun stepped down, Kay called expert witnesses to tell the jury that laboratory analysis had proved the photos bogus, and that they did not depict Sobek or a Lexus. Next he summoned Dr. Laura Slaughter, who expressed the opinion that Sobek's anal injuries, inconsistent with consensual sex, had been inflicted by penetration with a blunt object, which may have been Rathbun's Colt .45 handgun. The victim, Slaughter said, also had damage to her lips and gums caused by the forcible insertion of something into her mouth, possibly a liquor bottle.

In final arguments, the prosecution drove these points home with powerful logic. Tears filled Kay's eyes as he said, "She didn't deserve to spend the last minutes of her time on earth tortured at the hands of the human monster, Charles Rathbun."

The defense could only argue their theory of accidental death, and deny the sodomy evidence.

Jurors, nine men and three women, deliberated only six hours before returning with a verdict declaring Rathbun guilty of first-degree murder. They also declared the special circumstance of murder committed while the defendant sexually assaulted the victim to be true. In addition, they convicted him of anal penetration with a foreign object, using force and violence.

On December 16, 1996, superior court judge Donald Pitts sentenced Charles Rathbun to spend the rest of his life in prison without the possibility of parole.

Rathbun remained a suspect in the unsolved murder of Kimberly Pandelios, whose skull was found a short distance away from the site where he buried Linda Sobek's body.

CHAPTER 11

HE WANTED TO
SEE MY BODY

Since no evidence had turned up in the intervening years to connect Charles Rathbun to the murder of Kim Pandelios, investigators began wondering if Victor Paleologus might have been involved. But for now, they focused on a search for evidence that he had killed Kristi Johnson. So far, nothing conclusively linked him to either death.

Sometimes revealing facts turn up during autopsies of murder victims.

Before 8:00 A.M., Wednesday, March 5, Dr. Lisa Scheinen called Virginia Obenchain to announce that she would begin conducting the autopsy of Jane Doe 22 within an hour. Obenchain and Detective Nicols rushed to the L.A. County Coroner's Office.

This location would soon become well-known nationwide with the launch of a Court TV documentary series titled *North Mission Road*. It would present true-crime stories with emphasis on forensic science investigation by L.A. Coroner's Office personnel. (Episode number one was based on a Kensington book, *Body Double*, 2002, by Don Lasseter, and featuring the author commenting about the case.)

The expansive coroner's laboratory is responsible for conducting a scientific investigation into the cause and manner of any sudden, suspicious, or violent death occurring in Los Angeles County. That goal is accomplished through toxicological, histological (study of tissues), and scanning electron microscopy analyses of properly documented, collected, and preserved physical evidence. It's a huge responsibility, considering that roughly eighty thousand people die each year in the county, including a daily count of seven or eight murders. Of those deaths, the coroner's office conducts a staggering volume of autopsies annually, in the neighborhood of eight thousand. Twenty-six full-time pathologists perform these medical procedures, supported by thirty-five extra consultants.

Autopsies of homicide victims are always observed by at least two members of the investigating agency.

Dressed in scrubs, with masks and latex gloves, Obenchain and Nicols observed the entire process. Dr. Scheinen performed a visual preliminary exam, noting and charting significant observations. In this case, the facial features had been completely obliterated by decomposition, leaving only blackened remains of the flesh, while the rest of the body remained in relatively good shape. Since Kristi Johnson had been lying on the slope with her head downhill, blood had drained into the head causing accelerated decay. Even with that explanation, Dr. Scheinen said it was unusual to see such marked decomposition of the head as opposed to the body condition. A strange brown marking on the back and along the upper abdomen defied explanation.

The medical examiner stepped aside to allow Dr. Astrid Hagar to photograph the body and perform a sexual assault examination. She noted the presence of possible bruises on the outer pubic region and on both hips. Obenchain jotted down a note that these types of injuries are *similar to bruising seen on kids attending "Rave" parties*. It seemed odd, in view of the evidence that Kristi, even though she had purchased tickets to a rave event, had never shown up. Dr. Hagar observed markings on both ankles, probably made by the stiletto straps and by ligatures.

A "rim of estrogenized hymen" indicated sexual activity. Further examination revealed "no perianal trauma." Finally Dr. Hagar collected a cervical and rectal swab and preserved the specimens for evidence.

Resuming the primary autopsy functions, Dr. Scheinen noted a postmortem abrasion on the back of Kristi's right shoulder. A clear ligature mark could be seen on the right wrist, including a "striated" furrow, and a less distinctive mark on the left wrist. It appeared that someone had grabbed her upper left arm as indicated by a deep bruise near the bicep and at the elbow.

In all probability, Kristi had fought her assailant violently, suffering deep bruises on her right calf, left lower calf, on the upper left buttock, and on both knees. Other bruises Scheinen noted, also observed by Dr. Hagar, showed up on the left ankle and wrists, caused by ligatures.

One of the most gruesome aspects of bodies exposed to the elements over a period of several days to a couple of weeks involve insect activity. Maggots and eggs remained in the head hair, and in the eyes, nose, and mouth. The left ear, which had been separated from the scalp, also contained insects. The doctors collected the tiny creatures for preservation for use in determining when she died.

Using a scalpel, the doctor incised most of the bruises to verify hemorrhages instead of simple skin discoloration.

Scheinen removed a white metal tongue stud and bagged it to be stored with other property belonging to the decedent.

The next step would be extremely difficult for a lay person to observe, especially those weak of stomach. Obenchain and Nicols braced themselves, even though they had seen the procedure countless times.

The doctor applied a scalpel to the chest and made a deep Y-shaped incision from the sternum to the abdomen. She expertly removed each of the vital organs, weighed them, and spoke into a microphone to record the data. The stomach, she said, was almost empty, indicating that Jane Doe 22 had not eaten for some time prior to death, and that the minuscule contents could be nothing but secretions.

Next she flipped the switch on a circular Stryker saw, activating a shrill screech of noise, and cut through the perimeter of the upper skull. Removing the bone cap, she examined it and the brain tissue. A possible skull fracture became evident from radiating hairline injuries behind the left ear. Scheinen explained that it could possibly have been the result of blunt-force trauma, and was possibly perimortem, meaning inflicted while the victim was still alive.

Close scrutiny of the neck area revealed unusually dark frontal throat tissue. An incision showed signs of hemorrhaging. The horseshoe-shaped hyoid bone, which supports the root of the tongue, is usually examined in the case of violent death, because injury to it can be consistent with manual strangulation. Scheinen discovered no injury in this case, but commented that it might be due to Jane Doe's youth.

Enough evidence existed in the autopsy for Dr. Scheinen to conclude that this Jane Doe had been the victim of homicide, but the exact cause of death must wait for toxicology test results. If those were normal, she told the detectives, she could fix the cause of death as asphyxiation.

Any expectations or hopes that solid forensic links would

connect the crime to Victor Paleologus collapsed like sand castles in a high tide.

Yet, Virginia Obenchain had no doubts that Kristi Johnson's brutal end was directly related to Paleologus. The detective had mulled over all of the known facts, hour after hour, and formed in her mind the probable sequence of events that left Kristi lying on that steep slope. "I think she arrived up there, probably at the castle house, and saw Victor Paleologus standing outside waiting for her. She stopped, he gets in and directs her to drive up Skyline Drive, to the dead end. He steps outside and says, 'Okay, I want you to change into the clothes.' She begins to change, inside the car. He climbs in, and I think he attempts to rape her. I think he starts trying and she resists, fights back. He gets her in a choke hold, strangles her to the point where she's unconscious, perimortem. He panics, thinks he killed her. Some time during this struggle, he lashes her wrists and ankles with shoelaces. She has a sleeping bag, which was her brother's, in the car. Victor gets it, stuffs Kristi into it, and tosses her over the edge. On the tumble down the hill, she hits her head, causing the laceration and the radiating skull fracture. If she didn't try to change her clothes inside the car, she might have done it in the enclosed patio area of the house where they were supposed to meet. Victor had been there twice with the real estate agent, and had probably observed him dial the combination lock. Perhaps the attempted rape took place there, and when she lost consciousness, he put her in the car and drove up to the dead end. In either case, he dumped her, and she tumbled about eighty or ninety feet down the hill."

This all happened shortly after sunset, said Obenchain. "He pushed her over the side, and drove away in her car. And he called his friend Willie Craven."

* * *

Willie Craven had stalled when Detective John Henry telephoned him in late February, offering the feeble excuse that he would be out of town until March 3. As soon as that Monday morning dawned, Henry followed up, wasting no time, and met Craven at his place of employment, the drugstore on the corner of Santa Monica Boulevard and La Cienega.

Still nervous, as he had been when the two men first spoke, Craven told Henry that he'd first met Victor Paleologus on January 24. The pudgy little man, thirty-two, his face marred by acne scars, also worked part-time as a housekeeper, and often tidied up the nearby building where Paleologus had found lodging again after being paroled on January 20. Victor had spoken in a friendly manner to Craven, and they sometimes found mutual interests to talk about. Craven had heard the building owner complaining about Paleologus, and wasn't surprised when it flared into a strong suggestion for Victor to move out.

Detective Henry asked Craven how often he and Paleologus had seen one another in the three weeks between their first meeting and February 15. Stammering and faltering in his slow answer, Craven said they really hadn't shared any time, other than chatting now and then on the telephone. Somewhere around February 10, they had agreed to maybe hang out later in the week, but kept postponing it. Then, said Craven, on February 15, Paleologus had called and asked when they could get together. They settled on meeting later that Saturday night, about eleven-thirty, at a local pancake restaurant.

"So, did you meet him there?" Henry asked.

"Yeah. I got there right on time and stood outside near the front door. Victor called me on my cell phone three times between eleven-thirty and midnight to say he would be there." He finally arrived, on foot, walking south, not north from the direction where he lived, and they had dinner in the pancake house, sitting there for more than an hour. Hesitantly Craven volunteered something else to the detective. He said that Victor had asked if he could spend the rest of the night with him. Craven didn't have many friends, and thought it would be rude to deny the request. So they left the restaurant and boarded an eastbound city bus, headed for Craven's residence near Sunset Boulevard and Gower Street in Hollywood. For some odd reason, according to Craven, he sat in the front while Victor occupied a seat at the rear.

Before he went to bed that night, Craven said, Paleologus asked him for an early Sunday wake-up call so he could attend a 6:30 A.M. mass at the Good Shepherd Church in Beverly Hills. Victor slept on a couch in the living room, and Craven arose early to wake him. They both had coffee, and Victor walked out the front door between 5:00 and 5:30 A.M.

At 5:45 A.M. that Sunday, a Rambo-type man left Kristi's Mazda in a valet parking area at the St. Regis Hotel, about eight miles west of Craven's residence.

Detective Henry instinctively felt that this guy might not be telling everything he knew. He made it clear to Craven that it would be a mistake to hold information back. Obstruction of justice, he hinted, is a serious charge. Cringing and perspiring, Craven insisted that he hadn't lied. Henry suggested that he think about it and call if he wanted to add anything to the statement.

On Wednesday morning, March 5, it didn't surprise Henry when he received a call from Craven, who agreed to come to the Santa Monica Police Department and take a polygraph test. During the session, the polygrapher asked a few questions about a white Mazda Miata. Craven said that he had never known Paleologus to drive or be in possession of a motor vehicle, that he had never seen him near a white Mazda Miata convertible. Also, Craven denied that he had ever ridden or sat in such a vehicle. The results showed deceptiveness in Craven's answers.

Henry confronted him with it, and Craven admitted that he hadn't been entirely truthful. He still denied knowing anything about the Mazda, but said that there was something else he hadn't revealed. After they ordered dinner, he recalled, he had noticed something about Victor's face. Three red welts, with vertical scratches, looked fresh near his right eyebrow.

"Can you describe them?"

"Yeah. They were maybe an inch and a half long, about one-eighth of an inch apart. I asked him what happened." Paleologus, he claimed, had shrugged it off with a curt comment about a piece of furniture falling and striking him.

Henry continued to press, and elicited another tidbit of information from the reluctant witness. During one of Paleologus's three calls while Craven waited in front of the pancake restaurant, his friend had said something strange. "He told me he was in a car with someone else and was on his way. But when he arrived, on foot, he was by himself."

If Willie Craven knew anything more, he chose not to divulge it.

Lending a hand to Henry in checking the veracity of what had been said, Sergeant Robert Almada contacted the Good Shepherd Church in Beverly Hills. He wanted to know if Paleologus had, indeed, attended mass there early that Sunday morning. He found that the church conducts services at 6:30 A.M. on weekdays, but not on weekends. Nor did anyone named Victor Paleologus appear on their membership roster. Almada drove to the church and showed two priests a picture of the suspect. Neither of them recalled ever having seen him.

Detective Obenchain sorted out the information in her own mind, and came up with a theory. "I think that when Victor met Willie at the pancake restaurant, he drove Kristi's car and parked in the back lot, where Willie couldn't see it. The place has its own little parking lot just a short walk from the drugstore, where Willie worked. Behind that store is a two-level parking structure. We're surmising that Victor drove the Miata, parked it underneath, away from street view. He came down the hill, taking a route different from what he would have used if he had walked from the place he lived on La Cienega. The next morning, when Victor left Willie's residence, and caught the bus to supposedly go to church, there was nothing to stop him from going directly to the restaurant, picking up the car, and driving it to Century City. He dumped it in the valet parking, went into the Century Plaza, then a few minutes later caught the bus on Santa Monica Boulevard right back to La Cienega. It's a good bet that he intended to create an impression that Kristi had met someone at the hotel, spent the night, and was abducted from there. But Roberto Marquez saw him and shot holes in that plan."

A telephone call from the coroner's office to Obenchain finally and permanently set aside the Jane Doe 22 tag for the murdered young woman. Through dental records, she had been positively identified as Kristine Louise Johnson.

Obenchain wondered how many other women had heard Paleologus's James Bond scam, and if any of them would come forward. On Friday, March 7, an attractive, dark-haired woman walked into the Santa Monica Police Department and asked to speak to a detective. She carried a packet of clothing with her.

Detective Maury Sumlin interviewed Alice Walker. She told him that she had seen and read news reports about the death of Kristi Johnson, and that she knew a man who might be involved. He had invited her to audition for a role in a

James Bond movie. With that statement, she had the officer's undivided attention.

According to Walker, she had first met the man, who called himself "Victor Ippolito," in the Century City mall on Saturday, January 25, 2003. Sumlin marveled at the unmitigated chutzpah of this guy, obviously Paleologus. Here he was, hitting on another woman *the very same day* of his confrontation with Susan Murphy's companion, Mark Wilson, when he sobbed and mumbled promises to never do anything like this again.

The meeting with Alice took place in a mall restaurant, where she worked as a server. Victor, dressed in a blue business suit and tie, sat at a booth in her section and they began a friendly conversation. He commented to her that he had just recently moved to Southern California from New York and was staying at the nearby Century Plaza. Alice felt a sense of kinship, since she, too, was a transplant, albeit from Illinois, just a couple of months earlier.

"I asked him why he had moved here," said Walker, "and he said he was copyrighting a book and had come out here to pursue publishing it." To some, that might have sounded a bit odd, since the book-publishing center of the United States is New York. But Walker had found it fascinating. "I was an English major in college and I like talking about literature and art." She told Victor that the restaurant job was only to pay the bills and that her ultimate goal was to succeed in an acting career.

The exchange between Victor and Alice turned flirtatious, and he asked what she was doing after work. Would she like to have some coffee and continue talking about the book?

Yes, Alice had said. So he suggested they meet in the lobby of his hotel. Before he left, she gave Victor her cell phone number, but he said he didn't have a local one yet, and he had left his cell phone in New York. She agreed to join him in the Century Plaza lobby, only about three blocks from the restaurant. It would be late, she said, after the end of her shift at eleven o'clock.

Victor left and called her twice, once as she put finishing touches on her duties, and again as she drove the short distance, to let her know that he was waiting just inside the entrance. The hotel lobby is a lavishly decorated, expansive place, extending a city block in length. A row of huge columns support the high ceiling and the tan marble floor is impeccably polished to a mirror surface. Couches, tables, and round-backed wooden chairs invite patrons to relax in luxurious comfort, and a long, dark-wood bar offers refreshments, but was closed at that late hour. Potted bamboo trees create an ambience of tropical elegance, enhanced by a view of the Olympic-size pool through floor-to-ceiling glass panels. Alice arrived shortly before midnight and found Victor sitting in a lounge area, with two cups of coffee on the small circular table in front of him.

She recalled, "He had coffee already there waiting, but it was cold, so I remember he asked one of the people who was like a staff person working there if they could get room service to bring us new coffee or espresso." They sat and talked nearly four hours. Victor told her of trying to find some suitable real estate in the area, and that he planned to establish a business called Logus Corporation, utilizing computers in the restaurant food-ordering process. Uncertain just what that meant, Alice still suggested he look in Santa Monica because "it was a nice area."

In chatting about his book, Victor explained the plot to Alice. Detective Sumlin took notes as she summarized her recollection of what he said. "It was about a man named Vincent, who was in the process of trying to open a restaurant. His wife was divorcing him and had moved to Europe. In order to start the restaurant, he took out a lot of money. I think

he said something like three hundred fifty thousand dollars
he got from a loan shark. When he couldn't pay it back, they
came after him. In that process, he hired this lawyer, and one
night the lawyer and him were at a party and the lawyer had
met some girl. He took her to their car and started having sex
with her and somehow killed her while doing it. Vincent
ended up in jail and the thing that happened in the car with
the lawyer got pinned on him. The story just kept going on
with him and this string of bad events."

Sumlin said nothing, but recognized a lot of autobiograph-
ical elements to Victor's story of Vincent, especially the part
about divorce and a nefarious acquisition of money to open a
restaurant. The meeting between Walker and Paleologus had
occurred before Kristi Johnson vanished, so Sumlin mentally
reflected about this fictional murder story. Had Paleologus
been involved in previous events related to a young women
losing her life during a sexual encounter?

The detective wondered when Alice had been subjected to
the James Bond scam. She cleared that up with her next comment. "He said that he'd been friends in college, at the University of Iowa, with movie director Darien Serakian, and that
he was directing a new James Bond movie. They were looking for a girl who would sort of be the poster girl for the
movie. They needed a new face, someone who sort of resembled Jennifer Garner from *Alias,* a very strong woman."

Walker referred to a popular television series by that title
in which Jennifer Garner played CIA employee Sydney Bris-
tow, for which she won several Emmy nominations.

The mention of "Darien Serakian" may have been a mistaken reference to producer/writer/director Deran Sarafian.
There is no record, however, of Serafian ever being ac-
quainted with Victor Paleologus, or of being involved in a
James Bond film.

Did Victor offer Alice the opportunity to participate in the

James Bond project? She answered the question before Sumlin could ask. "Well, at first it seemed like he was just talking about it. And obviously in my mind, I was hoping he was offering it to me. So when it got to the end, it sort of came out like, well, 'I think it could fit you, but let's see.'" Her next statement was predictable. "So he had me walk back and forth and he felt my calves."

Why had he done that? "Well, his reasoning was that they were looking for a new face and especially wanted someone who is a strong woman character. He wanted to see my body. I assumed at the time that the reason he was feeling my calves was to see if I was strong. . . . . I had said that I was a ballet dancer."

Victor, said Walker, spoke in more detail about the James Bond film. It would cast Sean Connery, the first Bond, in a role alongside the current 007, Pierce Brosnan.

Detective Sumlin recognized the same lie Paleologus had used in his attempt to lure Susan Murphy.

According to Walker, Victor said that she would play a dominatrix in the film. Camera shots, she recalled, "would be about the legs. It's about the legs and butt. The opening shot of the film focuses on this woman walking—just walking basically away from the camera. It starts out at her feet and goes up the back of her legs." An audition would be required if Alice wanted to try for the role. And she would be paid well. "He said that it was a contract for two hundred thousand dollars. Also a Donna Karan, I guess, endorsement, and others that I can't remember." It could lead to contracts for greater movie opportunities.

Asked if she believed Victor, Walker snapped an unhesitant yes.

Did he offer an appointment for the audition? "He did, yes. And he said I needed to wear black high heels, stilettos. Also nylons that sparkled like diamonds. Those were his exact words. And I needed to wear a short skirt, either black or tan, and a men's button-down white shirt. He would provide a necktie." To the detective, these words had a ring of déjà vu.

Detective Sumlin had noticed the neatly wrapped package Walker carried in with her and asked about it. With a show of pride, she extricated the contents, and displayed the exact clothing she had purchased for the audition. Grateful, and impressed at her forethought, Sumlin arranged for the garments and shoes to be photographed.

Walker continued her narrative of the events surrounding her meeting with Victor Ippolito. She said they talked until almost four o'clock Sunday morning. Walker agreed to meet Victor that same day, at about 2:00 P.M., at an address near the corner of Santa Monica Boulevard and La Cienega. Sumlin recognized it as the spot where Susan Murphy had confronted Paleologus.

Walker had arrived promptly, bringing the required miniskirt, hose, stilettos, and white shirt in a bag from a Ross store, where she had purchased most of the clothing that same morning. As she approached in her car, she spotted Victor standing outside on the corner, wearing casual clothing in place of the blue suit. Alice pulled over and he directed her to park at the curb behind "his car," pointing toward a silver Mercedes. It puzzled Alice, since he had complained about taking taxis and limos because he didn't have any transportation. However, the discrepancy didn't set off any alarms in her mind.

Victor verified that Alice had brought the necessary clothing, then escorted her through the building entry and up a flight of stairs at the end of a short hallway. Describing the interior, she said, "It was somewhat like a loft, white walls, some of them like half walls that created—like a bar or separation divider, and there was counter space. The floor was like green Astroturf. Really dirty." The place appeared to her like an abandoned business, perhaps a dance studio or restaurant.

They walked past a worn black couch to a bathroom. Victor asked again about the clothing, especially the nylons, and Alice said she had brought several pairs. She laid all of the apparel out on a bench "that's sort of built into the wall. He picked the nylons he wanted me to wear. Then I went into the bathroom to change." Perhaps an element of suspicion had crept into Walker's psyche by this time. "I put my foot against the door so he couldn't get in."

"Were you afraid?"

"Well, I told a friend of mine at work that if I didn't show up for my shift at four-fifty, that she should just call the police." Walker had previous experience in changing her clothing speedily in tight quarters. "Because I was a ballet dancer, I have been accustomed to changing in the wings, sort of putting things on and taking things off at the same time." She emerged from the bathroom wearing what Victor had demanded. Seated on the black couch, he gave her an approving nod.

"You look great," he said, and added that she had a "really good" chance of being picked for the part.

In Walker's recollection, Victor explained how they would prepare for the next step. "He said that at this audition, I was going to be told to be in several different positions. And, in fact, what he said was that when I go into the audition, I should just immediately do these positions, so I needed to know all about them in advance, which is why we were at these rehearsals. They expect everyone just to know what to do."

"What did he tell you to do?"

"One thing was that I needed to be sitting on the edge of a chair—the very, very edge of it, with my legs crossed and my ankles really close together as if they were one. My arms must be behind me, and my legs tightly close together from my knees to my ankles, as tight as I could possibly get them. He was describing it, like through camera shots—'We're going to start at your ankles and we're going to ride up the side of your legs. So the position needs to show your legs, the sexiness of your body.'"

Victor instructed her, Alice said, exactly how to pose. "At first, he kind of walked around, looking at both sides of me, saying that they were going to see how I looked from different angles based on what would happen in the film. Then he asked if it was okay to touch me to get me into the right place. I said it was okay."

For the next ten or fifteen minutes, according to Walker, Victor manipulated her legs and ankles, squeezing her knees together. "He was saying that the muscles in my thighs would need to be showing in a certain way, so the way my legs were crossed was important."

Apparently satisfied with the sitting poses, Victor next asked her to walk around. "Like a model in a runway sort of saunter. The description he gave me was that I would be walking into this bar and everywhere I walked throughout the movie, I would have to saunter there, that I would have to just ooze sexuality."

Another requirement, said Alice, was to practice walking while holding a gun in her right hand, concealed behind her. "So I walked. He had me walk in a circle, slowly. Then I would have to stop, kind of have a hip out, like a runway pose, with the gun behind my back. I had to swoosh my hips back and forth."

The activity Walker described was clearly taking on gradual erotic tones. And it grew. "There was another pose. I had to crawl up on a countertop and was on all fours with my legs behind me in the air, crossed, and my back arched. And I had to kind of look behind me." Her description was difficult to visualize. It sounded like acrobatics.

All of this posing had been without a necktie, Alice said. Victor then produced one, and said he would put it on her and make the correct knot. Again, she must have felt a surge of suspicion. "He put it on me and attempted to tie it. I kept my thumb under the neck loop, though, because I was nervous about somebody tying something around my neck."

As the afternoon wore on, with Victor circling and instructing, Walker glanced at her watch and told him that she needed to go to work soon. But, if the actual audition was going to be held that day, she could call the restaurant and ask to be excused. Victor, she said, told her he would make a call and see if the producers could see them within the next hour or so. She went into the bathroom to change back into her street clothes, and when she came out, Victor had bad news. "He said that it was canceled because Sean Connery got sick." So they had to cancel everything for the rest of the day. "Victor said he was going out of town, and that when he got back, he would call me and we would schedule the audition later in the week."

Three days passed, said Walker, and Victor did, indeed, call her. She met him again in the same place on Wednesday, at about five that evening. "Once again, I went into the bathroom and changed into the clothes I brought. We talked about other people who had auditioned for the part, but were rejected. He said he felt that I had really a great chance. In fact, I remember him saying numerous times he thought I had an eighty percent chance of getting this role, and that he really believed in me."

Repeating the same routine, Alice recalled, she posed and moved around as directed by Victor. "He said that in the film [I] would walk up to Pierce Brosnan's character. And I have a gun once again, obviously behind my back. And I was attempting to kill him, so I would walk up to him, he would grab the back of my hair, pull me down, and kiss me, and I would try to shoot him and he would kill me instead."

The irony of her comments was chilling.

They rehearsed the scenario about fifteen times, said Walker, and the atmosphere grew tense. "It was really hot in there, and I got angry with him. The shoes were giving me blisters and I felt like we really didn't need to keep doing this over and over again. He wanted me to swish my hips more. I was frustrated because I felt like the character wouldn't necessarily be this outright raunchy."

Frowning now, Alice continued. "He was, I guess, playing Pierce Brosnan's character, so I was a little uncomfortable to have him grab my hair, over and over pretend to kiss me, because we weren't getting into that yet, but it was just uncomfortable. So I expressed that I didn't want to do it anymore. He said, 'Just a couple of more times. You know, you are going to have to kiss whoever is rehearsing with you in the actual audition.' So the last time that we did it, I walked over to him. He grabbed the back of my hair and he actually did kiss me. And I pushed him into the wall and yelled, 'That is not in the confines of our relationship and I don't feel comfortable with it.'"

Her anger flaring in retrospect, Alice recalled saying, "'I'm not a whore.' And he said, 'Yes, you are a whore.' I turned around and walked to the other side of the room and sat down. He flopped down on the black couch and seemed to be really hurt at the fact I was angry and frustrated. He said, 'I'm sorry. I just really wanted you to earn and get this role. I really believe in you.'"

His apology eased the tension, said Walker. They actually tried another couple of poses, but she began asking him for specific information about the timing and location of the audition. Victor "kept passing it off. So we parted ways and I left."

Fully expecting that to be the end of Alice's story, Detective Sumlin was surprised when Walker admitted to seeing Victor again. They met twice more, once to share a dinner, but she made it clear that she had no romantic or sexual interest in him. At one point, she pressed him for his full name. He repeated that it was Victor Ippolito. He had previously told her that he had started a business called the Logus Corporation. She asked where that odd title came from. Apparently forgetting their earlier conversation, he said it was part of his name. Alice challenged the explanation, pointing out that she couldn't see how "Logus" connected with "Ippolito." Victor recovered in a flash, saying that his full surname was "Ippolitologus."

Detective Sumlin had to suppress a laugh. This guy was the most outrageous liar anyone could imagine.

It became apparent that Alice Walker had come to the same conclusion. But she had continued talking to Victor, somewhat like poking a rattlesnake with a long stick just to see what it will do. He tried to impress her by claiming he had purchased a home up in the Hollywood Hills for $2.5 million, and he planned to move in right away. She asked how it could clear escrow that soon, and he instantly came up with a story about renting it in the interim. No, she said, she didn't want to go up there with him to see it.

When the last shreds of hope about a movie audition faded away, Alice ended any further contact with Victor Ippolitologus. He made one more attempt to call her, and left a message on her voice mail on February 15, the day Kristi Johnson vanished. Walker dialed *69 and wrote down the number from which Victor had called. Sumlin traced it to a public telephone in the Century City mall, near the men's restroom.

It took a while for Walker to convince herself that Kristi's abductor, and probable killer, might be the man who had so convincingly lied. Her conscience demanded telling the police of the experiences.

Sumlin placed a six-pack of photographs on the table in front of Alice Walker, and she had no trouble identifying number three, Victor "Ippolitologus" Paleologus.

CHAPTER 12

KILLING SPREE

Phony photographers luring young women into posing, then raping or killing them, is nothing new. It's been going on since the invention of cameras. Southern California, with the aura of Hollywood, movies, and celebrity glamor, has seen more than its share of these crimes.

One of the scam artists has been a kink in the convoluted system of justice for almost three decades. Rodney James Alcala had once been a contestant on television's *The Dating Game* show, and had won a date with a woman asking double-entendre questions. But at thirty-five years of age, Alcala's sexual interests were aimed at much younger females. He trolled the Huntington Beach sands in 1979, with a camera dangling from his neck, and persuaded twelve-year-old Robin Samsoe to pose for him. After she willingly climbed into his car, he drove almost forty miles into the mountains of the Angeles National Forest. A U.S. Forest Service employee found the little girl's ravaged remains five days later.

Witnesses at the beach who had seen a man talking to Robin and her girlfriend helped artist Marilyn Droz sketch a composite portrait of the suspect. And in a perfect foreshadowing of the events surrounding Kristi Johnson's death twenty-four years later, a parole agent recognized the features shown on the television news. He notified investigators, and they arrested Alcala. Like Victor Paleologus, Alcala's rap sheet revealed that he had been paroled after serving only a few years for a serious sex crime. He had raped an eight-year-old girl. At the time of Robin's death, Alcala was out on bail for sexually assaulting a thirteen-year-old.

A jury convicted Alcala of Robin's murder in 1980, partially based on the forest service employee's testimony. She stated that she had seen a man resembling Alcala lead a blond young girl into a mountain canyon on the day Robin vanished. Five years after the judge sent Alcala to San Quentin's death row, the California Supreme Court interceded. Because the jury had been allowed to hear of the defendant's previous crimes, the court overturned the verdicts and ordered a new trial. A second jury, in 1986, again found Alcala guilty and recommended a death sentence. Seventeen years later, in 2003, the U.S. 9th Circuit Court of Appeals, notorious for overturning death penalties, reviewed the case and found that its trial judge, Donald A. McCartin, had erred. The forest service employee who testified in the first trial had since experienced a nervous breakdown, rendering her unable to give evidence in the second one. McCartin allowed transcripts of her earlier testimony to be read to the jury. He also disallowed testimony from a psychologist who claimed that two detectives had used "inductive hypnotic techniques" in questioning the forest service witness. The "expert" went even further with an assertion that the prosecutor had also hypnotized the witness. Observers and experts applauded McCartin's decisions, but the federal jurists,

pointing to McCartin's "errors," ordered that Alcala be freed
or face yet another trial.

As this book is being written, Alcala, age sixty-two, sits
in the Orange County Jail awaiting his third trial. In this one,
though, he will face even greater problems. Cold-case investigations of homicides from the late 1970s have linked Alcala,
through DNA evidence, to the murders of three women. In all
probability, he will return to death row.

Another "photographer" earned worldwide notoriety for a
1984 killing spree. Christopher Wilder, a native of Australia
and a millionaire, couldn't resist a predatory urge for twisted
sexual adventures. At least eight women fell victim to his
heinous perversity.

After moving to the United States in 1969, he achieved financial success in Florida as a construction contractor. Os-
tentatious about his new wealth, he acquired a luxury home,
boats, race cars, show dogs, and expensive cameras. His photography "hobby" turned out to be the catalyst for his future
troubles. After several brushes with the law stemming from
his attempts to persuade women to pose in the nude, Wilder
grew bolder. Shopping malls were his hunting grounds, and
pretty young women his prey. He allegedly kidnapped a few
and sexually assaulted them, carrying out deviated rape fan-
tasies. Like Victor Paleologus, decades later, Wilder slipped
through the justice system with one jury acquittal of rape, and
several reduced charges via plea bargains.

On a visit to his homeland in 1982, the police accused him
of sex crimes against a pair of girls, both under sixteen. His
family came up with the necessary bail, and with the court's
permission, he returned to Florida while waiting trial, scheduled for April 1984.

A couple of months before that date, Rosario Gonzalez,

age twenty, a casual friend of Wilder's, vanished from the Miami Grand Prix racetrack. Elizabeth Kenyon, age twenty-three, left her Coral Gables workplace in March and disappeared. Wilder, who turned thirty-nine that month, had reportedly dated Kenyon, a former Orange Bowl Princess and beauty contestant, and even asked her to marry him, but she wasn't comfortable with the age difference. Neither woman was ever seen again. Publicity about the two mysteries evidently frightened Wilder into emptying his bank account and embarking on a cross-country exodus of death and destruction.

Within a few days, about one hundred miles away, Wilder strolled through a mall and told Terry Ferguson, age twenty-one, that she should be a model. A shopper observed her leave with a tall, balding man who wore a short beard. Terry's body was later discovered in a snake-infested canal. The witness picked out Wilder's picture from a six-pack lineup.

On Tuesday, March 20, 1984, three days before Terry was pulled from the swamp, Wilder trolled a mall near Florida State University and approached a beautiful coed in the parking lot. Saying that he needed a "fresh-faced" model for a photo shoot in a nearby park, he offered her $25 to pose for just a few minutes. When she politely rejected the offer, he slammed a fist into her stomach, punched her in the face, and wrestled her into his car. Later that night, a motel resident heard screaming from an adjacent room and rushed outside. He caught sight of a man, about six feet tall, carrying a suitcase and sprinting off into the night. A severely bruised girl stumbled into the reception office wearing only a bloody sheet, her hair caked with blood, and her eyelids closed and sealed with glue. She had been repeatedly beaten, raped, forced to dance nude, and tortured with electrical charges. At last she had made it to the bathroom, locked the door, and screamed as loud as possible. Her attacker hightailed it into the parking lot and drove away. The victim described the assailant and his car, a light-colored older Chrysler. He had paid for the room with cash.

Wilder made it all the way to Texas by the next morning, and resumed his tactics of terror after checking into a Beaumont motel. When nurse Terry Walden, age twenty-four, disappeared on Friday and was found floating in a canal on the following Monday, her stricken husband told police that she had spoken of being accosted a few days earlier. A "bearded, older man" had asked her if she would model for him. Absolutely not, she had said, and repeated it when he continued to press her. She and her orange-colored Mercury Cougar vanished soon afterward. Investigators found Wilder's abandoned Chrysler on the outskirts of town.

The fugitive's route apparently took him through Oklahoma City, where Suzanne Logan, age twenty-one, failed to keep an appointment after shopping in a mall. Her sexually abused and knife-punctured body turned up in a reservoir. Acquaintances of the victim knew that she had aspirations of being a model.

Within a few days, eighteen-year-old Sheryl Bonaventura didn't return home after visiting a Grand Junction, Colorado, mall. Witnesses had seen a bearded, well-dressed man chatting with several women, including Sheryl, asking them if they wanted to be models. Sheryl had already found limited success posing for photographers, and decided to join Wilder on his cross-country excursion. A waitress in Silverton heard her speak about heading for Las Vegas. A hunter found her dead body, filled with bullets, in a Utah forest.

In the gambling capital of the West, Wilder attended a fashion show, where he met seventeen-year-old Michelle Korfman. She, too, vanished. A photograph of the strutting models in the show later turned up, in which Wilder could be seen admiring Michelle. Witnesses subsequently told of him roaming

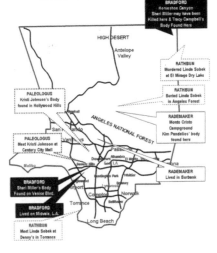

LOCATIONS WHERE MODELS KILLED IN LOS ANGELES COUNTY

Map depicting sites of model murders in Los Angeles County. Eerie connections linked five slayings. *(Graphics and photo by Ron Bowers)*

BRADFORD
Horseshoe Canyon
Sheri Miller may have been Killed here & Tracy Campbell's Body Found Here

HIGH DESERT

Antelope Valley

RATHBUN
Murdered Linda Sobek at El Mirage Dry Lake

RATHBUN
Buried Linda Sobek in Angeles Forest

PALEOLOGUS
Kristi Johnson's Body found in Hollywood Hills

RADEMAKER
Monte Cristo Campground Kim Pandelios' body found here

ANGELES NATIONAL FOREST

PALEOLOGUS
Meet Kristi Johnson at Century City Mall

RADEMAKER
Lived in Burbank

BRADFORD
Sheri Miller's Body Found on Venice Blvd.

BRADFORD
Lived on Midvale, L.A.

RATHBUN
Meet Linda Sobek at Denny's in Torrance

Kristi Johnson accepted a stranger's invitation to audition for a modeling job in a James Bond film promotion. She never returned home. *(Photo from Saugatuck High School yearbook)*

A department store security video camera caught Kristi on the last day of her life, shopping for the required sexy clothing to wear at the audition.
(Photo courtesy of the Los Angeles County District Attorney's Office)

Kristi lost her way while driving to the audition but knew it was near a "castle house." *(Author collection)*

Desperate, Kristi made her last cell phone call, which bounced from this cell site relay tower, placing her in the Hollywood Hills.
(Author collection)

Santa Monica P.D. Detective Virginia Obenchain led the team of investigators searching for Kristi, and later the hunt for her killer.
(Author collection)

Santa Monica P.D. Detective John Henry descended a muddy hillside to confirm the identity of a female murder victim. *(Author collection)*

Susan Murphy read a short news article, called the police, and helped break the case wide open. *(California DMV photo)*

Forensic artist Sandra Enslow, L.A. Sheriff's Office, drew this composite portrait of the suspect, as described by Susan Murphy and Mark Wilson. (Photo courtesy of the Los Angeles County District Attorney's Office)

Kristi's missing Mazda Miata turned up in a parking building of the St. Regis Hotel, adjacent to the Century Plaza Hotel and the Century City Mall. The valet attendant recalled that a "Rambo"-type man left it. (Photo courtesy of the Los Angeles County District Attorney's Office)

A department store security camera caught "Victor Thomas" in the mall where he first approached Susan Murphy. She instantly identified him from the videotape. *(Photo courtesy of the Los Angeles County District Attorney's Office)*

Model Jeanene Boscarino demonstrates apparel Paleologus required numerous women to wear in "auditioning" for the James Bond film promotion. *(Photo by Ron Bowers)*

Actress Cathy DeBuono, invited to audition, identified Paleologus as the scam artist. *(California DMV Photo)*

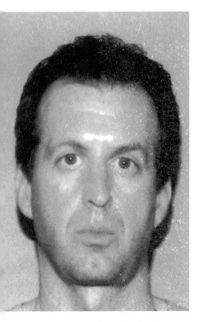

Victor Paleologus, arrested for trying to steal a new BMW. *(Photo courtesy of the Los Angeles County District Attorney's Office)*

Aerial view of the Skyline Drive dead end. Kristi's body was found down the slope from the parked vehicles. *(Photo courtesy of the Los Angeles County District Attorney's Office)*

Hikers spotted what they thought was a mannequin lying in thick brush. The tattoo on her lower back indicated that it was Kristi Johnson. *(Photo courtesy of the Los Angeles County District Attorney's Office)*

Under floodlights, the Los Angeles County Fire Department used a ladder truck as a boom. They lowered investigators to the body and then lifted Kristi's remains from the ravine. *(Photo courtesy of the Los Angeles County District Attorney's Office)*

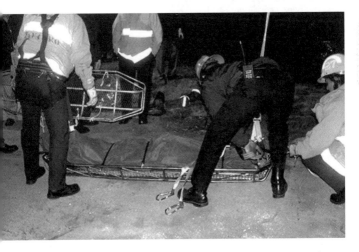

Gently, just as they would with an injury victim, firefighters recovered Kristi's body. *(Photo courtesy of the Los Angeles County District Attorney's Office)*

Victor Paleologus stood in a live lineup. Several women he had sexually assaulted or lured with the James Bond scam identified him. Midway through his subsequent trial, he astounded everyone. *(Photo courtesy of the Los Angeles County District Attorney's Office)*

For one lineup, Paleologus tried to change his looks with a beard, but was forced by court order to shave it off. *(Photo courtesy of the Los Angeles County District Attorney's Office)*

Charles Rathbun, a legitimate photographer, took former NFL Raider cheerleader Linda Sobek to a remote desert site for a photo shoot and murdered her. *(Photo courtesy of the Hermosa Beach Police Department)*

After frequent denials, Rathbun led detectives to this culvert where he had buried Sobek's body under the large chunk of concrete. *(Photo courtesy of the Los Angeles County District Attorney's Office)*

The LA Sheriff's CSI team examines and photographs the Sobek crime scene. *(Photo courtesy of the Los Angeles County District Attorney's Office)*

Sobek's lightly clad body gradually came into view as forensic technicians brushed away the rocks and sand. *(Photo courtesy of the Los Angeles County District Attorney's Office)*

Investigators erected a canopy over the site to sift carefully for evidence. *(Photo courtesy of the Los Angeles County District Attorney's Office)*

Sobek's body is removed and transported to the coroner's lab for autopsy.
(Photo courtesy of the Los Angeles County District Attorney's Office)

The district attorney arranged for reenactment of Rathbun's story of how Sobek died in the desert when he lost control of the SUV he planned to photograph. *(Photo courtesy of the Los Angeles County District Attorney's Office)*

The reenactment, with use of a dummy, showed the implausibility of Rathbun's story. *(Photo courtesy of the Los Angeles County District Attorney's Office)*

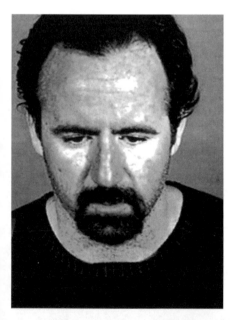

David Rademaker lured Kim Pandelios into the mountains for a photo shoot. It took investigators more than a year to link him to her death. *(Photo courtesy of the Los Angeles County District Attorney's Office)*

Hikers discovered Kim's skull in thick brush 200 yards off the mountain highway, not far from the location of Linda Sobek's burial site.
(Photo courtesy of the Los Angeles County District Attorney's Office)

Bill Bradford photographed Shari Miller at a remote desert site, killed her, and dumped her body near the 20th Century Fox movie studio.
(Photo courtesy of the Los Angeles County District Attorney's Office)

Shari's quilt-wrapped body was found in a Pico Avenue parking lot, along the route traveled by Kristi Johnson on the last day of her life.
(Photo courtesy of the Los Angeles County District Attorney's Office)

Investigators searched the desert where Bradford photographed Shari and were stunned to find the remains of a second victim on this site.
(Photo courtesy of the Los Angeles County District Attorney's Office)

Las Vegas streets soliciting women to be models, before he headed west again. By this time, a nationwide search was under way for Christopher Wilder, with FBI agents spearheading the hunt. Michelle Korfman's body was finally unearthed in Southern California's Angeles National Forest.

Wilder's next escapade with a victim turned out to be one of the most bizarre and unpredictable episodes of all. In Torrance, California, within blocks of the site where Charles Rathbun would rendezvous with Linda Sobek eleven years later, Wilder targeted sixteen-year-old Tina Newton (pseudonym) for his modeling scam. At a shopping mall, he asked her if she would be interested in posing for some ads, and collect $100. She agreed, accompanied Wilder outside, struck a few poses, then informed him that she had to leave. With a handgun, he convinced her to stay. Inside the orange Cougar, he tied her hands and ankles, then drove southeast to El Centro, near the Mexican border. In a sleazy motel room, after attacking Tina, he made an amazing decision.

Something about this girl convinced Wilder to spare her life and to use her as an accomplice in luring other young women.

A witness to Tina's abduction in Torrance had seen multiple news reports about the FBI's most wanted fugitive, and identified the man who took her as Christopher Wilder. The national search intensified as the fugitive and his teen slave headed east.

In Indiana, Tina helped attract another girl into the web. Wilder raped and tortured the newcomer in the Cougar's backseat while Tina drove. He repeated the assaults later in Ohio, Pennsylvania, and New York hotel rooms. Near Penn Yan, a rural town on the northern tip of Canandaigua Lake, Wilder decided that he'd used up the most recent captive and needed to dispose of her. He stabbed her repeatedly and left her lying in thick woods. Miraculously, she survived, was quickly rescued, and informed police that Wilder and Tina were on their way to Canada.

The lust still boiled deep inside Wilder, and he forced Tina to recruit another victim, this time with two objectives. He wanted not only another sexual conquest, but another car. The Mercury was a bull's-eye in everyone's target by this time. In a mall parking lot at Victor, New York, they spotted Beth Dodge, age thirty-three, stepping out of her Pontiac Trans Am. Tina used some excuse to bring Beth over to the Mercury, where Wilder subdued her, tied her up, and placed her in the backseat. Tina drove the Pontiac, staying behind Wilder and the captive in the Cougar. At an old rock quarry, Wilder killed the new victim, and left her along with the orange vehicle.

Driving as if obsessed, Wilder followed the coastline up to Boston, then made an inexplicable decision entirely inconsistent with his whole pattern of behavior.

At Logan International Airport, he handed Tina money to buy a ticket to Los Angeles, plus some extra cash, and sent her home. Back in Torrance, she also did something very odd. Tina took a cab to a lingerie store and spent the cash on personal items. She could never fully explain what had happened during those incredible eight days with a notorious killer.

Another opportunity soon presented itself to Wilder. On a lonely highway, he spotted a stalled car and a lone young woman standing outside it. The nineteen-year-old gladly accepted his offer of a ride to get a can of gas, but she soon saw that Wilder had no intention of stopping at a station. Frantic, she managed to open the passenger door, tumble out, and run away.

Speeding north, Wilder finally had to stop for gas himself, in the tiny burg of Colebrook, New Hampshire, on the Vermont border, just a dozen miles south of the Canadian border. While he chatted with the attendant filling his tank, a pair of passing state troopers thought he looked familiar and stopped. Wilder leaped into the Trans Am and grasped a .357 Magnum handgun. One of the officers dove on top of him. The sharp crack of two gunshots split the silence. One slug seared through Wilder's flesh and lodged in the trooper's body. The second bullet found its way into Wilder's heart, instantly killing him. The mystery of his destructive, murderous behavior died with him, along with several unanswered questions. Did he deliberately shoot himself? Why did he set Tina free? How many unsolved murders did he leave behind? No one will ever know.

Sensational national news coverage of Christopher Wilder using his camera as a magnet seemed to have little effect on young women dreaming of a career in modeling or movies. Ambition and glamor continued to overrule common sense. It might have given even more men, such as Victor Paleologus, ideas for improving on the age-old artifice.

CHAPTER 13

SICK AND DANGEROUS

SMPD chief James T. Butts Jr. wanted to keep the news media informed of progress in the mystery of Kristine Johnson. In press conferences on February 19, 20, and 25, he had provided only sketchy details of the events. Television and newspaper coverage had produced excellent results so far, especially with the response of Susan Murphy to a short article in the *Los Angeles Times*.

By March 4, ten days had passed since Butts last spoke to reporters. He decided they deserved an update, but still chose to be reticent about specific information relating to Paleologus.

Butts began with acknowledgments of hard work by detectives on the case, and by offering "heartfelt condolences and sympathy" to Kristi Johnson's family. Their strength and courage as the case unfolded, he said, deserved everyone's admiration. He paid tribute to LAPD chief Bill Bratton, to Hollywood Division officers, and to other agencies for their aid and cooperation. "Chief Bratton personally responded to the crime scene. Without the resources provided by L.A. Fire

[Department], we could not have processed the scene in a timely manner."

To reporters eager for important developments, Butts said, "As of yesterday, this investigation has turned from a search to locate and bring home this vibrant young woman to a potential kidnapping/murder investigation. We believe that we can and we will bring the person responsible to justice. The purpose of this conference today is to provide the public information into our progress in this case without compromising any future prosecution and without naming or identifying any individuals not yet charged with a crime related to this disappearance."

A collective sigh of disappointment could be heard in the gallery of newshounds. Ignoring it, Butts continued. "We have received over five hundred tips on our tip line that was established February 20, 2003. Of those, two hundred were deemed viable and followed up on by individual investigators. Two tips received weeks apart from independent sources were classified as strong and viable. Follow-up provided corroborative information that has led us to focus on a subject of interest. This [person] had been identified as the individual who lured a female to a corner in West Hollywood in late January under the offer of an audition for a photo shoot related to a specific movie production. This female witness and her boyfriend have positively identified him as the person they described in the composite."

A few of the reporters glanced at one another, as if they already knew the chief's secrets. Said Butts, "The subject lives within two blocks of the intersection where he met this witness, on foot, in January. Additionally, this subject has been convicted of crimes in which the victims were female and were lured to the location of the crime under the pretense of photographing them for publicity-type photos related to the entertainment industry. In one of the crimes, he stated that he was shooting photos for the same specific movie production that he mentioned to both the witness from January and Kristi Johnson. This subject was arrested shortly after Kristi Johnson's car was dropped off at the St. Regis Hotel and has been in custody ever since. Kristi Johnson, when found, was wearing an article of specific apparel that the subject asked both her and the female from January to wear in their purported photo shoots. We believe we have evidence that establishes his presence in the Century City Mall on the fifteenth of February, the day that Kristi met the individual purporting to be a photographer and subsequently disappeared."

Winding down, Butts added, "There are other pieces of information that we believe tie this subject of interest to Kristi's disappearance. We await the forensic processing of evidence secured from Kristi's Miata and locations searched pursuant to search warrants before making a final arrest decision. This press conference will be the last conducted by the Santa Monica police until an arrest has been made. I will take questions at this time, but will not discuss any subject matter that may jeopardize the reputation of uncharged persons or any future prosecution and justice for Kristi and her family."

True to his word, Chief Butts revealed nothing more during the following question-and-answer session. He did say about the subject being held in jail, "This person is a very convincing and very smooth predatory-type person."

Throughout the ages, reporters have devised techniques for finding sources of information to flesh out their stories. The *Los Angeles Times,* on Wednesday morning, March 5, stated in an article's opening sentence, *Police sources said the man investigators are focusing on in the kidnap-slaying of Kristine Johnson is Victor Paleologus, who was twice convicted of luring young women with false promises of acting jobs, and of assaulting them.* The piece also revealed that Paleologus had been released from prison on January 20, that he had been arrested on suspicion of auto theft, and that he had served time on six various charges.

Details of his criminal past followed, along with quotes of a court report stating, *Victims regard the defendant as being highly capable of repeating such behavior in the future.* While the article did not name Susan Murphy or her companion, it did cover details of the confrontation. It stated, *The boyfriend, a former police officer, chased down and frisked the man. He didn't find any identification and the man broke free.* It also asserted that Kristi's roommate had spoken to the police, telling that the missing girl had met someone at the Century City Shopping Center, where he offered her an audition. Finally the article gave the Skyline address of the home where Kristi was supposed to meet Paleologus, and noted that *a nearby home, recently the set of a pornographic film,* had been listed in a search warrant.

The *Santa Monica Daily Press* didn't name Paleologus, but featured a photograph of the home and stated that *actor Laurence Fishburne rented the house until six months ago.* Their coverage chided two local television stations for broadcasting *the suspect's photo and name on Tuesday night, despite a warning from police that making his identity public could jeopardize the investigation.* It quoted SMPD lieutenant Frank Fabrega saying, *"We are very disappointed that Channel 2 and Channel 9 decided to air the subject of interest. If this person turns out to be the suspect, other victims that come forward will have a difficult time proving anything in court because they have a preconceived notion that he is guilty."*

What Chief Butts or Lieutenant Fabrega did not say at the press conference was that forensic evidence to link Victor Paleologus with the murder of Kristine Johnson remained frustratingly elusive. Circumstances pointed a powerful finger of accusation, but Detective Obenchain and her team still needed something concrete, such as DNA, fingerprints, fibers, hairs, or witnesses.

A coroner technician had called Obenchain to report that the ligatures found on Kristi's body might be Converse shoelaces. He had initiated contact with the manufacturer to see if a particular style of shoe could be associated with the laces. Also, during the autopsy, minuscule fibers had been found on the body, and what appeared to be human flesh showed up on clippings taken from her fingernails. Another search warrant sent specialists to the home on Skyline Drive at which the "audition" was supposed to take place, this time to collect fiber samples from the carpets for comparison to a few fibers found on Kristi's body.

So far, the primary element connecting Paleologus to Kristi was the modus operandi, or MO—Victor's pattern of offering women the opportunity to be involved in a James Bond film promotion. Three of his targets—Susan Murphy, Dawn Cooper, and Alice Walker—had told of hearing the same pitch from Victor. Obenchain, like Fabrega, suspected more would turn up. She was right.

Cathy DeBuono watched a televised morning news show on March 5 while getting dressed for work and realized that she knew the man being pictured. She had met him at the Century City mall about four years earlier. Maybe too much time had passed for the police to still be interested, but it nagged at her as she finished grooming her long, dark hair and added a bit of makeup around flashing brown eyes. After checking her statuesque six-foot figure in a mirror, she left her residence, climbed into her car, and picked up her cell phone to call the Santa Monica Police Department. She agreed to come in on Saturday, March 8, for an interview with Detective Michael Cabrera.

DeBuono had elevated her career in the entertainment industry with roles on a television series called *Star Trek: Deep Space Nine*. A second-generation spin-off from the original Gene Roddenberry hit, *Star Trek,* this series ran from 1993 to 1999. The Internet Movie Database (imdb.com) notes that:

> *Cathy DeBuono played "M'Pella" on Star Trek series Deep Space Nine. She was originally hired as Dax's (Terry Farrell) photo-double. In addition to doubling Dax and playing the role of M'Pella, Cathy played The Breen, a Vulcan Baseball Player, and a Klingon Warrior for the last 3 seasons of the series.*

Even with blossoming success, Cathy still maintained strong interest in climbing higher, and kept an open mind about new opportunities. Sometime during the early part of 1999, Cathy stopped in the Century City mall to glance at a window display, and heard a man's voice say, "Are you an actor or a model?"

It's usually pleasant to be acknowledged for being attractive, and Cathy didn't mind the recognition. She looked up and saw a man with interesting facial features, about two inches taller than she was, neatly dressed in a gray suit. She gave him a simple yes, then added, "I am an actor."

He introduced himself as "Brian."

Recalling the incident, Cathy said, "I was wearing shorts and he started to talk about my legs. He thought I had great legs. And he said he was looking for girls to do posters for promoting the new James Bond movie and that he thought I had good legs for that."

Courteously responding to Brian, Cathy told him that she

would give him her agent's phone number, and that he could call and set up an audition or photo shoot, whichever he preferred.

His preference, he countered, was not to deal with an agent. "He said it would be more money for me. I wouldn't have to give the agent her usual ten percent. It would cut out a lot of red tape and make things a lot simpler."

Detective Cabrera wondered why a person experienced in the industry wouldn't immediately turn suspicious at the shady proposal. Perhaps fading ratings for *Star Trek: Deep Space Nine,* nearing the end of its six-year run, had created a need in Cathy to land a new assignment. There would be no harm in exploring the possibilities, and surely she had enough savvy to take safety precautions.

As if reading the officer's mind, DeBuono commented, "I was interested enough to keep listening to him talk. But I had also, I think, been in the business long enough to know that he was up to something. He didn't feel quite right to me." She asked Brian for a business card.

Describing it, Cathy said, "He took out a card. I distinctly remember it was sort of tattered and old. He let me look at it, but told me that he needed to take it back because it was the last card he had." She recalled seeing the name Brian on the card, but couldn't quite make out the surname. On the reverse side, she saw the Walt Disney Studio logo. He allowed her only a cursory glance before quickly retrieving it.

Did he suggest or mention an audition?

"Yes. He wanted me to leave the mall with him right away. I refused. I knew better than to do that. I told him we could make an appointment for another time."

Both Cathy and Brian used gambits and defensive maneuvers, as in a tight game of chess, pitting experience, skill, and intelligence against one another.

Agreeing on an audition two days hence, Brian explained that it would be held in the Hollywood Hills. In Cathy's recollection, he then said, "It's a private home, where they have a studio, right off the Lookout Mountain area." He gave her a specific address and instructed her to drive up Laurel Canyon, then make a left turn on Lookout Mountain Avenue. She had been up there before, making her reasonably familiar with the area.

If Cathy thought he would provide specific instructions regarding entry into the residence, or other details, she was wrong. "I was supposed to pull over in my car, park, and wait. Someone would come, get me, and take me to the house."

Were you advised to wear or bring any special clothing? "No. He said it would all be provided, that there would be wardrobe on location, and that it was to be all about my legs."

On the specified date, Cathy followed her own instincts of safety, and took a wise precaution. She invited a sturdy, powerful stuntman who worked on the TV series with her to ride along. "I went up Laurel Canyon, turned left on Lookout Mountain, and passed other streets that I can't remember the exact names of. Something like Wonder, or Wonderland, I think." She pulled over at the specified site and waited. Fifteen minutes passed, and Brian never showed up.

Several days later, Cathy spoke about the encounter with her agent. A man named Brian, the agent revealed, had left employment with Disney, and had thrown away his business cards months ago.

She never saw or heard from Brian until a televison news program on March 5, 2003, brought back odd memories.

To Cabrera, an important issue became clear. Paleologus's choice of the address up on Skyline Drive, when telling Kristi Johnson where to meet him, had not been by sudden impulse. He had planned it for years, probably mulling it over endlessly while lying in a prison cell. When Paleologus asked Charlie Simon, the real estate agent, to take him up there in search of a home to buy, he had a specific plan in mind.

Victor had premeditated the plan and mentally honed it for a long time.

The detective showed Cathy DeBuono a six-pack of photographs and she instantly identified Brian as Victor Paleologus.

Three days after Cabrera interviewed Cathy DeBuono, yet another victim emerged. Detective Larry Nicols, sifting through aging police reports, found one that caught his interest. It detailed a complaint lodged in early 1991 by a young woman who accused a man of spiking her cocktail with a drug. In the otherwise routine statement, something jumped out at Nicols, instantly grabbing his attention. It told of a suspect offering a young woman the chance to be in a James Bond project. Re-reading every word, Nicols saw yet another story of an oft-repeated fraud.

It took place in the final days of 1990, when a remarkably attractive twenty-seven-year-old model and actress, named Elizabeth Davis, arrived at Los Angeles International Airport. She exited the terminal on the lower-level concourse with other incoming passengers and carried her baggage to the curb in search of a taxicab. A man spoke to her, admiring her beauty, and mentioned his position as an executive with Disney. He was working on a new James Bond film, he said, and thought she would be perfect for a role in it. They chatted a few minutes and exchanged telephone numbers.

Davis had already broken into the business with several modeling jobs, as well as minor roles in film and television. She had her own agent, but the opportunity presented by this man calling himself "Joe Messe" appeared to be a chance to take an important step up. They spoke by phone periodically over the next few weeks and she finally agreed to go out with him to discuss his offer. She thought of it as a "professional date" in which this "vice president" at Disney promised her the opportunity to meet important people associated with the James Bond project. On February 19, Messe picked Davis up at her North Hollywood apartment in a white convertible and drove to a popular seafood restaurant on Ocean Boulevard in Santa Monica.

Inside, he suggested that they first have a drink in the lounge, and he guided Davis to a table. He made his way to the other end of the bar, ordered for them, and carried the glasses back to where Davis sat. After drinking about half of the fruity vodka-and-rum cocktail, while they conversed, Davis began to feel tired and a little queasy. Shortly after they moved to a dining table in the restaurant, with a view of Palisades Park on the other side of the boulevard, she noticed something strange about her drink. A powdery white substance formed a thin crust at the top, and fear gripped Davis. Worried about possibly passing out, she excused herself to go to the restroom.

Instead, she located a coin telephone, punched in the restaurant's number, and asked to speak to the manager. Explaining what had happened, Davis demanded that he call the police to detain the man sitting with her.

She returned to the table, planning to stall him until officers arrived. Feeling even weaker, she decided to take the offensive, and asked, "Exactly what was that white powdery stuff you put in my drink?"

Contorting his face into a perplexed expression, Joe said, "It's only salt."

"Why did you put salt in my drink?"

"No big thing. I just wanted to dissipate the taste of the alcohol."

"Well, then, let me see you taste it."

Joe said he didn't want to, rose, excused himself, and said he was going to the restroom. He promised that he would be right back. She watched him walk out the main entrance and turn right into a hallway leading toward the restroom facilities. He never returned.

Soon after Messe's departure, SMPD police officer Oscar Scolari arrived and Davis told him the full story, including the James Bond pitch. She gave him her glass, in which half the drink remained. The police filed a report on the incident, but lodged no charges against Joe Messe.

After reading the yellowing reports, Larry Nicols knew that Joe Messe was probably Victor Paleologus. He also found that the reporting officer had also retained the drink and filed it in a cold-storage evidence locker. Miraculously, it was still there in 2003. Laboratory analysis proved that the white powder residue was Dramamine, a brand name for the chemical dimenhydrinate, used for prevention and treatment of motion sickness. A heavier dose can cause drowsiness and even hallucinations. Usage directions recommend that it should not be mixed with alcohol.

It took a while for investigators to find Davis, but when they did, she eventually confirmed their suspicions by identifying the man who had spiked her drink as Victor Paleologus.

Detective Nicols added the report to Virginia Obenchain's growing "murder books," the binders of accumulated information about Paleologus.

Another similar incident took place within a few weeks after the Davis episode. Paleologus singled out Julie Kruis in a department store and claimed to be an executive at 20th Century Fox. She agreed to meet him for coffee in Marina del Rey. After Victor went into his spiel offering her an opportunity to pose in promotional media for the next James Bond film, Kruis accompanied him to a cabin cruiser docked nearby. His access to the boat would remain a mystery.

In the galley, Kruis felt a sharp blow to her head. Blood seeped from the wound. Victor denied striking her, made apologetic sounds, and tried to soothe Julie with promises that Fox would pay for any medical expenses. Furious and confused, she left and went to an emergency clinic, where a doctor closed and sutured the cut on her head. Kruis filed a police report, but never saw or heard from the "Fox executive" again.

In 1993, Paleologus dated a woman for several weeks while pretending to be a doctor. Before long, her suspicion of him turned into abject fear. Finally contacting the police, she described him as "sick and dangerous," and said she had stopped seeing him due to his proclivity for wanting to tie her up.

To the investigative team, the picture of Paleologus's long-term planning of his James Bond scam came through in high definition. No wonder he had perfected it so well, since he'd been using the ploy for at least a dozen years.

Discovery that Paleologus had scammed one woman by claiming to be a doctor brought to mind another extreme con artist. Could Victor Paleologus be another Frank Abagnale Jr.? The general public learned all about Abagnale in the 2002 film *Catch Me if You Can,* starring Leonardo DiCaprio in the main role, with Tom Hanks as a pursuing detective.

The real Abagnale, a New Yorker born in 1948, carried out a fantastic international impostor/forger career during the 1960s. Using eight different identities, he passed himself off as a doctor, lawyer, airline pilot, and university sociology instructor. Exceptionally intelligent, Abagnale not only pretended to be active in those professions, he actually performed them in several instances. His motive, though, was money, not sexual conquests. Reportedly, he wrote bogus checks for more than $2 million in two dozen countries, comparable to $20 million in the twenty-first century. Abagnale served prison time in France, Sweden, and the United States. Ultimately he turned his skills into a successful career as a consultant in fraud detection, and earned far more than his illegal activities ever produced.

If Paleologus was no Abagnale, he still could be regarded as a remarkably prolific liar.

News coverage carrying a tip line telephone number yielded new information on March 12. It helped Obenchain reconstruct Kristi's trip in the Hollywood Hills on her last day of life. A man named Douglas Kirkland left a message and Obenchain responded that same evening.

Kirkland said that he had been watching the news, saw Kristine Johnson's picture, and realized that he had seen her on the day she disappeared. "I was getting the mail from my box just before dark, and saw her in a white convertible, a Mazda. She drove up to me and asked for directions to a place that looked like a castle."

Describing her behavior as "desperate," Kirkland said the girl told him she had been driving "all over the place" trying to find a particular location. "She seemed really nervous because she was late." It struck Obenchain with a touch of irony when Kirkland mentioned that he was a photographer, and that he figured the girl was going to a photo shoot. From his vantage point, standing at the entry to his driveway, he could see inside the car and noticed a white blouse on a hanger.

At first, Kirkland said, he couldn't think of a "castle-type" house in his neighborhood but recalled it with his wife's help. "It's on the corner of Green Valley and Skyline," he explained. It had saddened him to hear of her body being found on a slope below the spot where Skyline Drive dead-ended.

Obenchain asked Kirkland if he could recall what Ms. Johnson was wearing, but he said he couldn't. He thought it might have been "something white." The detective thanked him for his call.

So many references had been made to the "castle house." The next afternoon, Obenchain drove up to the intersection and knocked on the door, but got no response. She snapped several photographs of the place, and observed a sign advising NO OUTLET on Skyline Drive.

Dead end, in this case, took on a whole new and deeply sorrowful meaning.

CHAPTER 14

MODUS OPERANDI

Although it made investigators unhappy to see news coverage naming Paleologus and featuring his photo, it helped another young woman recognize the man who had approached her outside a Century City mall theater.

On February 12, 2003, at 5:00 P.M., Mary Beth Licudine left the downtown Los Angeles office where she worked in the legal profession. She drove through the mad tangle of commuter traffic across town to the Century City mall, planning to meet a girlfriend for an early dinner, then enjoy a current film in the movie complex. Both the food court and the theater were located within a few steps of a restaurant at the mall's north end, where Victor Paleologus often hung out, and where Susan Murphy had dined after meeting him.

When the film ended after 9:30 P.M., Mary Beth said goodbye to her companion and stopped at a pay telephone kiosk to call another friend in the San Fernando Valley. During her conversation, in which she said the movie hadn't been very good, someone interrupted her. A man muttered something inaudible, then stepped back until Mary Beth hung up and, still holding the handset, started to key in another number. "I was holding the phone, pushing buttons, and digging through my purse, all at the same time." He spoke again. She recalled, "I can't remember exactly what he said, but it was something about looking for a James Bond poster girl, that they really needed one right away—that I have the look. And that I could think about it."

Her curiosity slightly titillated, Mary Beth asked him for a business card. "He fumbled through some credentials that he had attached to his pants, and then said he didn't have a card."

Skeptical and annoyed, Mary Beth hissed, "Well, sorry, then we can't do business." The number she tried to call was busy, so she hung up and walked away.

Over three weeks later, a television news story about the disappearance of Kristine Johnson caught Licudine's attention. She watched and saw a composite drawing that resembled the man she had seen at the pay phones. The next night, more news came on after a press conference by the Santa Monica chief of police. This time, a photograph appeared on screen, showing the face of Victor Paleologus. Mary Beth unequivocally recognized it. She called the police.

One more episode in the long history of Paleologus's James Bond fraud was added to the record. This one, finally, registered an encounter in which the intended victim used common sense and brushed him off.

Sometimes, even when the photographer turns out to be legitimate, and young women who are dying to pose actually find the fame they seek, the original connection can eventually lead to serious problems.

In 1992, a pretty nineteen-year-old woman who had done some modeling in high school looked for a way to jump-start her career and make the transition into film acting. Not yet well-known, but successful enough to have signed with an agent, Cameron Diaz held high hopes of becoming rich and famous. By 2003, she would act or star in twenty-six movies, including *There's Something About Mary* and two *Charlie's Angels* films.

Long before that, her agent called one day with an offer from a photographer who had been published frequently, mostly in European magazines. John Rutter had a reputation for "edgy" work, leaning a little more toward explicit material, but certainly nothing close to hardcore pornography. Diaz hesitated, but with the hope that international exposure could create the desired breakout experience, she told her agent to submit her name. Rutter selected several young hopefuls, including Cameron Diaz.

He arranged for the photo shoot to be held in an abandoned warehouse located in the City of Industry, about ten miles east of downtown Los Angeles. The location didn't alarm Diaz. Top-ranked photographers usually have an artistic eye for offbeat backgrounds, which might include the rustic interior of an ancient factory or a warehouse offering unorthodox angles and light beams filtering through dust. Rutter liked to shoot in black and white for a film noir look.

Cameron showed up with a few other models in the dilapidated building, not knowing quite what to expect. A crew of lighting experts, makeup artists, and hairstylists had preceded them. High-wattage floodlights, reflectors, and oversize white umbrellas mounted on telescoping tripods stood everywhere. Miles of thick electrical cords snaked across scarred floors. Assistants to Rutter rushed about, eager to satisfy his every whim. Obviously a professional setup, the ambience set all of the models' minds at ease, including Cameron's.

Wishing to excel in this session, Cameron readily donned fishnet and leather outfits and posed as directed by Rutter. At first, he snapped a number of shots portraying her as a "tough woman," with grim facial expressions and wearing a leather bra, high-cut leather shorts, and boots. In one hand, she held a threatening bullwhip; in the other, a lit cigarette.

If the image bothered Cameron, she didn't let it show. She simply played a role for the camera's benefit.

Gradually Rutter ordered her into more sensual postures. For the sake of art, she was asked to shed some of the clothing and exhibit more flesh. The urge to achieve success can rationalize almost anything. Rutter used masterful skills at relaxing the models, making it a fun, playful experience. None of them objected.

It didn't take long before cleavage shots evolved into even more exposure: "Hey, let's try it without the tops and see if it works." His camera seemed to be clicking more rapidly. It has been said that young women feel a sense of power and control when they realize how men react to nudity.

On this day, even nudity didn't seem to satisfy the photographer, and he began to demand gymnastic poses. The models acquiesced, not wanting to appear prudish or unprofessional. Bowing to peer pressure, they fell into the mode of rationalizing: "If she can do it, so can I."

Cameron didn't take off all her clothing, but did agree to pose topless. It hadn't been in her plans to do so, but she knew that she looked good, and maybe this would be the pivotal point of her career, even though the pay wasn't particularly good. In one shot, she held a heavy chain attached to the neck of a beefy male model.

After the shoot ended, it surprised Cameron to see that Rutter didn't follow the usual routine of asking her to sign release forms for marketing the photos. Nearly all photographers routinely require the signatures to prevent models from demanding more money if the pictures are used in major publications. Maybe it meant that Rutter thought hers weren't sellable. Arty but commercially unusable, most of the photos wound up in one of Rutter's files. A few appeared in German magazines, including one showing Cameron clad only in a leather vest and shorts, but the experience didn't produce her big breakthrough.

Fast-forward ten years, and a strange reversal of positions had taken place. Rutter's career faded into obscurity, while fame and fortune embraced Cameron Diaz. Photos of her appeared everywhere and she signed multimillion-dollar contracts for her acting skills.

Rutter dug out the old topless pictures and saw a possible gold mine. Surely, this world-famous woman would compensate him generously for the negatives so they could be destroyed, never to be seen by the public. Only there was a big problem. Without releases signed by Diaz, the pictures could not be sold or published. Perhaps, he hoped, she had forgotten about the release oversight, and would pay him anyway. Probably not. The other alternative would be to forge her signature on release forms and gamble that she would be unable to prove it.

Forgery, in the twenty-first century, often utilizes modern technology in the form of computers. Rutter went to work. First he scanned a blank release form, then searched the Internet for photos autographed by Cameron Diaz. Using digital manipulation software, he inscribed the signature on his blank forms and even filled out the witness signature with another forgery. The printed-out final product, he realized, wouldn't pass for an original document, so he made a photocopy, planning to say that he had lost the original but had retained a copy in his files. A new flash of ingenuity came to him. He created another release through the same process, using the name of a male model he had photographed in 1992. Photocopying both forms on the same page, he figured, would add to the authenticity.

Examining the forms, Rutter still thought something was

missing. Realizing that many older documents usually showed damage, often torn, and frequently had staple marks in the upper left corners, he reworked the forgery to enter similar blemishes. To him, they looked truly genuine.

With the "proper" documents now in his possession, should he attempt to sell the topless photos to well-known skin magazines? Tentative probes made this idea unworkable, so he moved on to plan B. Rutter knew that Diaz had done the voice of Princess Fiona in the Dreamworks animated feature *Shrek,* and signed a lucrative contract to repeat it in *Shrek 2* and *Shrek the Third.* Negative publicity arising from topless photos, and especially the sadomasochistic poses, might severely damage box office returns, and ruin her chances for other jobs.

Furthermore, she had already started work in *Charlie's Angels: Full Throttle,* based on the popular television series that ran from 1976 to 1981. Rutter gambled that the producers wouldn't be happy to see sadomasochistic, topless photos of their star turning up in tabloids worldwide or on the Internet. Publicity is usually welcome for new movie releases, but not necessarily that type.

Calculating the maximum amount he might receive by peddling the pictures, Rutter weighed the infinite public appetite for sensational dirt on celebrities, the potential harm the photos might inflict, and the high salary Diaz currently commanded for movie roles. He figured he might make as much as $5 million in the underground market. On this basis, he would offer them to Cameron Diaz, or her legal representatives, for a bargain $3,300,000. Taking a deep breath on Wednesday, June 19, 2002, he telephoned her agent. In the spirit of Marlon Brando's Don Corleone, Rutter made an offer they couldn't refuse.

In the initial stages of his gambit, the deal looked solid. A conference call hooked him up with Diaz's attorney, Marcy

Morris, her manager, Rick Yorn, and Cameron herself. Articulate and thorough, Rutter explained that he had in his possession some painfully embarrassing photos of Ms. Diaz that he really didn't want to sell to unethical people, and being a nice guy with her best interests at heart, he would make them available to her for a reasonable sum. Rutter suggested that other potential buyers had made offers, so he needed to settle the matter within a couple of days. The manager agreed to meet Rutter personally the next day to examine the merchandise.

As soon as the call ended, Cameron huddled with her representatives and assured them that the photos couldn't be all that bad. It had been ten years since she posed for Rutter, but in her recollection, the shots were artistic.

In the Thursday meeting at Yorn's office, he saw not only a stack of photos picturing Cameron topless in sadomasochistic poses, but also a low-resolution videotape made at the same time. In it, Cameron could be seen engaging in those poses with two other models, male and female. No doubt existed that it was, indeed, young Cameron Diaz. The video's poor quality would probably preclude sales at porn video shops, but it might draw interest on the Internet.

Rutter left, convinced that he would soon reap the rewards. They had agreed to a meeting of all principals on Sunday, June 23.

At the outset, Rutter quoted his price, two-thirds of the $5 million offered to him by underground buyers. Asked what right he had to sell the photos and video, he cited release forms signed by Diaz at the time. Eyebrows shot up in surprise, since Diaz had always followed instructions never to sign releases without running it by her agent.

To prove his point, Rutter produced what he claimed was a copy of the original release. Cameron Diaz asked to have a closer look. She scrutinized it for several minutes, looked up at Rutter, then dropped a bombshell. "This is not my signature!" She added that Rutter knew very well that she hadn't signed the documents.

Tension filled the room. How could she be so certain? Couldn't her handwriting have changed somewhat in ten years?

The explanation was quite simple, and everyone in the room understood it, except perhaps Rutter. Celebrities, especially those with poor handwriting, frequently pay someone with calligraphy skills to sign photographs requested by fans. Rutter had made a disastrous mistake by forging a signature from a publicity photo. Yet, he tried to bluff his way through. Before departing the meeting in a huff, he said that he had done everything in good faith, and that he expected a decision from Diaz and her team no later than the next day, Monday.

Even though the release had been deemed a forgery, could Diaz risk fighting the issue in court? With such publicity, the photos would skyrocket in public curiosity, and so would their monetary value. Wouldn't it be easier just to pay the guy off, perhaps bargain with him for a reduced price, and sweep the entire episode under a rug?

No, said Diaz. Her righteous indignation erupted. She felt proud of her high moral values and personal dignity, and refused submission to raw extortion.

With guidance from the Los Angeles County District Attorney's Investigation Bureau, Diaz and her representatives planned a meeting. Rutter was invited to discuss the matter in more detail on Wednesday.

He agreed, attended, and once again presented his request for more than $3 million in return for his photo collection, and the signed release forms. Other buyers would pay more, he stated, and public dissemination of the pictures would be of immeasurable harm to Cameron Diaz's career. He had even prepared mock-ups of billboards to be posted in Japan, showing her topless in suggestive poses. He repeatedly emphasized the urgency created by competing offers.

The Diaz team requested names of potential buyers and told Rutter that they needed a little more time to consider the matter. He departed, hopeful that he had made the sale.

On June 30, Rutter heard a knock on the door of his Venice apartment. He opened it and faced DA investigators who produced a search warrant for all of the photos and videotapes of Cameron Diaz, related documents, along with Rutter's tower and laptop computers. It took two hours to collect everything.

When they left, Rutter smiled to himself. He had anticipated something like this, and placed all of the originals with a friend for safekeeping.

It's not that easy to outsmart law enforcement or prosecutorial agencies. On July 16, they summoned Rutter to sign a declaration stating, under penalty of perjury, that "the model release is not a forgery or phony." At that point, Rutter should have asserted that he actually thought the release was valid, and after hearing Diaz's denial, he had reconsidered and wished to withdraw his offer to sell the photos. Instead, he signed the declaration.

The district attorney promptly filed charges of extortion, attempted grand theft, forgery, and perjury. At a court hearing, the judge dropped the extortion count, but set a trial for the remaining three charges.

The trial opened in August 2005. Salivating tabloid reporters and Internet entrepreneurs showed up, probably thinking they might be able to see, and perhaps copy, the pictures and videos without paying one cent for them. To avoid making the images public, Deputy District Attorney (DDA) David Walgren introduced only three pictures, two of which showed Diaz properly covered. The third one, a topless shot, was discreetly shown to the jury, and to Diaz on the witness stand, out of the gallery's view. They were later sealed by the judge with orders prohibiting their distribution forever.

Walgren called experts to demonstrate how Rutter had used his computer to perpetrate the forgery.

Rutter's attorney built a defense on the proposition that his client had the prerogative of giving Diaz first "right of refusal" to the photos. Diaz testified, stating that she felt no shame for the poses, and that she thought her breasts looked good. She also adamantly denied signing any release forms. The defense countered by having Rutter take the stand and assert that he had not forged anything, nor did he have any knowledge of how it happened.

Jurors didn't buy it. After two weeks of testimony, it took the seven women and five men only a few hours to find Rutter guilty on all three counts. On September 15, the judge sentenced him to serve four years in prison.

Prosecutor David Walgren had carried the day, but would face a much tougher courtroom battle ten months later.

A final victim of Victor Paleologus's James Bond scam came forward on March 14, 2003. Laura Hayden, like most of the other women, caught sight of his face on a television newscast, and it jarred her memory. Speaking to Virginia Obenchain, Laura couldn't remember exactly when the event took place, in 1999 or 2000. But exactly as it happened with Cathy DeBuono, Susan Murphy, Alice Walker, Mary Beth Licudine, and Kristi Johnson, Paleologus had singled out Laura from all the female shoppers strolling through the Century City mall. He presented the same claims of working on a James Bond movie and the opportunity to participate in it.

Hayden couldn't recall what name he used, but listened to his generous compliments about her legs, and his desire to photograph her. His pitch sounded valid, and she accepted his

invitation to meet at a house in the Lookout Mountain neighborhood of the Hollywood Hills. He told her to wear "really high"
black heels. Hopeful and excited, Laura kept the appointment.

Something apparently went wrong for Paleologus, wreck-
ing his chance to be alone with Laura. Another man stood
next to him when she arrived and Laura could see a 20th Century Fox logo on a clipboard carried by the stranger. She
never heard his name, and had no chance to talk to him, since
he spoke to someone on the telephone the whole time of her
stay at the house.

Her host had brought a short black skirt and nylons. He
asked her to put them on for the audition and a photo session.
The shoes she wore were the wrong kind, he complained, so
maybe they should postpone the session for a few days until
she could find the necessary stiletto heels. A little disappointed, she left and never heard from him again.

Obenchain asked Laura if she recalled the address or street
name of the home where the appointment took place, but she
couldn't recall. She did remember seeing a FOR SALE sign
posted in front of the house.

After thanking Hayden for her cooperation, Obenchain entered the sparse report in her ever-growing records of the
complex case, but knew that it would be of little use, due to
the woman's hazy memory.

Still, with reports from nine different women revealing the
consistent James Bond modus operandi used by Paleologus,
the distinctive pattern of behavior could be regarded as his
own brand of fraud over a period of exactly twelve years,
from February 1991 to February 2003.

A huge problem loomed over the whole case, like the black
clouds of an approaching thunderstorm. The ongoing absence
of any real forensic evidence still undermined the possibility
of charging Paleologus with Kristi Johnson's murder.

CHAPTER 15

WITH MALICE AFORETHOUGHT

By March 2003, as Virginia Obenchain and her team continued probing for evidence in the death of Kristi Johnson, the 1992 murder of Kim Pandelios remained unsolved. No one had yet ruled out Charles Rathbun as her possible killer, but investigators remained open to identifying other suspects as well.

Could Paleologus have been involved?

He had established residence in Southern California by that time, and had already launched his James Bond scheme a year earlier with Elizabeth Davis. His rap sheet showed an arrest for rape in 1989, and he targeted beautiful young women who sought careers in modeling or show business. The files on Pandelios revealed her burning ambition to be a model. Could an examination of the facts surrounding her death implicate Paleologus?

* * *

A native of Cuba, Kimberly grew up in a middle-class Florida family. During her teen years, they moved to Reading, Pennsylvania, where Kimberly graduated from Wilson High School. She soon fell in love and entered into an early marriage. She and her musician husband, Peter, returned to Florida. Petite, with a perfect figure, brown eyes, and dark blond hair, Kim drew the attention of photographers, and enjoyed modeling swimsuits and lingerie for local advertising media. The birth of her little boy interrupted her budding career, but she worked hard to restore her body in order to resume it.

By 1991, she and her husband decided that greater opportunities for him as a drummer and for her as a model existed in Southern California. They moved to a small apartment in Northridge in the upper San Fernando Valley. No drummer work developed, so Peter went into the vending-machine business. A few stints at posing came Kim's way, but nothing like she had imagined. Still persistent, she searched through magazines and newspapers, including a few featuring ads for some exotic photography.

In late February 1992, a listing in a free weekly tabloid caught her attention. She called and left her telephone number. On the same evening, someone identifying himself as "Paul" contacted her and said that he needed a model to pose for a layout in an off-road vehicle magazine. He stated that he had been in the photography business for a long time, paid well, and needed to complete the shoot right away. It would take place somewhere up in the mountains for dramatic background scenery.

Kim sensed that something might not be quite right and replied that she would have to think it over. The idea of going any distance to meet a stranger bothered her, so she discussed it with a friend. He expressed skepticism, saying that it sounded too vague. Kim agreed and called Paul again to ask a few questions. His answers gave her more confidence, and she didn't want to waste a new chance for an entry into modeling. She agreed to meet him on Thursday morning, February 27. It pleased Kim's husband to see her so enthusiastic about this job, and he agreed to watch their thirteen-month-old boy until a babysitter would arrive at eleven o'clock. He shifted his work schedule to complete his rounds during the late night and early morning.

Leaving early, Kim allowed extra time to stop by a Sherman Oaks beauty salon to perfect her hair. The cool winter air might make it frizzy and she wanted to look her absolute best. She even wore her favorite earrings with three pearls dangling from each one. The hair appointment took longer than expected, keeping Kim at the salon until noon. She called home to tell the babysitter that if she heard from Paul the photographer to assure him that she was running late but would definitely arrive at the appointed place shortly. Paul did call, at about 1:30 P.M., and the sitter gave him Kim's message.

Expecting Kim to return home that evening, the sitter grew concerned when, well after sunset, she was still out. At 8:00 P.M., the phone rang. Relieved and expecting Kim's excited voice, the sitter rushed to answer it. She heard Paul's voice, instead, asking her to tell Kim that she had left her appointment book at his place. He said that he and his wife had gone to dinner after the photo shoot, and when they returned home, they found the calendar. Responding to the sitter's frantic questions, he denied having any idea where Kim might be, since she had left his place at about 4:00 P.M.

Peter arrived home, and immediately began calling acquaintances. None of them had seen Kim. He contacted the police to ask if she might have been involved in an accident. No, the officer replied, no reports had been filed regarding that name. In that case, Peter said, he wanted to file a missing persons report. The dismaying reply left him frustrated;

the department wouldn't file such a case unless the subject had been missing at least forty-eight hours.

The longest night in Peter's life followed, with him racking his brain trying to figure out exactly what he could do to find his wife.

That same evening, at nine forty-five, a female deputy sheriff for L.A. County motored along the Angeles Forest Highway toward the city on her way to begin her graveyard shift. Traffic was light. Few people wanted to risk the dangerous highway curves on a winter night. She passed a yellow two-door vehicle parked at one of the turnouts, and idly wondered why anyone would leave it there. It seemed strange that the driver wouldn't have turned into the Monte Cristo campground, just a short distance down the hill, on the same side of the road.

Almost four hours later, at 1:40 A.M., an off-duty deputy driving the highway approached the same spot, and promptly called the fire department. Smoke and flames engulfed a yellow car parked in a turnout. The female officer who had seen it earlier heard the call and rushed up there. It was the same vehicle.

After firefighters extinguished the blaze, and a tow truck had deposited the burned-out vehicle in a storage garage, investigators examined and photographed it. No one searched the site until two days later, when a deputy climbed down the slope and found a thirty-two-ounce metal container of Kingsford charcoal lighter fluid. A few feet away, he picked up a cigarette lighter.

Why would someone torch a car that had apparently been abandoned? It didn't make sense. The mystery deepened when a check of the license plate number led to Peter Pandelios, whose wife, Kim, had been reported missing. An investigator decided to have another look at the turnout, and discovered a handcuff key in the dirt a few feet behind the scorched gravel and sand where the car had burned. Even though the key appeared to be the type fitting cuffs for sale in specialty shops, and not police-issued, all of the officers who had been at the scene checked to make sure they hadn't lost it.

A search of thick brush and rocky terrain along a stream that ran through the Monte Cristo campground turned up nothing.

Four weeks passed before anything new developed. In a preview of the near-miracle discovery of Linda Sobek's planning calendar three years later, this find was even less probable. A hiker trudging along a meandering creek at the bottom of a deep canyon, not even following a trail, stopped under a bridge arching nearly two hundred feet above. The span on Angeles Forest Highway, built in 1941, supported by towering square columns on either end of the half-circle arch, provided a breathtaking view from above.

The hiker spotted something small and black near a column base and scrambled through heavy brush to check it out. He picked up a loose-leaf planning calendar/address book someone might have tossed from the bridge. Glancing through it, he noted listings for several modeling agencies. Since it didn't have any obvious value, the finder dropped it where it had lain and walked away.

Later he couldn't get the calendar off his mind, and contacted the local sheriff's station. An investigator asked the hiker if he could point the way to the book's location. Incredibly, they found it again, and brought it up the treacherous canyon wall. Discovery of Kim Pandelios's name raised hopes that it might be a clue to finding the missing young woman whose car had been burned just a few miles up the highway.

Peter Pandelios instantly recognized her calendar and

stated that Kim never went anywhere without it. It contained all of her contacts and appointments.

An odd thing had happened the previous day, said Pandelios. He had found a slip of paper with a name, Paul, along with a telephone number, written on it. A quick check revealed that the number had been disconnected. The police did find that it had belonged to someone named David Rademaker, but no one named Paul could be associated with that number. Of course, years later, Paul turned out to be David Rademaker.

One investigator commented that it seemed as if Kimberly "had slipped off the face of the earth." Her mother, in Pennsylvania, thought that Kim had perhaps been in an accident and lost her memory. "I nearly went crazy," she later said.

The missing persons hunt and the arson of a motor vehicle faded into cold-case status.

That all changed eleven months later on March 3, 1993, after a heavy rainstorm. A pair of hikers, exploring an old gold mine road in the north end of Monte Cristo campground, veered off the path into a thicket. One of them struck something odd with his foot. Bending over to brush away the leaves and mud, he realized that he had uncovered a good-size bone, perhaps from a long dead animal. Both men poked around in the brush to see if they could find more of the skeleton, then drew back in horror when they spotted a human skull.

Surprised and perplexed, they wondered what to do next. Should they collect the remains and take them somewhere, or leave them in place? Was this a crime scene or perhaps an ancient burial ground, maybe for local Indians?

They continued the search and discovered a dark piece of turquoise-colored fabric. Not wishing to touch it, they hoisted it into the air with a long stick, observed that it had straps, and finally realized it was a bra. The material seemed to be in pretty good condition, so they couldn't be certain it had any connection to the bones.

Deciding to leave all of their findings in place, the two young men exited the campground, contacted the sheriff's department, and agreed to lead investigators to the site.

After officers photographed the skull, bones, bra, and some other remains of cloth, they conducted an intensive hunt. A team of forensic specialists, joined by a pair of large fawn-colored search dogs, scoured the area. Recognizing that wild animals can tear apart a human body and scatter the remains over long distances, the team spent days rooting along the meandering creek and the old road. A jungle of brush and trees in the canyon, about one hundred yards wide from the highway to the opposite rise, created not only adverse but dangerous conditions.

Twenty-five feet from the skull, they found the lower jaw, or mandible, which would be useful in identifying the victim from dental records. They also turned up a clump of hair, more clothing, and a pair of handcuffs. The key previously picked up near the car burning site fit the manacles perfectly.

A technician, examining the artifacts in a laboratory, found that the bra had apparently been sliced with a sharp blade and stripped from its owner. Both shoulder straps had been incised, and a cut could be seen near the back hooks. It evoked an image of forcibly removing the bra from a woman bound with handcuffs.

The skull and pieces of bone proved inadequate for determining cause of death. Investigators initiated a new search on March 27, hoping to find more clues. Using anthropologist techniques, the hunters sifted dirt and sand through strainers. This new effort turned up a pair of earrings, three pearls dangling from each of them, and a gold ring mounted with a green stone.

Detectives understood that they had probably found the remains of Kimberly Pandelios, missing since February 27, 1992, thirteen months ago. But they needed positive identification.

Peter Pandelios confirmed that the ring and earrings belonged to his wife, and that the bra certainly resembled one she wore. He provided photos of Kim, one in which a big smile made a flaw visible—one of her eyeteeth slightly protruded. This looked exactly like the alignment of upper teeth in the skull. Dental X-rays made it final.

Nothing in the collected material provided any clue about how Kim had died, or who caused it.

Due to obvious similarities with the murder of Linda Sobek, and the close proximity of the body discoveries, L.A. County sheriff Sherman Block in 1995 announced Charles Rathbun as a prime suspect in the death of Kim Pandelios. One reporter noted, "They were both brunettes posing as blondes, they were last seen alive going to photo shoots, and they were both found in the Angeles National Forest."

America's Most Wanted, the popular television show hosted by John Walsh, ran an episode on the mystery, requesting help from anyone who might have information. Nothing else, though, turned up to positively link Rathbun to the murder.

Kim's remains had been found March 3, 1993, after a rainstorm, exactly ten years before the discovery of Kristi Johnson's body, also after a rainstorm. Could Victor Paleologus be the one who killed both women?

Detective Obenchain doggedly pursued every possible hint of a clue. Paleologus's computer had been seized during a search of the cubicle in which he lived on La Cienega. Specialists examined the contents and found hundreds of photos of young women in poses ranging from sexy to salacious. One series of shots featured a beauty with long brown hair in the setting of a schoolroom, complete with desk and an old-fashioned blackboard. She wore Victor's favorite ensemble: long-sleeved white blouse with necktie, black miniskirt, hose with garter belt, and black stiletto heels. In eleven photos, she gradually bared more of her body. A group of bondage pictures featured a naked, short-haired young blonde tied and gagged in various poses on a red chair.

Nothing in the erotic images provided data to reveal their source, identity of the models, or when Paleologus acquired them. The schoolroom sequence led investigators to interesting possibilities. Since Victor had been asking women to wear the specific clothing at "auditions," starting with Dawn Cooper in 1998, it could be argued that these photos inspired his requirements. Of course, they could also be of an unknown woman he had lured to one of his James Bond auditions, and actually photographed. Only Paleologus knew the answers, and he declined to comment. Still, the pictures lent even more credence to the modus operandi portfolio.

Computer users are sometimes frustrated when they accidentally delete text or photos, and can never recover them. However, the data must remain hidden somewhere, since experts can seem to find every e-mail, Web site visited, photograph viewed, or any other activity performed during the computer's lifetime. Technicians traced Paleologus's long-term habit of visiting pornography sites featuring nudity and bondage.

Still seeking clues, Obenchain spoke with Kristi's mother again. Terry Hall remembered that she had given Kristi a white gold necklace with an oval-shaped pendant, and stated that she wore it most of the time. It hadn't been on her body, and a search of her possessions failed to turn up the jewelry. If it could be found among Paleologus's property, an important connection might be made.

New telephone calls landed in Obenchain's electronic in basket. A former girlfriend of Paleologus's, frightened and insisting on remaining completely anonymous, told the detective that Victor often tied her up, using neckties, and was "into bondage." Even after almost a decade, she remained in abject fear of him.

Another call came from a police detective in Modesto, California. He inquired if there might be any similarities between the murder of Kristi Johnson and a case they were investigating. A woman named Laci Peterson had vanished under suspicious circumstances, and on March 5, the missing persons case had been reclassified to homicide, even though the body hadn't yet been found. Her husband, Scott Peterson, had admitted having an affair, but denied knowing anything about Laci's disappearance. Obenchain discussed circumstances with the Modesto detective, but they found nothing to interconnect their respective investigations. (The bodies of Laci and her unborn son, to be named Conner, were found the next month in San Francisco Bay. Scott Peterson's arrest, trial, conviction, and death sentence filled news media for months.)

A hotline tip from a U.S. Marine told Obenchain that he and another marine, currently in Iraq, had known Kristi. The caller had spoken to her around February 1. He wanted to report that she had not mentioned any appointments planned for February 15. Obenchain already knew that the "audition" had been spontaneously arranged that same day, but thanked the military man for his help.

The news remained negative for Obenchain regarding forensic evidence. Criminalist Steve Schliebe informed her that hair comparisons from samples seized at Victor's residence, and examined alongside hairs vacuumed at the Skyline Drive house, resulted in no matches. Tire tracks at both locations were not made by Kristi's Mazda.

By the end of March, efforts at building a forensic case trailed off into dead ends. The beginning of April showed no improvement. On April 7, Terry Hall told Obenchain that she had found Kristi's pendant necklace stuffed away in a backpack. One more potential lead crumbled.

A different new development looked hopeful. LASD criminalist Flynn Lamas notified Obenchain that biological material had been found inside the sleeping bag in which Kristi's body had been recovered. It would be subjected to DNA analysis. Meanwhile, a separate DNA test resulted in bad news. Tiny fragments of flesh under Kristi's fingernails turned out to contain only her own DNA.

Toward the end of April, even the hotline calls dwindled down to nothing. And scientists traced the sleeping bag DNA to Kristi's brother.

Jailers escorted Victor Paleologus into Beverly Hills court on April 22 for arraignment on the charge of illegally taking the BMW and related infractions. A judge imposed bail of more than a million dollars, in view of the defendant's previous record of probation and parole violations. That evening, Obenchain gritted her teeth at television news reports speculating about Victor's chances of facing trial for the murder of Johnson. One reporter stated, "Obviously, Santa Monica Police Department doesn't have enough evidence to charge Paleologus."

The Los Angeles County District Attorney's Office, the detective knew, was working long hours on the case, trying to decide that very issue.

At last, Obenchain received a call from Dr. Scheinen, coroner's office, inviting her to a meeting for review of various postautopsy lab tests. She attended on April 29, and learned that toxicology tests conducted on Kristi's body came back negative. No alcohol or drugs had been found in her system. The coroner ruled Kristi's death a homicide caused by trauma to the head and neck. Compression of the neck had led to asphyxia and hemorrhaging.

The first week of May produced very little encouraging progress in the ongoing search for evidence. Criminalist Flynn Lamas reported a list of negatives regarding DNA:

- The "scrunchy" on Kristi's wrist had some biological material on it, but not enough to type.
- A minuscule semen stain was found on her jacket, but not enough to type.
- Swabs taken from the Miata interior were not enough to type.
- A drinking straw taken from the vehicle—DNA typed to Kristi.

Despite the paucity of physical evidence, the L.A. DA chose to forge ahead. On May 12, Deputy District Attorney Eleanor Hunter filed charges against Victor Paleologus for violation of Penal Code 187 (a). It states that murder is the unlawful killing of a human being . . . with malice aforethought. The DA also tacked on two "special circumstances" that would make Paleologus eligible for the death penalty or life in prison without the possibility of parole, if pronounced guilty of murder. Lying in wait, and attempted rape, if found true by the jury, would earn him a trip to death row or permanent residence in state prison.

Sandi Gibbons, spokeswoman for the district attorney, told reporters that, although special circumstances were included in the official charges, the decision had not yet been made whether the prosecution would actually seek capital punishment during the trial. A preliminary hearing would be scheduled, and all of the factors would be discussed after that process.

Now the pressure heated up. Could Paleologus be brought to trial for charges without the traditional forensics customarily used in first-degree murder cases? Would he walk free, scoffing at the specter of prison, much less death row?

CHAPTER 16

SMILE, YOU'RE DEAD

California's death row already held another inmate, in addition to Rodney Alcala, who had lured young women by wearing the mantle of professional photographer. It took one of the greatest detectives of all time, the legendary John "Jigsaw" St. John, of the Los Angeles Police Department, to spearhead investigation of two blood-curdling, barbarous murders committed by this shutterbug killer.

The condemned inmate had previously served time for sex crimes in the early 1980s, and targeted younger women by appealing to their aspirations for being models or in movies, exactly like Victor Paleologus would do nineteen years later. Both spent a lot of time in Marina del Rey and bought cars from the same dealer there. Each of them drew headlines in the new century—Paleologus from 2003 to 2006 on suspicion of killing Kristi Johnson, and the inmate midway through 2006 when fifty photographs surfaced, all portraying women who had posed for him. Sheriff's detectives searching old files stumbled on the collection, and wondered how many of the smiling faces might have been murder victims. Officials arranged for the photos to appear nationwide on television and in newspapers, with appeals for anyone who recognized them to come forward with information about each of the women's current status.

The killer's two known victims, Shari Miller and Tracey Campbell, like Kristi Johnson, died of savage strangulation in 1984.

Shari Miller, at twenty-one, the same age as Kristi, hadn't had the same upbringing or advantages in life. In the summer of 1984, a failed marriage and pending divorce had left her homeless and often sleeping in her car, staying overnight with various girlfriends or crashing at her mother's apartment. Even some of her clothing came from generous friends. One pal sometimes scavenged trash bins for undamaged clothing. He found a long-sleeved black blouse decorated with multicolored flowers and tiny cartoons of snails, gave it to her, and it became one of Shari's favorites.

Not beautiful, but attractive, with long, middle-parted brown hair, blue eyes, and a well-formed five-nine, 120-pound figure, Shari sometimes dreamed of being a model. More pragmatically, though, she often spoke of going to college to become a graphic artist. Perhaps her interest in art motivated the inking on her body of three tattoos: Harley-Davidson motorcycle wings on her left ankle, Winnie the Pooh on her lower abdomen, and an *S* on the bottom of her right foot. One unique ring she wore had been crafted out of a silver spoon, and another bore the carved head of an Indian chief.

The vagaries of Shari's existence, and the people she hung out with, sometimes led her into scrapes with the law. But for the most part, she avoided serious trouble and kept her dream alive of achieving some level of success.

By serving drinks part-time in a bar near Culver City, called the Meat Market (and by many patrons, the "Meet"

Market), Shari earned enough to feed herself and to buy gas for her battered, ten-year-old brown Dodge Dart hatchback. Men in the bar appreciated her good-humored chatter, interpreted by some as flirtatious, and kept coming back for more. Shari counted among her male friends the ragpicker who gave her clothing, a housepainter, a motorcyclist, and a bearded beer drinker. The painter kept saying he might employ her as a helper. The biker, age thirty-seven, often dropped in at the bar, seemingly flattered that a twenty-one-year-old girl would engage in banter with him. The beer drinker sometimes joined his rowdy buddies in kidding around with Shari. She met another man in June 1984, and took him as a lover.

Late that same month, Friday, June 29, Shari telephoned her mother from a hospital and asked if she could come over to stay the night. She had slipped getting out of a shower, fallen, and cut her left arm badly enough to require five stitches just below the elbow. The next morning, Shari made a call, overheard by her mother, inquiring if "the job was still available." Asked about it, Shari told of being invited to pose for a photographer, modeling leather jackets and boots for a magazine.

On Sunday, she shared the same news with a girlfriend. Shari remarked that she was looking forward to modeling leather outfits within a week for a photographer, who "had a lot of money" and lived on a boat in the marina. The guy, she said, would supply all the clothing. With a knowing look, the confidante asked if there would be any nude shots. "Absolutely not," Shari insisted.

The next night, after arriving late, clad in cutoff jeans and a flimsy, sleeveless white peasant blouse printed with red and blue flowers, she stayed with another girlfriend. In the morning, the two women made lists of things they planned to do. Shari scribbled on notepaper, *Meat Market, 6 p.m.* She also bubbled to her hostess about the upcoming modeling job.

That afternoon, the housepainter came by to inquire if Shari wanted to help him with a job in the San Fernando Valley right away. They left together in her Dodge, squeezed by overflowing cardboard boxes, piles of clothing, and a white quilt with small red patterns imprinted on it. It would later be revealed that he injected methamphetamine during the trip, and she tried but couldn't get the needle into a vein.

Working all afternoon, they slapped yellow paint on a house and left at 6:30 P.M. On their way to the Meat Market, she told the painter of her plans to model. At the bar, a man arrived, and Shari introduced him as the photographer Bill Bradford. The painter realized that they'd met before in the bar, and recalled that this man was a biker, age thirty-seven, who was frequently seen talking to Shari.

Arrangements were made for Shari to show up on Tuesday, July 3, at the photographer's apartment on Midvale Avenue in the Palms area of Los Angeles, about two miles from 20th Century Fox Studios. If she had known very much about Bradford's background, Shari would never have kept that disastrous appointment.

Bradford didn't live in a boat at the marina, as Shari had mentioned to her girlfriend, nor did he have a lot of money. An inveterate drifter, who fancied himself a photographer and took countless pictures of willing young women, Bradford worked sporadically as a handyman. All three of his marriages had ended in vitriolic bitterness. He wasted a moderate inheritance from a relative, and produced income through a variety of sources, legal and illegal.

Like Victor Paleologus's future dance with justice, Bradford magically eluded punishment for a long history of criminal and sexual violence. Beginning in his early teens with several incidents of indecent exposure, he escalated in 1972 to something even more serious, assault to commit rape, for which he received a suspended sentence. That same year, the nude body of a young black man was found strangled in an alley. He had last been seen inside a Culver City bar talking to Bradford, whose motor home was parked nearby.

Bradford's pattern continued with more sex charges, batteries, and suspicion of murder. One woman suffered torture from him for three years, from 1975 to 1978. At age sixteen, she moved in with him and produced a son—despite constant abuse. She fled to Michigan, but he pursued and convinced her to marry him. It only escalated the beatings and she left again, to California. Bradford followed, and, using subterfuge, cornered her once more. He ramped up the violence, and his use of fists and unspeakable sexual torment left her with temporary blindness, permanent hearing loss, and a partially severed finger.

In late August 1978, a strikingly pretty mother of two, Donnalee Duhamel, age thirty-two, chatted with a man while her boyfriend played pool in a Culver City bar. Men couldn't help but notice her lustrous shoulder-length brown hair, dimples when she smiled, and an eye-catching figure. She sometimes spoke of ambitions to model. Witnesses overheard the conversation in which the stranger bragged of his skills as a photographer, and showed her some snapshots. Donnalee told her boyfriend she was going outside with the photographer so he could take a few pictures of her, and she would be back in a few minutes. Hours passed, and a subsequent search failed to turn up any clue of Donnalee's whereabouts.

Eight days later, hikers found her nearly decapitated body, wrapped in plastic, on a rural brushy slope in mountains about twenty miles west of Culver City. Someone had strangled her to death and mutilated her torso. Homicide investigators interviewed all of the bar patrons, but found nothing to identify the photographer.

Bill Bradford soon left the state.

He migrated to Florida in 1980, the same year Ted Bundy faced trial there for his final murder. Resuming the same pattern, Bradford couldn't resist violating more women. One victim endured beatings, rape, insertion of a coat hanger in every bodily orifice, and threats to cut off her nipples with scissors. Charged with sexual battery, he served a short jail sentence, then left the state.

Back in Southern California, Bradford lured even more women with his camera. He moved into a trailer court near Marina del Rey in 1982. Riding a motorcycle, camping out in his rattletrap motor home, or carousing in local bars occupied most of his time. One of Bradford's drinking pals showed him the way to a special place in the Mojave Desert he found particularly appealing. Near Edwards Air Force Base, an outcropping of jagged rocks slopes up into a bowl-shaped valley at a place called Horseshoe Canyon. It offers a primitive camping site in absolute solitude.

The dry, windswept region is pockmarked with evidence of broken dreams—abandoned, disintegrating shacks, rusting skeletons of dead vehicles, decayed homesteads that someone had once seen as a paradise of blue skies and sanctuary from the evils of urban crowding. The pitiful dwellings are miles apart, isolated, and lonely. But there is something mystical about the place, too, offering communion with hardscrabble survival, a sort of competition with the elements. The desert's fierce power is palpable, and Bill Bradford loved power. Especially over young women.

In April 1983, he invited Stephanie (pseudonym), age twenty-two, to ride out to Edwards Air Force Base and join a group of friends to watch the NASA space shuttle landing. He had known her about a year, lived with her for a while, and she had modeled for him a few times. They all camped out at Horseshoe Canyon that night and departed the next morning. After driving only a few miles, Bradford suddenly turned his motor home around, complaining of uncertainty about the campfire being properly extinguished, and returned to the isolated spot.

Alone with Stephanie, he pulled a knife and repeatedly raped her in the most vile manner imaginable, involving beatings, oral abuse, sodomy, insertion of foreign objects, and forced ingestion of excrement, urine, and unidentified drugs. Back in Los Angeles, she reported the horrific assault to the police, who soon arrested Bradford. After serving a few weeks in jail, a judge inexplicably reduced his bail and he walked away, free to do anything while he waited for trial.

Relocated in 1984 to an apartment in Palms, Bradford ran into an old pal he had befriended in the marina trailer court. Mark, now coupled with a girlfriend, Nicole (pseudonym), age twenty-one, agreed to testify in Bradford's behalf in the pending rape trial. In return, Bradford said, he would pay the couple's living expenses.

Bradford told his pal that Nicole would make a great model, and he wanted to photograph her. In June 1984, she posed for a few shots while Mark observed, after which the trio visited several bars. Drowsiness suddenly overtook Mark and Nicole, and they both passed out. When she regained consciousness, while Mark still slept, they were all in the desert, under late-night stars. Pointing a rifle at her, Bradford ordered Nicole to strip and orally copulate him.

Mark woke up, tried to intercede, but backed off when Bradford fired the rifle into the sand. The next words from Bradford amazed and frightened the couple. He said that he'd been paid by a mutual acquaintance, with whom Mark had some legal disputes, to kill both of them. But, Bradford cackled, he was going to have some fun first. Again he forced Nicole into deviant sexual acts with both Mark and himself. Sated, Bradford offered to release them if they would agree to leave the state and never tell anyone he hadn't carried out the execution. With their agreement, Bradford drove the couple to San Diego and dropped them off. Apparently believing the "hit man" claim, they didn't report the rape.

Shari Miller had no inkling of her photographer friend's horrific record of behavior, and showed up at his apartment on July 3, just one month after he had assaulted Mark and Nicole. Bradford told her to relax in his late-model white Chevy Camaro while he and his bearded beer-drinking buddy from the Meat Market completed a motorcycle repair job. She complied, and fell asleep in the passenger seat. Bradford snapped a Polaroid picture of her, arms crossed, mouth open, peacefully sleeping, while his pal stood next to the open car holding a bottle of booze close to her right ear, in a clumsy joke indicating she had passed out from drinking too much.

The motorcycle repair evidently superseded Shari's expected modeling session on that day. Before sunset, she accepted Bradford's offer to accompany him to West Hollywood for something to eat. As they pulled out onto Midvale Avenue, he spotted a young male neighbor walking, pulled over, and invited him to ride along. The youth lived in an adjacent apartment building with several relatives, including his pretty cousin, Tracey Campbell, age fifteen. Bradford introduced him to Shari, who sat quietly in the passenger seat.

Only one more person could recall seeing her alive. Shari arrived at her lover's apartment late on Tuesday, slept with him a few hours, then left before dawn on Wednesday, Independence Day, July 4.

Early Friday morning, a motorist pulled into a small parking lot near the corner of Pico Boulevard and Elm Street, a few blocks from 20th Century Fox Studios. Kristi Johnson would pass the spot nineteen years later on the last day of her life. After parking, and exiting his car, the man caught sight of a bulky bundle lying on the pavement next to a wooden barrier near the back of a store. Perhaps it was just trash tossed there by some jerk irresponsibly disposing of his household detritus. But a little closer look revealed a scarlet stain. Also, a powerful odor filled the air. He called the police.

The first officer on the scene peeled back the red-patterned white quilt and saw the nude, mutilated body of a young woman. He secured the scene and called for the homicide team.

One of the most revered detectives on the LAPD force inherited the case. John "Jigsaw" St. John, called legendary by many, had been an investigator in scores of high-profile cases, including the notorious "Black Dahlia" murder of Elizabeth Short. He carried a detective's gold shield, badge number one. Unimposing in appearance, St. John still wore a fedora hat, reminiscent of movie detectives from 1940s film noir thrillers.

He observed while a coroner's technician unveiled the naked body, and he could see that the killer had used a razor-sharp knife on her. A few inches of flesh at the front of her left ankle had been neatly sliced off, along with a larger section from her lower abdomen, and both nipples had been severed from her breasts. A long leather thong held her ankles together, looped around the left thigh, and ended in tight knots binding her wrists below her stomach. Maybe the tattoo of an *S* shape on the bottom of the victim's right foot would help identify her, or perhaps the Indian head silver ring she wore.

At the subsequent autopsy, the coroner concluded that "Jane Doe 60" had died from strangulation by a ligature around her neck, possibly like the leather thong used to bind her. At least she hadn't suffered torture from the incisions of her flesh, since they occurred postmortem. The examiner estimated that she had died on the evening of July 5. A yellow substance from under her fingernails turned out to be paint.

Jigsaw St. John had seen more than his share of mutilated young women, harking back to Elizabeth Short, the Black Dahlia. In 1947, her body was found eviscerated and sliced into four parts. Her slayer had also removed a tattoo from the body with surgical precision. The case had never been solved. Viewing the autopsy of Jane Doe 60, St. John made a silent vow to himself that he would find the killer of this young woman.

It would take several weeks to discover the identity. Her old car, minus a quilt friends had seen inside, was towed from the parking lot of a bar within a few blocks of an apartment building where Bill Bradford lived, next door to fifteen-year-old Tracey Campbell.

Tracey's mother, along with an older sister and brother, had moved from Montana to the apartment on Midvale Avenue early in 1984. In spring, Tracey and her cousin Todd, age twenty, had followed.

While sunbathing on the front lawn in the first week of June, Tracey watched Bill Bradford washing his motorcycle. It fascinated the junior-high student when he told her that he often did professional photography. Maybe she could become a model.

Todd had the same idea for himself. On Monday, July 9, he posed for Bradford at a construction site, and later that day viewed the pictures in Bill's apartment. Some other snapshots caught his attention, too. He recognized the image of a girl he had met a week earlier when Bradford had pulled over to the curb, given Todd a ride to West Hollywood, and introduced him to the passenger named Shari.

The following Wednesday, while Todd visited Bradford in his apartment, Tracey appeared at the door to inform him that dinner was ready. She gave Bradford a coy smile, said she wanted to become a professional model, and suggested that she could pose for him. He recommended that she submit a portfolio to a magazine for people who shared that ambition. Tracey asked if he would help her prepare it.

"No," Bradford replied, surprising her. "I don't work with minors." His suddenly elevated ethics may have been primarily for Todd's ears, since he had never before shown any reluctance to aim his camera at younger girls.

Temperatures soared in Southern California on July 12, and Tracey dressed as if she planned a trip to the beach, wearing a blue-and-white two-piece bathing suit covered by white shorts and a floral-patterned lightweight blouse. At eight o'clock that morning, after all of the family except her brother had left for work, a knock came at the apartment door. The brother, preparing to leave for his job, would later recall hearing Tracey greet Bill Bradford and talk briefly to him. Bradford said something about a job for Tracey.

An hour later, another resident of the building noticed the closed door to Tracey's apartment, which struck him as odd, since the youngster always left it open while at home alone, especially on warm days.

Todd, too, couldn't believe it when he returned home from work that afternoon and found the door not only closed, but locked. He waited for Tracey's mother to show up, then pried open a window to get inside. The deadly still interior had apparently been unoccupied all day, as evidenced by Tracey's uncompleted housekeeping chores and the presence of a sandwich she had planned to have for lunch. Most worrisome of all, she had not taken her purse with her.

Questioning of neighbors didn't help. Todd rushed over to Bradford's apartment, but no one answered the doorbell. The underground garage parking space reserved for his Camaro remained empty. The family searched in desperation for Tracey, and filed a missing persons report the next morning. Frequent checks of Bradford's apartment, and the parking garage, indicated that he didn't return home until early evening, Friday, July 13.

After learning of the missing girl, an acquaintance of

Bradford's repeatedly attempted to call him that day, and finally connected that night. Bradford said that he had given Tracey a ride on Thursday morning to Venice Boulevard, about one mile away, and dropped her off where she could hitchhike to the beach.

The neighbor who had noticed Tracey's closed door paid a visit to Bradford and asked if he had seen the girl. No, Bradford replied, explaining that he had gone to the desert to do some photography. He added that she had dropped by on Thursday morning to use his phone, and then left.

Perhaps alarmed by the questioning, Bradford visited Tracey's family. They noticed him trembling, appearing agitated, and failing to make eye contact with any of them. He repeated the story about Tracey coming over, asking to use the phone, and said that he heard her call a girlfriend, after which he gave her a ride to Venice Boulevard. It took place at about 2:30 P.M., he said, and described the clothing she wore. Accounting for his own time, Bradford told the relatives that he had gone to Orange County, thirty miles down the coast, after dropping Tracey off.

An LAPD investigator, fielding the missing persons report, visited Bradford and heard the same tale. With Bradford's permission, he conducted a brief search of the apartment and his freshly washed Camaro, which turned up nothing.

Two weeks elapsed with no sign of Tracey Campbell. Bradford's behavior, past record, and inconsistent stories of his whereabouts—the desert and Orange County—put him in the sights of police investigators. At the end of July, they executed a warrant for his arrest and for a thorough search of his vehicle and apartment.

Detective John Rockwood, a close colleague of Jigsaw St. John's, took Bradford into custody at the Meat Market, and had the Camaro towed to an impound garage. Officers scouring the apartment found several items of women's jewelry. The vehicle yielded more: a Polaroid photo of a young woman asleep in the car's passenger seat, a razor-sharp knife, numerous keys on rings connected by a key chain, and a camera bag containing photography equipment, pictures, and several negatives.

One of the keys, for an older Dodge Dart, subsequently turned out to fit Shari's car.

A technician examined the photos and negatives, including the Polaroid shot. Prints made from the negatives showed the same young woman who was asleep in the Camaro's passenger seat. In other photos she stood posing on a boulder, wearing a blue dress with flower patterns, against a background of rugged brown-and-tan rock formations under a deep blue sky. In yet another picture, apparently in the same remote site, she wore cutoff jeans and a lightweight white peasant blouse also decorated with imprinted flowers. A black watch band encircled her right wrist.

Detective Rockwood scrutinized the photos, using a magnifying glass like Sherlock Holmes, and could see a bandage on her left arm, just below the elbow. He spotted something else that made his skin crawl—a small tattoo of Harley-Davidson motorcycle wings on her left ankle.

Good detectives have near-photographic memories, and Rockwood remembered the body on Pico Boulevard being investigated by his colleague John St. John. The female victim had recent sutures on her left arm, below the elbow, and a patch of skin had been excised from her left ankle. Within minutes, he shared the exciting find with St. John.

Clearly, the pictures were of Shari Miller. To confirm it, St. John pulled records of Shari's 1980 arrest, found her fingerprints, and had them compared to those of Jane Doe 60. With the identification made, he could close the missing persons case. Now St. John intensified his investigation into the murder of the mutilated girl.

Bradford's photography, so often used to lure countless

women, now made him the target of suspicion in Shari's murder. St. John and Rockwood interviewed him for hours on end. He admitted that he had met Shari in the Meat Market about two years ago, and had generously satisfied her request to take pictures of her as a present for her mother. She had posed for them, he said, in late June at Topanga Canyon, about ten miles west of Bradford's apartment.

"When did you last see her?"

"Oh, it must have been about the end of June, or maybe July first. That's when I took the Polaroid of her in my car."

"Where were you on the Fourth of July?" The detectives referred to the last day Shari had been seen alive.

Bradford didn't hesitate. "I went down to Huntington Beach, in Orange County, to watch the tall ships. But I didn't take any pictures of them."

In the picture of Shari wearing cutoff jeans, she wore a necklace that strongly resembled one seized from Bradford's apartment. Asked where he got it, he claimed that Shari had given it to him a couple of months ago, with the request for him to have it repaired.

The detectives switched directions to ask about Tracey Campbell. Bradford denied any conversations with the girl about her ambition to model. On the morning of July 12, the day she vanished, he had performed maintenance work at a camera shop in nearby Culver City. In the middle of the afternoon, he came back to the apartment and Tracey showed up, dressed for the beach, asking for use of his telephone to call a girlfriend. "I gave her a ride to the corner of Midvale and Venice Boulevard." He couldn't be certain where she went after that.

"Where did you go?"

His answer flummoxed Rockwood and St. John. Bradford said he had driven around the rest of the day, to Santa Monica Airport, Marina del Rey, Century City, back to Santa

Monica Airport, the LDS Mormon temple on Santa Monica Boulevard in West L.A., Loyola University, El Segundo near Los Angeles International Airport, King Harbor in Redondo Beach, Malibu Beach—fourteen miles west of his residence, Leo Carrillo State Beach—eighteen miles beyond Malibu, back to the Culver City camera store, and finally to his apartment. In normal Los Angeles County traffic, that sounded like about thirty hours of driving.

Shrugging off the long-winded travel report, the detectives zeroed in on another location. They had already learned that one of Bradford's drinking buddies had steered him to Horseshoe Canyon, near Edwards Air Force Base, back in 1982, and the men had camped out there in April 1983. St. John asked him about it. Bradford acknowledged the group camping trip, but he denied ever going there with anyone else.

Little doubt existed in the minds of St. John and Rockwood that Bradford had some connection to the murder of Shari Miller and to the missing girl, Tracey Campbell. But more evidence would have to be found before he could be charged. They set Bradford free after only three days in custody.

St. John wondered if the background in photos he had seen of Shari Miller standing on a boulder might be in Horseshoe Canyon. In midsummer heat, on Saturday, August 11, he led a task force of seventy-five law enforcement officers on an expedition to the Mojave Desert. Bradford's old drinking buddy, who had first pointed out Horseshoe Canyon to him, led the way. St. John brought the photos of Shari Miller with him. On horseback and on foot, the searchers crisscrossed scores of sandy acres, looking for uniquely shaped rocks depicted in the pictures. It took some time, but they found the site, exactly where Shari had stood. A police photographer took new photos, to be scientifically compared, for use as evidence.

As they began to wrap up for the day, a few of the men

explored an adjacent outcropping of boulders about four hundred feet from the spot where Shari had posed.

They made a horrifying discovery.

Partway up the slope, a "severely decomposed and partly skeletonized body" reposed on the rock-strewn dirt and sand. It had apparently been savaged and moved after death by animals, as indicated by bloodstains several yards away. Both hands, as well as other bones from the limbs, were missing. The leg bones had been pulled from the torso. From the waist down, very little skin could be seen, and remains of flesh on the upper parts looked like ancient leather. Severe damage to the genital area made it impossible to even guess the corpse's sex. The only clothing in sight, wrapped around the face, was a long-sleeved black blouse decorated with multicolored flowers and tiny cartoons of snails.

Transported back to the coroner's lab, the body underwent autopsy. Dental records identified her as Tracey Campbell. She had died from ligature strangulation, and deep imprints of a rope could still be seen on her mummified neck. Exact date of death could not be determined, but according to the examiner, the body's condition indicated that she had expired approximately July 12, the day Tracey vanished.

Detective St. John learned that the snail blouse had belonged to Shari Miller. It provided a powerful triangle, linking Bill Bradford to both Shari and Tracey. With a new warrant, the detective arrested him the second time on August 16.

Initially Bradford refused to answer questions without the presence of an attorney. But when he couldn't reach the lawyer by phone, and another detective helping St. John spent about ten minutes alone with the suspect, Bradford changed his mind.

Speaking readily, Bradford still had no intention of confessing. He stubbornly maintained that the photos of Shari had been snapped in Topanga Canyon on June 28. They had gone to a drive-in theater later, he insisted, and he had dropped her off afterward at the Meat Market bar. Regarding Tracey, Bradford stuck with his story of giving her a short ride, after which he had never seen her again. Confronted with the fact that her body had been discovered close to the site where Shari had actually posed, Bradford could only hang his head and say, "I can't explain it to you." Now, he decided, he needed an attorney after all, and the interview came to a halt.

A new warrant to search the apartment produced crucial evidence, including a section of rope matching the marks found on Tracey Campbell's throat, and a black band wristwatch flecked with yellow paint, exactly like the one Shari wore in the desert photos.

It took more than three years to finally bring Bradford to trial in the fall of 1987. The courtroom battle lasted several weeks, during which the jury boarded a bus for a trip to Horseshoe Canyon in the high desert. They viewed the sites where Shari had posed, where Tracey's pitiful remains were found, and compared the backdrop in Shari's photo with the snapshots taken during the massive desert hunt.

Back in the Los Angeles courtroom, after final arguments by the prosecution and defense, twelve jurors retired to deliberate the case. A day passed, then two, four, and then seven. After a couple of days off, the jury went back to work while the court principals, reporters, victims' families, and Bill Bradford waited and wondered.

Another week passed, and the prosecution team realized that hopes for conviction looked awfully bleak.

At last, five days before Christmas, the jury foreman sent a note out to announce they had arrived at a verdict. Not only was Bradford guilty on both counts of first-degree murder, but they also found true the special circumstance that he had committed multiple murder, which made him eligible for the death penalty or life in prison without the possibility of parole. The same jurors would next sit through a penalty phase of the trial to make that decision.

In this phase, prosecutors brought to the stand a series of women who had suffered brutal sexual assaults and beatings by Bradford. The testimony couldn't have been more disturbing or gruesome.

Before it ended, Bradford fired his attorney and received permission from the court to represent himself. Still, he rested his case without having called any witnesses or presenting any evidence of mitigation.

The prosecution presented closing arguments requesting jurors to recommend the death penalty. Deputy DA David Conn wound up by saying, "These two innocent victims— Sentencing Mr. Bradford to death doesn't even compensate for their lives . . . but it's the least you can do."

Bradford's closing statement, spoken directly to the jury, consisted of fourteen chilling words: "Think of how many you don't even know about. You're so right. That's it."

The jury set the verdict at death, and the judge made it official on May 11, 1988.

Bill Bradford's name resurfaced in news headlines during the summer of 2006 when cold-case detectives rummaged through old evidence and found fifty-three photos of fifty women who had posed for him. The pictures received wide coverage in television and print media and generated over one thousand telephone calls, confirming that twenty-eight of the women were alive and well. Two, though, turned out to have been murdered. One, whose body was found in the high desert in 1980, had been strangled, fitting the pattern of Tracey and Shari's murders. The other was Donnalee Duhamel, the woman who had been seen leaving a Culver City bar with a photographer in 1978, and whose murder had never been solved.

All of the others remained in question.

In 1998, Bradford appeared ready to accept execution when he announced that he planned to cease all appeals. A judge set the date for him to die by lethal injection. Five days before the scheduled event, Bradford changed his mind, starting the slow-grinding gears of justice once again. With the population of California's death row creeping toward seven hundred, and executions subject to frequent moratoriums, it is more likely that he will die of natural causes than lethal injection.

CHAPTER 17

THE DEFENDER

Defense attorney Andrew Reed Flier spoke to a *Los Angeles Times* reporter in February 2004. He said that his client Victor Paleologus, charged with first-degree murder and facing a possible death penalty, was innocent. In a cryptic way of indicating that no evidence had been found to connect Paleologus to the murder, Flier stated, *"There is not any way that anybody could have been this clean,"* apparently leaving off "if he was guilty." No DNA, no hair samples, nor any eyewitnesses had been found by the prosecution, all of which, according to the defender, pointed directly to innocence.

Flier, who bore an uncanny resemblance to the late John F. Kennedy Jr., with full dark wavy hair and handsomely chiseled features, had worked on numerous high-profile cases. In December 2003, he had defended a reputed gang member being tried for shooting a Burbank police officer to death. A month later, Flier triumphed when an appeals court overturned another client's conviction for second-degree murder.

Headquartered in Encino, a few miles northwest of downtown Los Angeles, Flier knew his way around the legal system and demonstrated willingness to defend a broad spectrum of clientele, from celebrities to crime lords.

Victor Paleologus, Flier said in May, "is adamant—one hundred percent not guilty—about not doing injury to the young lady in question." To find him culpable, Flier explained, a jury would have to believe that his client had committed the perfect crime. Possibly, Flier suggested, investigators had targeted Victor because of two previous convictions in which similar allegations of luring young women had been charged.

Deputy DA Eleanor Hunter agreed that no forensic evidence had turned up, but rationalized that Kristi Johnson's body "was out there in the wilderness forever. Any evidence that might have been around, I'm sure, got washed away by the elements."

Meanwhile, Andrew Reed Flier started building his plans to defend Paleologus while simultaneously trying to anticipate the prosecution's main thrust. He knew that the exact time of Kristi's death could be a pivotal point, especially in view of his client's presence in jail two days after she vanished. He chose to fight with an especially gruesome weapon—maggots!

The dispute was just the first salvo in the coming barrage.

At least, Flier wouldn't have to defend his client in the murder of Kimberly Pandelios, whose remains had been discovered in March 1993. On March 3, 2004, David Rademaker had been arrested for that crime. Cold case investigators had located one of Rademaker's former girlfriends. She told of having sex with him when she was only fifteen after falling for his ruse of being a photographer on contract to Hollywood producers. During their three-year relationship, she had moved in with him, shared drugs, and helped him operate a phone sex business.

Now twenty-eight, the woman informed detectives that she

had accompanied Rademaker in February 1992, on a drive into the mountains and watched as he torched a car. She examined a photo of Pandelios's vehicle and thought it closely resembled the one Rademaker had burned.

By monitoring telephone calls the cooperative informant made to Rademaker, investigators gathered enough incriminating statements to charge him with the murder of Pandelios. Trial was set for February 2006, just a few months before Victor Paleologus would face a jury.

CHAPTER 18

AN INSIDER'S VIEW

Ronald E. Bowers, a member of the Los Angeles County DA's Office for four decades, has been involved in countless major cases. Working for the largest prosecutorial agency in the world, he has witnessed every conceivable twist and turn in the jurisprudence system. Some of the people with whom Bowers worked have included renowned legal personalities such as author Vincent Bugliosi, who prosecuted Charles Manson and his gang, Judge Lance Ito, who presided over the O.J. Simpson trial, and former LAPD officer turned author Joseph Wambaugh.

Bowers worked closely with the retired chief deputy Curt Livesay for years. During more than two decades, Livesay shouldered the awesome responsibility of personally deciding which murder defendants would face a possible death penalty in their trials. He processed over fourteen hundred cases, and earmarked about one-third of them for capital punishment, including "Nightstalker" Richard Ramirez, "Hillside Strangler" Angelo Buono,

"Freeway Killer" William Bonin, "Sunset Strip Killer" Douglas Clark, and founder of the Crips street gang, Stanley "Tookie" Williams.

Following his 1966 graduation from the University of Southern California School (USC) of Law, Bowers joined the LADA Office the next year. After serving as a trial prosecutor, he advanced up the ladder to supervisory positions and helped form policy in various landmark issues. CBS's *60 Minutes* once called on his talents to help research and write a segment on traffic-stop search and seizure. In 1984, he launched one of the first volleys, eventually resulting in voters removing three justices from the California Supreme Court, including Chief Justice Rose Bird. Four years later, Bowers created a new leg of the DA's office, the Prosecution Support Division, which included the hiring and training of all attorneys in the office, and ran it as head deputy. Following the O.J. Simpson debacle in 1995, he spearheaded another creation called Trial Support Division, for the purpose of providing trial prosecutors with timely and effective visual aids to be used in jury presentations.

Bowers wrote two books, *Visual Aids for Prosecutors* and *Visuals for Today's Prosecutor,* both of which are widely used references in national legal circles. In 2006, the Japanese Ministry of Justice invited him to lecture and train prosecutors in that country.

Retirement from the L.A. office in 2002 didn't change his life much. The district attorney rehired him on a part-time basis in the Major Crimes Division as a senior deputy.

In that function, Bowers observed early steps in the murder case of Kristi Johnson, and became actively involved as it progressed toward trial.

He vividly remembers the emotional roller coaster.

* * *

Ron Bowers's Recollections

For years, I have developed a routine of watching the nightly news before going to bed. Car chases and gang shootings don't necessarily induce sleep, but I have grown so numb from seeing death and destruction that these images don't shock my sensibilities any more. Conversely, being briefed about the most recent twenty-four hours of tragedy and turmoil in our incredible City of Angels allows me the satisfaction of at least being well-informed.

Often, news affects me personally, especially when reporters stand in front of the courthouse and announce a verdict in one of the many cases I have worked on behind the scenes. The nightly television broadcast is often the first time I am aware of the outcome. People might ask why I am not among the first to know. The reality of the situation is that the Los Angeles County District Attorney's Office is so large, it might take days before the result of a verdict filters its way down to everyone. In an office of one thousand attorneys and sixty thousand annual felony cases distributed over twenty-one courthouses, it is understandable that television news is sometimes the best source to find out what happened in court each day.

February 19, 2003, was no exception and I turned on the local news to see if all was well in L.A. Partway through the program, a photo of an attractive young woman flashed on the TV screen. Her smile and long hair, as well as the sparkle in her eyes, caught my attention. I grabbed the remote control and turned up the volume to hear what the story was all about. Kristi Johnson, the reporter stated, had left for a photo shoot audition on Saturday, four days earlier, and never returned. Her roommates and family expressed concern about her safety. An appeal for public help had been announced at a press conference: "If anyone knows the whereabouts of Kristi, you are urged to contact the Santa Monica Police Department."

The brief coverage, no more than one minute of airtime,

somehow riveted me. The missing young woman looked like the typical girl next door. My gut reaction: this story wasn't going to have a happy ending.

The following evening's news provided an update, but a full week passed before the story took on a more somber twist. SMPD chief Butts held another press conference and revealed that Kristi's Mazda had been discovered in Century City. This fact jolted me. In a missing persons situation, it's nearly always a bad sign to locate the abandoned car. When the chief showed a composite drawing of a "person of interest," I automatically shook my head, knowing that Kristi Johnson would probably not be found alive.

Over the next couple of days, broadcasts continued to show video of friends, family, and even strangers searching everywhere for Kristi, from city streets to mountain ravines. Reporters interviewed volunteers, who, for the most part, simply wanted to reunite the missing girl with her family. I thought, *These people need a reality check. Are they ostriches with their heads in the sand? Don't they remember what happened just a few years earlier to model Linda Sobek—killed by photographer Charles Rathbun and buried in the mountains? Have these searchers forgotten the young women that Bill Bradford took to the desert for photo shoots, then raped and murdered?*

My initial reaction was to marvel at the naivete of people painting a happy face by believing Kristi would be found alive. Then I stopped and refocused my thinking on what the family and friends must be going through. In my experience related to so many homicide cases, I noticed a big difference between missing persons and murder investigations. In a homicide, the victim's fate is known, and the family or friends have the opportunity to grieve and move on with their lives. Depending on their beliefs, they may even be comforted by the idea that their loved one has gone on to a better place in the afterlife. With a missing person, though, the family is faced with tormenting uncertainty. Some will recognize that the absent individual will not be coming back, while others persistently cling to hope that everything will someday be all right. The range of emotions and behavior can set up an internal tug-of-war—guilt for giving up, or self-admonishment for ignoring reality.

There is often a reference in tragic situations to seeking "closure." I'm not certain there is such a thing as closure when a loved one is lost to a violent predator.

On February 27, a candlelight vigil was held for Kristi at the Santa Monica Episcopal church and part of it showed up on the nightly news. They announced a celebration of Kristi's twenty-second birthday. I had mixed feelings about celebrating the birthday of someone who, in all likelihood, was dead. The coverage concluded by showing Kristi's mother singing "Amazing Grace" as the audience joined in.

The sights and sounds of the church vigil, and the outpouring of mixed hope and grief, struck a deep chord inside me. It was one of those moments you don't forget. I might be somewhat jaded after four decades of dealing with an endless chain of violent criminals who have littered the streets of L.A. with human carnage. Yet, it surprised me to feel so deeply touched at seeing this strength in Kristi's mom, and her determination to maintain hope for her daughter being found alive. I reflected on my usual cynicism and searched deep within myself for an explanation to Kristi's disappearance. Did any real hope exist for her survival? For once, my attitude changed, and I took on the approach of a glass half full, not half empty.

On Monday night, March 3, I worked at home, sorting my financial papers, and covering my entire kitchen table, in preparation for next week's dreaded appointment with the income tax man, and with my thoughts focused, I was barely conscious of the droning television news in the background. Yet, the voice seemed to rise in volume, and grabbed my undivided attention when an anchor announced that a female body had been found in the Laurel Canyon section of the Hollywood Hills. I dropped my W2 forms on top of expense receipts and swiveled toward the screen. It showed emergency vehicles clustered against the dark sky, surrounded by rescue personnel. A large truck had telescoped its ladder out over the blackness of a canyon to lower technicians, and raise the body.

I asked myself, *Oh my God, could it be?* I listened to the reporter, using typically cautious language, saying it couldn't be confirmed that the remains were of Kristi Johnson until the coroner made a final determination. No doubt existed in my mind. This was the body of Kristi. In those few dramatic seconds, her sad fate had been announced to the world. Before I had time to digest what I had just seen, the commentator veered off into describing the next story and then to a tasteless commercial about erectile dysfunction, which annoyed me even more than usual.

My first reaction was to mentally kick myself for being such a softie and for thinking that everything would turn out okay. Clearly, handwriting had been on the wall for quite a while. My experience had taught me that young women who go alone to isolated locations with seedy photographers sometimes don't come home.

The Kristi Johnson story added just one more to the long list of unfortunate situations I have seen firsthand over my career as a prosecutor. It was, in Yogi Berra's immortal words, "déjà vu all over again." I knew these types of cases are some of the most problematic to prosecute. The reason for such difficulty is that model killers take their victims to isolated areas in the mountains or desert to avoid eyewitnesses. Too often, any workable leads quickly dry up in the rural air and the homicide folders end up in the unsolved file.

Still, I could see a slim possibility that Kristi's killer might be caught. The killer may have thought he had pulled off the perfect crime, but he didn't realize that an extraordinary police department was going to take over the case.

The city of Santa Monica is unique in many ways. Situated on a high cliff overlooking the Pacific Ocean, it has its own distinct personality. Thought by some to be one of the most broad-minded communities in the country, it is often referred to as the city of "left-coast liberals," who are soft on crime and are more tolerant of lawbreakers. Perhaps this accounts for so many homeless people drifting into Santa Monica's parks and playgrounds. On beautiful summer days, tourists sometimes have difficulty walking along the picturesque bluffs, the pier, and the strand, trying to step over or circumnavigate slumbering transients.

At the same time, Santa Monica takes pride in the fact that it has one of the lowest homicide rates in the nation. When a slaying occurs within city borders, civic leaders expect and demand the police department to put in countless hours and track down the killer.

Kristi Johnson didn't die within Santa Monica's city limits. Her body turned up in the Hollywood Hills, within the city of Los Angeles and the jurisdiction of the L.A. Police Department. Kristi's death would never be reflected in the homicide statistics for the city of Santa Monica, since it didn't happen within its borders, and her only connection was that she had been a resident for about two months. This turned out to be the main reason for the Santa Monica Police Department conducting not only the missing persons case, but also the subsequent search for her killer.

For years, I have been involved in the debate as to which agencies do the best homicide investigations. Are the biggest law enforcement agencies the best just because of their size and resources available? The Los Angeles Sheriff's Department Homicide Division has an excellent reputation for quality work, as does the sheriff's crime lab. LASD handles all the unincorporated parts of the county, as well as providing services to cities requesting their help. Their Homicide Division has always been willing to provide assistance to the smaller communities who have their own police departments but need additional resources to successfully resolve "whodunit" murder cases.

The Los Angeles Police Department Robbery-Homicide Division is equally effective. Older TV viewers will recall that the LAPD was made famous by Jack Webb with his *Dragnet* series in which he always asked for ". . . just the facts, ma'am." Other similar series followed, demonstrating fictional LAPD cops and sleuths. Real-life investigators have also been highly publicized, such as homicide detective John "Jigsaw" St. John. Personally, I remember working with him and several other members of LAPD's old-fashioned detectives, known as "the Hat Dicks." They wore their fedora hats everywhere, while chomping on unlit cigars, and enjoyed a reputation of "always getting their man." I don't know how true that was, but when I asked them to find a witness, they seemed to magically come through. Those were the days when the detective bureaus had a network of informants who knew everything going on in every street and dark alley.

During my tenure as a prosecutor, I worked with both LAPD Robbery-Homicide Division and LASD Homicide Divisions on thousands of murder cases. Both are extremely professional. Yet, like most law enforcement agencies across the nation, they sometimes have slightly off-kilter understanding of the DA's requirements when it comes to filing murder charges.

When they feel that they have enough evidence, the detectives will bring the homicide case to the DA's office with expectation that murder charges should automatically be filed. The prosecutor reviews a stack of police reports to see if there is sufficient evidence to justify the next step, and if so, the case is filed. Afterward, the homicide cops are ready to move on to the next murder investigation assignment, and forget about the ones in the DA's hands.

When the DA's office asked Detective Virginia Obenchain, from the Santa Monica PD, to do additional investigation in the Paleologus case, she complied with a spirit of willingness to meet the requests. Because of Santa Monica's proactive approach, Chief Butts scheduled a news conference to update the public while Kristi Johnson was still a missing person. This worked to the detriment of Victor Paleologus even before anyone considered him a suspect. A large city like Los Angeles has so many missing persons in one day, news conferences are seldom held.

Paleologus couldn't have anticipated that the *L.A. Times*

would carry an article about Kristi being missing, which would be read by Susan Murphy, who, in turn, called the detectives to report the incident, and set off a landslide effort to find her.

After the discovery of Kristi's body, optimism soared that Paleologus would be easy to prosecute for her murder. In what would usually be construed as unfortunate, his booking photo appeared on TV in news reports. Revealing an arrested person's photo to the news media strikes at the right to a fair trial, possibly prejudicing witnesses. The practical result, though, turned out to be a great help to the police. A series of young women saw Paleologus's picture and contacted the detectives about being approached by him regarding auditioning for a James Bond movie.

Before the DA filed murder charges against Paleologus, Beverly Hills had already initiated proceedings for his attempt to defraud a BMW dealership. Since he had two prior serious felony convictions, he faced a sentence of twenty-five years to life if convicted.

After countless phone calls and meetings regarding the Paleologus case, DA administrators considered multiple issues regarding the sufficiency of evidence and public interest. The final decision as to filing murder charges would be made by the Major Crimes Division.

Detective Obenchain carried her police reports and the coroner's autopsy findings to a deputy DA for full review. The assistant head deputy of Major Crimes shepherded the case through its beginning stages. Ethically, the DA's office can file criminal charges when there is sufficient evidence to believe that a reasonable jury would convict the defendant of the charges.

Even now, after all my years of courtroom work, I still can't predict with any degree of certainty how twelve jurors will react to the presentation of evidence. Actually, trying to have a dozen people agree on *anything* is quite a task. In criminal justice, a verdict must be unanimous. The defense needs only one ringer who will be the contrarian unwilling to go along with the majority. Henry Fonda played that role in the classic 1957 film *12 Angry Men,* and Jack Lemmon repeated it in a 1997 television version. The character was the only one voting not guilty in a murder case, and gradually persuaded the other eleven jurors to acquit the defendant.

Nearly every prosecutor remembers the experience of a hung jury or an outright acquittal. Those losses shape future decisions. Once burned, prosecutors tend to be more cautions about filing similar cases. It must be realized, though, that the trial's outcome may not have resulted from insufficiency of evidence, but by the composition of the jury. Many believe this was the issue in O.J. Simpson's notorious acquittal. Preferring to avoid costly and embarrassing losses or mistrials, quite a few prosecutors set extremely high standards for evidence requirements, while others are willing to file charges with less evidence in hopes of getting a good jury.

When a weak case is sent to the Major Crimes Division, the top administrators in the DA's office like to believe that something magic will happen. The Paleologus matter had monumental issues for the filing prosecutor to consider, primarily the key question of what evidence linked him to Kristi's murder. To the general public, based on publicity about Paleologus's efforts in luring women to isolated places on the pretext of a photo shoot, it seemed quite obvious that he had killed her. To a DDA looking at the evidence available, the picture wasn't quite that well focused.

Detective Obenchain performed additional investigation above and beyond the call of duty in order to get the case filed. The reviewing parties in the DA's office didn't want to rush the process, though. They preferred to wait, hoping that more forensic results might turn up. After all, Paleologus wasn't going anywhere, since he was in jail on the automobile fraud charges, as well as having a parole hold preventing him from being released.

The nice guy DDA who lets the investigative agency talk him into premature filing learns the hard lesson. The end result of filing a weak case is that the prosecutor is faced with the difficult choice of either dismissing the case or accepting a plea bargain to get rid of it.

Excruciating pressure crashes down on the DA when a case is dismissed after the filing of the charges. It's unpleasant for the prosecutor to ask a judge in open court, in front of the public, to dismiss the case. The media, victims' relatives, and various rights groups swarm the DA, making noises about being soft on crime. In the Paleologus case, the DA's office knew the dangers of prematurely filing charges.

The general public had heard about the body being found, about Paleologus's arrest, and assumed that plenty of evidence must exist to connect him to her death. They didn't know that forensic testing and analysis takes time. Even insiders who had heard about the victim's clothing, the sleeping bag that should have some trace evidence in it, or her car, which must be loaded with fingerprints and DNA, expected quick action. There had to be prints, fibers, hairs, or other trace evidence somewhere. Unfortunately, TV programs about crime scene investigations don't always reveal that forensic testing is never quick and easy. On those shows, the actor places the piece of evidence into a machine, pushes a button, and within a few seconds something flashes on the computer monitor claiming there is a match.

In most felony cases, a preliminary hearing is conducted to determine if enough evidence exists to take the accused to trial. A magistrate, who is a judge, presides. The defendant is present with his attorney, who may cross-examine all witnesses called by the prosecution. Testimonial evidence can be proffered by the prosecutor in two ways. The actual witnesses may take the stand, or the process can be accelerated by having the investigating officer testify to what civilian witnesses would be expected to say, as recorded in interviews and police reports. This second method benefits the prosecution in two ways. Civilian witnesses don't have to be inconvenienced by coming to court, and the defense attorney doesn't have the opportunity to vigorously cross-examine the witnesses. Defenders like to elicit detailed testimony from prosecution witnesses at the preliminary hearing, and then use it in the subsequent trial to bring out inconsistencies.

Conversely, by putting only the investigating officer on the stand, prosecutors suffer the disadvantage of not being able to question the actual witnesses. Thus, a chance for testing their ability to stand up under stiff cross-examination is lost. Also, when the prosecutor evaluates the case for trial, it is important to know if the witnesses can positively identify the defendant in court, or recall events clearly.

The magistrate listens to all the evidence presented at the preliminary hearings and decides if there is sufficient reason for advancing the case to a jury trial.

In the case of Victor Paleologus, intense pressure built up for the DA's office. They had to either fish or cut bait. Finally the Major Crimes Division decided to file the murder charge and consolidate it with the Beverly Hills fraud charges. At that moment, the die was cast and officials crossed their fingers in the hope that everything would fall into place. Paleologus faced a charge of first-degree murder with two allegations of special circumstances. In potential capital cases, the defendant is not eligible for release on bail. The court appointed Andrew Reed Flier to defend Paleologus, at taxpayer expense.

The preliminary hearing was held on June 25, 2005, using the accelerated method. This meant that Detective Obenchain had to testify to what various witnesses would say. In such a complex case, she needed to remember an incredible amount of information and accurately recall all of it under oath. It didn't surprise Obenchain's boss or colleagues that she accomplished it with admirable clarity. Judge Robert J. Perry, as the magistrate, heard the testimony and ruled that Paleologus would face trial for first-degree murder. Furthermore, he said, the jury would hear evidence about two special circumstances: lying in wait and attempted rape.

The "special circumstances" procedures were instituted in 1977, after the U.S. Supreme Court had overturned death penalty statutes across the country, with the provision that

they could be reestablished under newly defined laws. In two
elections, Californians overwhelmingly approved capital punishment, including twenty-two special circumstances. Two of
them, numbers 15 and 17, would apply to Paleologus. The
new law stated:

> *Paragraph 190.2. (a) The penalty for a defendant who is
> found guilty of murder in the first degree is death or im-
> prisonment in the state prison for life without the possi-
> bility of parole if one or more of the following **special
> circumstances** has been found . . . to be true: (15) The
> defendant intentionally killed the victim by means of
> lying in wait. (17) The murder was committed while the
> defendant was engaged in, or was an accomplice in, the
> commission of, attempted commission of, or the imme-
> diate flight after committing, or attempting to commit,
> the following felonies: (C) Rape.*

The argument for charges of "lying in wait" against Paleologus stated that he set up the audition ruse to lure Kristi to a
secluded area, and waited for her there with criminal intent.
Attempted rape was indicated by her clothes being pulled
down, as well as the binding of her hands and feet, without evidence of sexual intercourse.

Conclusion of the preliminary hearing signaled the start in
a formidable chain of activities. First the prosecutor reviewed
all the aggravating and mitigating evidence and prepared a
memorandum recommending death. The supervisor added
his comments, and the documents moved all the way up the
chain of command in the DA's office. It landed in the Special
Circumstances Committee, where a group of experienced
prosecutors listened to a presentation about the facts of the
case, the witnesses, and how the evidence would be presented at penalty phase. Next the defense attorney, Andrew
Flier, was invited to discuss any evidence that would go to mitigation and thereby spare Paleologus's life. Ultimately it is up

to the chairperson to listen as the issue is debated, then make the final determination.

The discussion brought up Paleologus's two prior convictions and continual propensity for taking women to isolated areas where he could sexually assault them. Even though the murder charge applied to only one victim, his behavior toward so many women made him not only more than a mother's nightmare, but a dangerous predator. The committee concluded, with the chairperson's concurrence, to seek the death penalty.

In my ongoing part-time work with the Major Crimes Division, helping the prosecutors prepare their cases for jury trial presentation, I followed every step of the case against Paleologus. Although busy with various other cases, I could never completely forget Kristi's mom and others singing "Amazing Grace" at the candlelight vigil.

The DA's office recognized the importance of assigning one of its top prosecutors to handle the Paleologus trial. It had landed in the Major Crimes Division for that very reason. The supervisor had originally assigned the case to a DDA who left the office soon afterward. Eleanor Hunter took it over and worked the preliminary hearing stage. She left the office for a judgeship. This became an embarrassment to officials— handing off this important case from one prosecutor to another. Detective Obenchain observed a pattern that anyone assigned to the case would leave, forcing her to start all over and bring the new prosecutor up to speed on the facts.

Finally a particularly talented, seasoned veteran accepted the challenge. DDA Doug Sortino had graduated from Boalt Hall School of Law, at the University of California, Berkeley, which certainly attested to his intelligence and top level of legal training. His career started in the attorney general's office, where he honed his writing skills, enabling him to craft well-reasoned legal briefs. In addition to possessing a keen knowledge of the law, Sortino demonstrated superior litigation talents. Blessed with the deep resonant voice of a stage actor, he used it to effective advantage. Since my office adjoined his, whenever he spoke on the phone or met with witnesses, I couldn't help but hear every word he said. They echoed down the hallway. At times, this annoyed me, especially when I needed to concentrate on my work. However, it kept me aware of everything going on in the Paleologus case.

By midway through 2005, while Paleologus sat in jail, the case against him worked its way through the maze of justice. DA investigators supplemented the Santa Monica PD accomplishments by exploring existing aspects and looking for new evidence. With the hope that cell phone records might help, senior investigator Brian Bennett assisted Doug Sortino in interviewing an engineer for a major cellular network.

With copies of Paleologus's and Kristine Johnson's cell phone records in hand, reflecting activity during the crucial days and nights in February 2003, the engineer provided explanations. All of the calls made and received by both individuals traveled and were relayed through cell sites. These are towers covering areas of service, he said. Most cell sites in the Los Angeles region are triangular, consisting of three sides. The north sector is called Alpha, the southeast sector is Beta, and the southwest sector is Gamma.

Focusing first on Paleologus's nine-page report, the engineer said that on Saturday, February 15, the day Kristi vanished, Victor had made a call at 13:09:35, thirty-five seconds after 1:09 P.M. The north (Alpha) sector of cell site 34 was accessed to initiate and complete the call. Bennett and Sortino understood the importance of this when the engineer added, "The north-Alpha sector covers the majority of the Century City Shopping Center." It scientifically placed Paleologus, or at least his cell phone, in that narrow slice of geography shortly after one o'clock on the afternoon that Kristi Johnson shopped in Century City.

On that same date, someone had used the phone to make several outgoing calls, and received about the same number between 10:06 and 11:12 P.M. These were processed through a cell site covering a large sector of Hollywood. The next calls from Victor's phone, a few minutes before midnight, confirmed his presence in that area, probably as he drove toward the pancake restaurant to meet Willie Craven, with whom he spent the early-morning hours, according to statements made by Craven.

The engineer turned to the four pages reflecting activity of Kristi Johnson's cell phone. At about five-thirty and five thirty-seven that afternoon, two calls had been made from it, bouncing from a cell site in the Laurel Canyon area of the Hollywood Hills. Both attempts connected with information telephone numbers.

Sortino and Bennett next sought out a corporate security officer for the cell phone company that provided service for both Paleologus and Johnson. With his help, they examined billing statements, matching them to the calls traced through cell sites. Both sets of records dovetailed perfectly, further establishing the trails left by victim and predator.

While these efforts did add to the circumstantial case against Victor Paleologus, they did not provide rock-solid forensic evidence.

As the months went by, I could tell by Doug's many conversations with Detective Obenchain that his early optimism regarding the Paleologus case had turned to stinging pessimism. By nature, Doug always had a critical eye in evaluating cases. It wasn't just his perfectionism, but he could see legal and factual problems missed by most people. Doug and Paleologus's defense attorney, Andrew Flier, had earned reputations as aggressive advocates and neither of them liked to lose a single point during the pretrial motions. Watching them, I couldn't help but think of a heavyweight championship boxing match, in which the opponents jabbed, parried, danced away, and used masterful strategy. With scarcity of evidence in Doug's corner, though, he seemed to be fighting with one hand tied behind his back. Las Vegas oddsmakers would probably have rated him a ten-to-one underdog.

For quite a while, many of us in the office wondered if Victor

Paleologus had killed Kimberly Pandelios back in 1992. It came as a surprise when David Rademaker was arrested in 2004 for that murder and subsequently indicted. His trial ended in February 2006, with a first-degree murder conviction. In March, the same jury deliberated less than one day before recommending a sentence of life in prison without the possibility of parole rather than sending him to death row.

Now, we hoped that another jury could be convinced of Victor Paleologus's guilt.

CHAPTER 19

SEVERE OBSTACLE

Ron Bowers's Recollections

From overhearing Doug's booming voice, I could tell it was getting close to the date set for the jury trial, better known in the office as "showtime." I told him I would help prepare his opening statement and create any visual exhibits he would need in the trial. Some attorneys are able to use powerful oral skills to their advantage in court, and Doug certainly fell into that category. So, he didn't think much of using graphics to get his point across to jurors. He looked upon charts and diagrams as gimmicks and believed that real lawyers didn't need them. One day, I saw Detective Obenchain walk by my office to meet with Doug and I heard him complaining to her about the status of the case. He seemed frustrated at not getting the good news he wanted to hear. After a while, I overheard him say that he needed evidence he could use in court. He snapped off a list of demands to interview additional witnesses and write up supplemental reports.

As Doug stepped out into the hall with Obenchain, he

stopped and escorted her into my office. He asked me what I needed her to do to start preparing the exhibits for the case. This caught me by surprise, since he hadn't taken me up on my earlier offer to help him with the visual aids. Then I realized that asking for my help meant Doug must be feeling the onset of desperation. I tried not to appear dumbfounded and immediately gave Virginia a list to help me get started. Initially I needed pictures of the other women Paleologus had ensnared with his James Bond lies. Driver's license photos issued by the Department of Motor Vehicles would be fine. I told Doug that I needed the police reports to better understand the details of the case.

Detective Obenchain left the DA's office with an extensive list of things she needed to do for him, bloated by my requests. Doug retrieved extra copies of the police reports and handed them to me. This provided my first real opportunity to see what the Paleologus case was all about. I had been curious why Doug complained so long and loudly about problems. I began reading about the available evidence, and understood his frustration. I found plenty to prove that the defendant was the biggest jerk alive. However, when it came to evidence proving that he killed Kristi, I saw nothing but holes in the case, like gigantic craters in the moon. The case looked like Swiss cheese. I continued to examine facts, and saw certain fundamental problems that raised a huge question in my mind. *Why the heck did we ever file this murder case?* When our organization first debated filing charges, everyone recognized that the case relied entirely on circumstantial evidence. From the get-go, we all knew that no eyewitnesses could place Paleologus in or anywhere near Skyline Drive and the hill where Kristi's body had been discovered. Not one person ever saw Paleologus and Kristi together at the Century City mall or, as a matter of fact, could place them together at any time.

We desperately needed some forensic evidence to help link the suspect to the victim. Initially the prosecution had been overconfident that with so many potential forensic samples collected, at least some of them would come back positive and make that essential connection. After conducting extensive tests, we had no blood, semen, or fibers. We had nothing with his DNA. No usable evidence had been found on Kristi's body, on her clothing, or even on the sleeping bag wrapped around her lower body. Kristi's car and its contents yielded none of Paleologus's fingerprints. No collected hair or skin particles could be traced to Paleologus. Two thorough searches of the vacant house near the location of Kristi's body produced nothing. Investigators had found dusty tire tracks in the vacant house's garage. Hope that they would match tire prints from Kristi's Miata melted like a Popsicle in a microwave. They didn't even match in size, let alone tread pattern.

Since the forensic evidence failed to materialize, the basis for prosecuting the case started to unravel. No one looking at the available facts really believed Paleologus innocent of the murder. But it had to be proved to a jury beyond a reasonable doubt, and that didn't look very promising.

As if we didn't have enough bad news, Andrew Flier provided more. It became apparent that he planned to challenge Kristi's time of death by introducing her reservations to attend a rave concert on the night of her disappearance. Flier claimed that she had actually attended the concert held in a downtown Los Angeles converted warehouse, met someone there, and continued to party with drugs and booze into the next week. Corroboration of this, the defender claimed, could be seen in the sleeping bag in which Kristi and some guy possibly had sex.

In the minds of the jurors, the rave concert implications and the sleeping bag just might imply that Paleologus couldn't have done it.

Detectives had contacted the operators of the rave concert and came away convinced that she had never shown up at the event. Review of the reservation list showed that Kristi's name had not been checked off, as had the names of other attendees. However, the concert issue still bothered

Doug Sortino. He worried about the limited evidence of Kristi's disappearing and never being seen or heard from after 5:32 P.M. on that Saturday, February 15.

To settle his fears of the case crumbling beneath his feet, Doug called the rave promoter to talk to her personally about the guest list. She cooperated and spoke at length with him, reiterating how hosts at the door wouldn't let anyone in unless their names were on it. Upon entry, at least two people verified that the person had arrived, and used a yellow felt tip highlighter to cross the name off. Doug made more inquiries, but the woman couldn't give detailed answers. He asked her to please look at the list again to verify her statements. After a short silence, she said she didn't have the list any longer. In Doug's deep penetrating voice, he asked, "What do you mean you don't have the list?" Her answer might as well have been a fist slamming into his stomach. She said that a defense investigator had dropped in and asked to see it. Thinking the court had mandated his actions, she had turned the papers over to him, and he took them with him.

I could hear Doug growling out a litany of expletives, expressing his frustration. If I had gone into his office at that moment, I would've had to peel him off the ceiling. That list represented one of the keystones of the prosecution's whole case. He contacted Andrew Flier and asked that it be immediately turned over to the police or to the DA's office. The defender claimed that his secretary and the investigator looked through all their files and couldn't locate it. Doug practically flew to the judge and demanded that the original rave concert guest list be turned over to the prosecution. The defense continued denials of having it in their possession. Judge Perry patiently applied a little more pressure. It worked. The defense magically found the list and turned it over to the DA. Flier didn't apologize, but thanked the judge for not imposing sanctions.

Doug had been naturally losing his hair, but the rave list problem turned him almost bald overnight. His paranoia made him believe that the defense was playing fast and loose with evidence regarded as essential by the prosecution.

As I continued to read everything available on the case, I came across the name of a defense alibi witness named Willie Craven. He claimed to have met the defendant at a pancake restaurant and eaten dinner with him on the night of February 15. According to the report, the two of them remained together all evening and then took a bus to Craven's home in Hollywood.

Examining this, I kept shaking my head. To me, his story involving the whereabouts of Paleologus immediately after Kristi's disappearance had absolutely no credibility. But I wondered how jurors would evaluate such a bizarre tale. Could his statements create reasonable doubt in at least one of their minds?

In the thick binder of police reports, I came across statements from another important witness, real estate broker Charlie Simon. He had told the police of showing houses to Paleologus on Saturday, February 15, up until early evening. That would provide the defendant with a solid alibi at the exact time when Kristi arrived in the Hollywood Hills expecting to audition for the James Bond movie. When I saw that, I jumped out of my chair, rushed into Doug's office, and pointed out the paragraph in the police report. In a disgusted voice, Doug said that if I read farther down I would see that Simon had later realized his error about the date and corrected it. I still worried that the defense would make a big deal out of the discrepancy. They might infer that the DA's office had persuaded Mr. Simon to change his statement to fit the prosecution's scenario. Doug smiled, nodded, and agreed, saying that the defense probably would make a mountain out of this little molehill. He would look for a way to avert any damage.

Something else troubling had popped up, said Doug. Eleanor Hunter, the previous prosecutor, had conducted a preliminary hearing using only Detective Obenchain's testimony to support the murder charge. Obenchain had stated that calls made by Paleologus around the time Kristi arrived in the Hollywood Hills came from a cell tower in the Laurel

Canyon area. This had been based on an assumption that the call had bounced off a tower near the location of Kristi's body. Doug said that some doubts entered the picture because cell phone tracking had been complicated by the multiplicity of phone companies using the various towers involved.

Even though the mistake hadn't been intentional, the defense could turn it into an attack on the detective's credibility. This exemplified why it is best to bring all the witnesses into court, so the investigating officer isn't placed in the awkward position of testifying for other people. We had no way of knowing how much damage this error might do to the prosecution.

The sobering reports I read, along with Doug's comments, shook me. In my wildest imagination, this case could not be regarded as a slam dunk. I took the remaining reports home to mull over during the weekend. My routine for Sunday is to try to read the newspaper before *Meet the Press* airs on television. When Tim Russert comes on at 8:00 A.M., I place all the unread newspaper sections on the coffee table and I tell myself that sometime later in the day I will get to them. I don't think I have ever managed to completely read a Sunday paper. It certainly didn't happen this time.

From my briefcase, I pulled out a stack of police reports and found the one describing recovery of Kristi's sports car. I knew about valet attendant Roberto Marquez's testimony in which he saw the white Miata being parked at the front entrance to the St. Regis Hotel in Century City. I thought this could be strong prosecution evidence. A lone white male had parked Kristi's car around five o'clock on the morning after her disappearance. The prosecution could argue that Paleologus had dropped off the car in the Century City area, where he was known to hang out. I continued to thumb through the pages and started to realize that everything isn't what it seems at first glance.

Marquez knew when and where the car was parked, even though a full week had passed since he had seen it left in the valet area. When asked about the event, Marquez had good recollection. He had rushed over to the driver and explained that he couldn't self-park a car in the valet area. The guy threw him the keys, said, "Then valet it," and walked toward the Century Plaza Hotel. It had all happened in only a few seconds. Several weeks elapsed before he looked at a photo lineup.

Roberto wanted to be helpful to the police, so he carefully studied each of the six photos. Skipping over Paleologus's picture, he commented that the driver resembled Rambo, then pointed to another photo and said this looked like him. He repeated the disappointing error later when detectives asked him to attend a live lineup at the county jail. Again he looked at all six males standing on the platform, passed over Paleologus, and selected another man.

I couldn't believe what I read. He totally identified another person. If that wasn't bad enough, it turned out that person he selected was a registered sex offender! I knew that the defense wouldn't miss that point and would somehow try to infer that this sex offender identified by Roberto Marquez had probably killed Kristi.

Monday morning, I showed up at the office full of questions for Doug. He didn't arrive until later, having been in court on another case. At my request, he came into my office, scowling as if in a bad mood. So I hesitated, wondering if I should postpone my interrogation. Yet, without some answers, I couldn't get started on the exhibits and other visual aids. I decided to wade right in. "How did Paleologus get up to the vacant house on Skyline Drive?"

Doug said he didn't know. I told him that I looked at city bus routes and no buses went up Laurel Canyon. I asked him if Paleologus had any history of borrowing cars from friends around that time. No evidence pointed to that, said Doug, nor had anything else turned up to explain how he got up to Skyline Drive. He speculated about the possibility of a taxi, although no record of that had surfaced from any of the companies servicing that area.

Then I asked Doug about the cell phones of both Kristi and Paleologus. Was there any indication that she had his phone number and may have called it? He said that neither cell phone had been used to call the other one. So that point couldn't help the prosecution. I asked if any security cameras at the Century City mall might have captured an image of Paleologus talking to Kristi or walking around the mall at the time she shopped there. Doug relied, "No."

When Doug left my office, a feeling of abject hopelessness gripped me like a huge vise. Paleologus's track record as a sexual predator of young women cried out for locking him behind bars. But how do you prove a murder case when the DA can't even pinpoint where the slaying occurred? Nor could we substantiate exactly when it took place. And we had no way of proving how the killing actually happened. Bottom line: no eyewitnesses and no forensic evidence that could link the defendant to the victim.

After reviewing the Paleologus file, I had a gut reaction that this predator was going to slither out from under the murder. Back in 1991, he convinced at least one or more jurors to hold out, allowing him to escape a guilty verdict of assault and attempted rape. The victim Carol Newman had testified about being assaulted in the Bonaventure Hotel, and backed it up with evidence of her injuries. Yet, the jury let him slide. As a con man, Paleologus had earned the reputation of being one of the most devious. It repulsed me to think that he might escape justice again by using lies and deceit.

Close to lunchtime, I looked up from my desk and could hear several prosecutors in the hallway trying to decide where to eat—Phillippe's, originator of the French dip sandwich, Chinatown's Jung Chow, or Mexican food on historic Olvera Street. Some of these lawyers' best arguments are reserved for food debates. As they walked by my office, someone yelled to me, "Do you want to join us for lunch in Chinatown?" I thanked them for asking and said that I had to work on some exhibits. If they had agreed on Phillippe's, I would have gone, but MSG in Chinese food always gives me migraines.

Leaning back in my chair, I brooded over what appeared to be an insurmountable problem: What would it take to shore up the crumbling Paleologus case? Was it possible to convince a jury of his guilt and prevent him from beating the criminal justice system again? I thought of advice in an old song to "accentuate the positive and eliminate the negative." Maybe we couldn't eliminate many negatives, so I figured we needed to focus our efforts on the positive. The system has drastically changed in the last few decades, and we as prosecutors had to take a new approach on presenting our cases to jurors. In the days of William Jennings Bryan and Clarence Darrow, attorneys relied on silver-tongued oratory. I remember when I started with the DA's office in the 1960s, the emphasis was still on using verbal skills to persuade jurors of a defendant's guilt.

Two things have caused us to change our litigation style: how people retain information and how they accumulate it.

Research has proved that people remember more of what they see than what they hear. The brain processes visual images differently from auditory input, so eyes can be more important than ears. Visual impressions tend to be lasting and easier to recall at a later time. The greatest impact comes from appealing to a combination of these senses, both visual and auditory, producing optimum retention.

The first five to eight minutes of any speech are like a magic window in which the jurors are keenly tuned in to every word spoken. This is the time when the jurors' curiosity is aroused and they are eager to understand the differences between the two sides. However, this interest span is relatively short. If the attorney lapses into a droning presentation, jurors sometimes zone out and only comprehend a small portion of what is said. Effective attorneys use visual aids, such as charts, diagrams, photo displays, or even slide presentations, to continually refocus each juror's attention. In using the visuals this way, an attorney can significantly increase jurors' interest span, so they get the message loud and clear.

For prosecutors, the job becomes even more difficult, particularly when evidence is circumstantial. I worried that

Paleologus might benefit from this, even though the Santa Monica PD had a sterling reputation.

The L.A. District Attorney's Office, recognizing increased problems in trying defendants, and low morale among prosecutors, decided to take a proactive approach to improve the situation. The DA commissioned a study to identify methods for improving efficacy and boosting attitudes. One of the recommendations for change directly affected me. Officials decided to form an in-house service to create visual aids for trial prosecutors to use in court.

One day my supervisor summoned me, and I wondered just what the heck I had done, right or wrong. In these situations, it can be a little unnerving when the boss starts showing great interest in your well-being and your family's latest vacation. Where was this leading? Somehow I sensed bad vibes.

He seemed awfully gratuitous in compliments about my use of visual aids in trials, and how well I had performed in the Training Division. Was this leading up to a golden handshake and forced retirement, or worse? But I started to relax when he praised a video I had written and produced on how to prepare visual aids. Then he got to the point with a stunning statement: "We have selected you to head up the new Trial Support Division."

Listening to his every word, I began to wonder about the ramifications. His voice and manner, though, left no room for negotiation. I had been "selected," and that was that.

Realizing right then that I could be miserable with my new assignment, or I could actually do something constructive for the DA's office, I made a decision. I would seize this opportunity and make a positive impact on the criminal justice system. Helping prosecutors improve their presentations to juries had always interested me. Personally, I had experimented with various approaches in courtrooms, trying to find what did and didn't work. I had learned that the best way to make facts understandable for them involved the use of charts and diagrams. In this way, jurors could use their eyes, not just their ears, to comprehend it all. Visuals can dramatically improve a prosecutor's impact. It's like hearing a radio report of the USC Trojans winning a football game, versus being in the Coliseum and watching it happen. All of the noise, color, and drama is palpable, in dimensional proportions, etched permanently in the memory.

Prosecutors tend to use visuals most often in their opening statements. This is an important time to explain the facts of the case in a logical, sequential manner. Trials, like the production of movies, do not move in chronological order. Witnesses are called according to their availability. Their testimony offers piecemeal facts that must be reassembled for the jury in some logical sequence, just as a motion picture editor splices together scenes shot completely out of order. The prosecutor can lay the time framework out in his opening statements, giving the jury a chance to fit subsequent testimony into a meaningful chain of events.

During the trial, exhibits such as photo board displays may be used to assist the witness in explaining their testimony to the jurors.

Finally, effective charts and diagrams can be a powerful tool in summation arguments, when the prosecutor takes his last shot at persuading the jury to convict.

Evolving technology has helped to change the manner of preparing and using visuals in the courtroom. The electronic age offers up-to-date methods for presenting a case to the jury. Years ago, attorneys hand-printed "bullet points" on butcher paper, and dangled it on an easel for jurors to see. Today computers are a common tool, providing PowerPoint presentations or enlarged professional poster-size charts. Laptops came along, connecting to LCD projectors, enabling any attorney to present a slide show for use in opening statements or final arguments.

Observers wonder why prosecutors rely on visuals more than defense attorneys do. Veteran court watchers understand that prosecutors are saddled with the burden of proof, requiring them to convince all twelve jurors. The defense attorney has a different role in the proceedings—to plant a seed of reasonable doubt. Charts aren't useful in the attempt to create a warm, fuzzy feeling for the defendant, since they tend to focus the jurors' attention on details. Visuals bring facts into focus, while dramatics might succeed in arousing emotions. And, unfortunately, some jurors are persuaded by emotion.

During that lunch hour, I mulled over the facts of the Paleologus case and tried to imagine visual aids designed to accentuate the positives. First I grappled with the idea of creating indelible mental images to help jurors understand the power of circumstantial evidence pointing to his guilt. Next I wanted to see how I could use those exhibits as the basis of a slide show presented during the opening statement. The complexity of the case cried out for some way to explain evidence and at the same time convey the importance of every vital element. Each step had to be logical, memorable, and highly persuasive.

In the pending Paleologus trial, the central issue would be his modus operandi, the repetitious use of his James Bond scam. We had a list of nine women, including Kristi Johnson, who had heard his incessant lies—three of whom had been sexually assaulted, and one murdered. I tried to envision how best to clearly illustrate all of the similarities, and worked out exactly how a chart would depict it.

The far left column would contain a picture of each victim, along with her name. They would be presented chronologically, beginning with Elizabeth Davis in February 1991, and ending with Kristi in February 2003.

Column 2 would depict the location where Paleologus made his pitch, the last six being in Century City.

Column 3 would reveal how he characterized, or boasted, of phony status in the film industry.

Column 4 would drive home the point of his repeated use of the James Bond scheme, in eight of the nine cases.

Column 5 would list the clothing he wanted them to wear: a white long-sleeved shirt, a black miniskirt, stiletto heels, and panty hose.

Column 6 would tell what happened to the women, from "drugged by a drink," to "killed."

This concept should give jurors an easy, yet memorable, summary showing the horrifying progression, with repeated lies, perversion, and finally murder.

I realized that the repetition of this pattern could be the most convincing evidence available to the prosecution for proving Paleologus guilty of killing Kristi. The jury must understand the crucial importance of the similarity in this chain of events. By placing all of this information on one large chart, any reasonable person viewing it could unequivocally see that the same con man must be involved in each encounter. The pattern stood out so patently obvious that it might as well have been a personal signature, as good as the killer leaving a fingerprint behind.

When I finished completing this similarities chart, I knew that we could build a convincing case against Paleologus, but we had to do it one step at a time. Next I grappled with the challenge of finding a way to illustrate the pivotal dates. The jury had to have each one etched into their minds. The final phase started with Susan Murphy, just a few days after Paleologus walked out of prison on January 20, 2003. Two other women met Paleologus, one on January 25, and one on February 12, before Kristi's life tragically ended on February 15. Just forty-eight hours later, the police arrested him for stealing a BMW.

I could visualize a great deal of confusion if the prosecutor tried to rattle off this many dates and events in a monologue. He had to have something clear and easy to understand for the jurors to see. My simple solution: a one-page calendar beginning with January 20 and ending with the first week of March when Kristi's body was discovered on the hillside.

The next obstacle for me to overcome related to a clear way to show Paleologus's and Kristi's cell phone records. The locations where they made or received calls on that fateful day might tip the scales. So I came up with a map showing cell sites, or towers. We could prove that Paleologus's cell phone was used near the Century City mall while Kristi shopped there. This would support the prosecution's theory of Paleologus meeting Kristi there on that Saturday afternoon. By showing jurors a large map pinpointing cell phone sites, they could follow telephone company experts' testimony explaining where the cell phone would have to be in order to receive or send each call.

Without visual aids, jurors would be required to go through ponderous stacks of paper containing voluminous lists of telephone numbers, plus coded designations of towers, and figure out complex connections between them. It is human nature to shy away from complex technology. To me, simplifying this evidence could be extremely important.

I developed drafts of a few key visuals on my computer and made hard copies for Doug Sortino to review. Several pending legal motions, all quite important, consumed most of his attention. When I realized Doug couldn't get back with me, I used my various computer-generated exhibits to create a slide show for use in his opening statement. I knew that time was running out, and he would need the material soon.

I tried to identify something positive about the case, but kept running into frustrating negatives. I didn't envy Doug's position in the role of prosecutor. A not guilty verdict in such a high-profile case could do irreparable harm to his career in the DA's office. He hadn't smiled for weeks, and I thought he must be a nervous wreck.

That's why it startled me when I arrived at the office one morning and could hear Doug next door in a jovial mood. I had never heard him sound so happy. In that deep voice, he said to someone on the phone that he had to get going for his swearing in. Right then, I knew that Doug had been appointed as a superior court judge. A few minutes later, I watched as John Monaghan, one of the "top gun" prosecutors, came by to tease Sortino. He said, "Doug, you wanted out from under the Paleologus case so badly, you took a judgeship." Doug Sortino didn't say a word, but a huge smile on his relieved face spoke volumes.

CHAPTER 20

GAMBITS IN JUSTICE

Ron Bowers's Recollections

I realized that losing Doug Sortino this late in the proceeding struck a potentially devastating blow to the likelihood of convicting Victor Paleologus. Pat Dixon, head deputy of Major Crimes Division, reviewed each of his attorneys' workloads to see who could take over the assignment. The nod went to the most recent addition to Major Crimes, youthful David Walgren.

Soon after Walgren had joined the DA's office in the Van Nuys branch, he earned admiration for willingness to take criminals to trial rather than find easy dispositions. Before long, supervisors sent him to the Hardcore Gang Division, where he excelled by tackling tough cases in which witnesses, fearing retaliation, often failed to show up at trials. Somehow he seemed to do his magic in court, convict numerous gangsters, and send them off to prison. His exceptional talent propelled him to the coveted Major Crimes Division. One of his first cases there, the *People* v. *Rutter,* drew public attention due to the defendant's attempt to blackmail movie star Cameron Diaz.

In the courtroom, Walgren showed a boyish, but athletic presence. Dressed in dark blue suits, with pure white starched shirts, he projected the image of a young professional. His masculine facial features, topped by short, dark hair, always appeared somber—no matter how well his case went. The serious countenance probably reflected his driving desire to prove himself worthy of the task before him. He wasn't the type who smiled and showed any emotion even when talking to familiar people, such as the courtroom clerk or reporter.

Walgren's quiet, reserved demeanor took a backseat at showtime, though. His voice would deepen in front of juries, commanding the attention of everyone within hearing distance. Characteristic of most successful professionals, Walgren placed great value on advance preparation. He studied police reports, all available photos, and every piece of evidence, then organized it all by name, date, or by subject. As a litigator, he was ill at ease with last-minute surprises.

Finding himself suddenly assigned to an extremely complex, highly publicized case with gigantic evidentiary problems, Walgren rolled up the sleeves of his immaculate white shirt, and went to work. It didn't seem to faze him that the trial was set to begin within just a few weeks. The first lesson any attorney learns in law school is not to let anyone see you sweat when you are under tremendous pressure. Dave wanted to make certain that no one doubted his ability to handle the Paleologus case. I saw him come over to Doug's old office and cart off countless boxes of material, along with piles of loose-leaf notebooks, and line them up in the hallway just outside his office.

The cardinal rule in Major Crimes is not to complain. Just be willing and able to take on whatever is thrown at you. For the first week, Dave kept especially quiet and stayed in his office well past quitting time. It bothered him that short time frames in his preparation for pretrial motions didn't allow him to study every page, or even every box of material. He worked hard to familiarize himself with dozens of previous motions argued by the original prosecutors over a three-year period.

Andrew Flier, Walgren's opponent, had the advantage of being personally active in all of the concluded hearings and those still outstanding.

Pretrial motions may seem boring or superfluous by laypersons, but they are crucial to the final outcome of criminal trials. That is why attorneys on both sides strenuously argue these issues.

A highly controversial legal point would play a big part in the upcoming trial of Paleologus. Judges and law experts fear that if a defendant's previous criminal or antisocial behavior is revealed to jurors during a trial, it will have a prejudicial effect and they will jump to a conclusion that the defendant is probably guilty of the current charge. Appeals courts have ruled that it isn't fair to judge a defendant's guilt based on his past record. As a result, evidence codes in most states preclude prosecutors from presenting information regarding the defendant's prior bad acts, with narrow exceptions.

Legislators have modified the codes, enabling prosecutors to reveal defendants' prior acts to juries for proof of certain patterns, such as identification, modus operandi, or intent to commit the crime. Jurors are allowed to consider the prior bad acts only for these limited purposes, and not in determining the ultimate guilt of the defendant. The big question is whether jurors can follow such instructions.

The prosecution believed they could prove Paleologus committed the murder of Kristi Johnson by showing that he had a distinctive pattern of conduct, or modus operandi. The trick would be to convince the judge to allow MO evidence. For Dave Walgren, the road to success would lead through this maze. He must find and demonstrate every possible similarity in Paleologus's repetitious scam. Unless he could convince the judge that this MO fit legal exceptions, jurors would never hear of it, and Paleologus would walk away from the murder charge.

In court, Walgren argued that the defendant's prior acts

included claims to be working in the entertainment industry, lies about making a new James Bond film, and his requirement for the women to wear specific clothing. While these similarities sounded convincing, Walgren had to acknowledge a few dissimilarities. Paleologus's early use of his scam didn't involve meeting the victims at a mall, as did the later ones. The defense tried to emphasize these differences in order to prevent testimony from women the defendant met elsewhere.

Argument from both sides grew tense. Walgren knew the extreme importance of allowing jurors to hear about Paleologus's con man pattern. The defense worked equally hard to keep this information out of court. If the judge approved testimony from these women, the defense would probably resort to attacking their motives by suggesting that a desire for publicity led them to make up these stories. But that tactic would likely be a tough sell to the jury.

The judge listened, well aware that admittance of prior acts often resulted in subsequent reversals by appeals courts. He also understood that a ruling against the prosecution would leave little hope of a conviction.

After hearing intensive arguments from both sides, and carefully weighing it, the judge was convinced that prior acts at the Century City mall were similar enough to allow into evidence through testimony. However, an incident in a San Fernando Valley mall offered by Walgren failed to meet the judge's admissibility standards and had to be excised. As to earlier criminal acts, he saw enough of a similarity with the James Bond line to justify testimony from Dawn Cooper and Annie Olson about their encounters with Paleologus. The toughest decision related to Elizabeth Davis. Paleologus's claim to be in the entertainment business and working on a James Bond sequel fit the pattern, but spiking her drink did not. Finally, after heated debate between the prosecutor and the defense attorney, the judge said that enough similarities existed to allow the jury to hear it.

Early on, the judge also indicated that the incident involving Carol Newman at the Bonaventure Hotel would be allowed. This ruling elated the prosecution, and infuriated the defense. Paleologus had allegedly tied the victim to the bedposts and forcibly attempted to have sex with her. Without a doubt, this exhibition of violence could be a devastating blow for the defense. They maintained that the matter had been tried and ended with a hung jury. Later the defendant had entered a plea of guilty to a lesser charge and was never retried for the attempted rape. Andrew Flier fought doggedly, arguing that the elapsed fourteen years made it impossible to find original witnesses who might exonerate his client. After much discussion, the judge agreed with Flier and reversed his original decision. It would be unfair to Paleologus, he said, to defend himself against charges with the witnesses no longer available. The prosecution would be prohibited from introducing evidence about this aggravated attempted rape.

The defense had won an important battle in keeping the Bonaventure Hotel assault from the jury. On the other hand, the prosecution claimed victory in several other clashes. Most important, the judge agreed to allow presentation of Paleologus's repetitious pattern in trying to lure all of the "other women" via his bogus James Bond ploy.

In further motions, the defense vigorously fought to sever the auto fraud case from the murder charges. Originally, when Eleanor Hunter filed the murder case, she lumped them together, which would allow witnesses to testify in only one trial rather than two. It could all be decided by one jury, saving money and court resources. Combining multiple offenses into a single trial inures to the prosecution's benefit since juries tend to find collective guilt on subsidiary counts, when they might be unable to convict in smaller, separate trials. Defenders argue, of course, that joining weak charges with stronger ones is guilt by association.

Criminal law has recognized the problem in joinder of charges and set up rules to avoid unfairness. One provision states, *Offenses are properly joined in a single complaint where they are connected together in their commission or are of the same class of crimes.* Case law has further defined it: *Offenses committed at different times and places against different victims may nevertheless be connected together in their commission when there is a common element of substantial importance among them.*

Obviously, the murder of Kristi Johnson and the fraudulent taking of a BMW three days later could not be regarded as the same class of crimes. The prosecution had to find some way to show a connection in their commission with a common element of substantial importance. Walgren's efforts to prevent the charges from being severed appeared hopeless.

During argument in the pretrial motion, tension resonated in Judge Perry's courtroom. Doug Sortino, the previous prosecutor, had prepared a lengthy legal brief containing a novel argument. He maintained that the murder charge and the auto fraud shared a common element of substantial importance—the defendant's distinctive modus operandi in which he impersonated someone he was not. Sortino supported this with reference to the defendant's pretension of being someone else when he met Kristi, as well as all the other women. In the auto fraud charges, Paleologus used stolen documents and the name of a Laurel Canyon resident, thus continuing his impersonation pattern.

Doug knew that the judge might not accept this unconventional argument, so he added a second "common connection" theory in which the defendant possessed stolen property at the time of his arrest. Most of it had been taken from the Century Plaza Hotel, directly across from the Century City mall, where Kristi had met the defendant. The "connection" of these locations might just tilt the balance in the prosecution's favor.

The judge read the motions, heard the arguments, and denied Andrew Flier's severance motion, ruling that charges of murder and auto fraud were properly joined. One jury would hear both cases.

The criminal justice system has long required prosecutors and defenders to provide one another with all the evidence they intend to present before the jury. Called "discovery," it is intended to level the playing field by preventing the use of surprise witnesses or last-minute evidence. In a great many trials, one side or the other is accused of trying to circumvent the rule.

While Doug Sortino was still assigned to the case, he pressed repeatedly for the defense to provide its witness list in the Paleologus case. Finally he received it and quickly understood Andrew Flier's intended strategy. It appeared that the defense planned to hint that someone else had killed Kristi. Having been down this road before, Doug immediately initiated what is called a "third-party culpability" motion.

In 1986, the California Supreme Court carved out this new legal concept that gave the prosecution some protection from the defense muddying the waters by suggesting dozens of other possible suspects. This age-old tactic had often placed prosecutors in the untenable position of trying to prove that all of these other "suspects" couldn't possibly have committed the crime. Newer case law stated that the defense could present evidence of third-party culpability only if it is capable of raising a reasonable doubt about the defendant's guilt.

In Sortino's scrutiny of the defense's witness list, he saw a clear pattern aimed at third-party culpability. One group of witnesses would be called to testify about Kristi's lifestyle, apparently probing for possible contacts she had made with people who might have harmed her. A second group of witnesses would testify to Kristi's relationship with her former boyfriend and infer that he may have been the killer.

Relying on a specific provision, Sortino prepared a motion emphasizing that *evidence of mere motive or opportunity to commit the crime on another person, without more, will not suffice to raise a reasonable doubt about a defendant's guilt; there must be direct or circumstantial evidence linking the third person to the actual perpetration of the crime.* In a hearing, the judge grasped the defense's plan to launch a fishing expedition, hoping to hook at least one juror who might be sufficiently distracted enough to rationalize reasonable doubt. Perry asked the defense for a cogent argument to clarify how these witnesses could possibly show that someone else killed Kristi, but they failed to satisfy the requirements for third-party culpability. The prosecutor effectively blocked a potentially damaging flank assault.

After Dave Walgren took over the prosecution, the defense initiated a flurry of lengthy motions raising a broad spectrum of issues, apparently trying to delay the trial. One of the main attacks tried to exclude Kristi's roommate from testifying. They didn't want the jury to hear what Kristi told her about meeting the man at the Century City mall and the James Bond audition. Andrew Flier claimed that Kristi's statement to her roommate was hearsay evidence, thus inadmissible. American jurisprudence prohibits hearsay statements made by witnesses. But, like most courtroom rules, exceptions found their way into the law.

If the judge ruled in favor of Flier's motion, the prosecution would have no case. Unless the jury could hear about Kristi's meeting a man at the mall who wanted her to audition for James Bond modeling, and his demand for specific clothing, the testimony from several "other women" would be completely irrelevant. The defender, though, may have underestimated the new prosecutor. Realizing the extreme importance of prevailing on this issue, Dave Walgren hit the books and found a 1944 exception to hearsay that allowed statements regarding a person's intent to do something in the future.

Walgren cited the ruling made six decades earlier, and asked the judge to reject Flier's proposition. The judge listened, reviewed all the facts, and said he thought that Kristi's statement to her roommate about going to a James Bond audition expressed something the decedent planned to do in the immediate future. He ruled in favor of the prosecution.

The most heated and maybe the most grotesque pretrial motion revolved around insects found on and around Kristi's body. The defense attorney saw the opportunity to attack the prosecution's position that Kristi had died on February 15, two days before Paleologus's arrest. Flier chose maggots as his weapon for creating a reasonable doubt about her time of death. If he could show that the repulsive creatures had invaded her body after February 17, it could very well exonerate his client.

Maggot evidence, or the proven age of the nasty little creatures, is a fairly reliable way of determining when a person died. Because Paleologus had been arrested two days after Kristi's disappearance, the day of Kristi's death could be crucially important. Otherwise, he had a perfect alibi. Kristi's decomposed body had been found sixteen days after her disappearance, and fourteen days after Paleologus's arrest for taking the BMW in Beverly Hills. Therefore, if the maggots were younger than fourteen days, the defense would argue that Paleologus couldn't have committed the crime. They planned to tell the jury that Kristi had been alive for several days after her disappearance, proving that someone else had killed her.

Flier found an expert entomologist, who would examine the maggots collected during the autopsy, and at the body discovery site.

But was there anything in the insect collection worth examining? Flier filed a motion for the coroner's office or the sheriff's crime laboratory to turn over any and all insect and insect-related evidence regarding Kristi Johnson's death. The prosecutor immediately contacted both laboratories to see what they had collected at the scene and from Kristi's body at the autopsy. Both agencies told him that very little had been found or preserved.

A broad range of factors caused this—questions of jurisdiction, difficulty in collecting anything on a steep muddy slope, the body being perched in a precarious position, and heavy rainstorms preceding the discovery.

The coroner's office had three vials containing insect-related evidence removed from Kristi's body at the crime scene and by the medical examiner who performed the autopsy. Because of the small amount collected and saved, the prosecutor worried that if he turned it over to the defense expert, it would all be consumed by their tests. He didn't want to say that the defense would deliberately destroy evidence handed over to them, but he felt concern about recovering a usable sample.

Of course, he knew that the defense had a right to examine any evidence the people planned to present, along with the right to have their experts analyze exculpatory material controlled by the prosecution. The prosecutor suggested a compromise in which entomologists from both sides would simultaneously examine contents of the three vials.

His solution seemed reasonable, but the defense objected, claiming that case law permitted them to independently conduct their own tests and keep the results confidential. The judge grasped the dilemma and ruled that the prosecution and defense could hold a joint meeting with the coroner's office at which their respective entomologists could conduct the necessary tests. This meeting took place and neither side came away with any usable evidence for pinpointing the exact age of the maggots and insect life. Like battles in real war, this skirmish used up resources, time, and money—yet accomplished nothing.

The success and failures of pretrial motions will mold and sculpt the case well before a jury is seated. Few cases have been more vigorously contested during this phase than the *People* v. *Paleologus*. Both sides recognized the importance of every piece of evidence. Like a pendulum, the advantage swung back and forth, with both sides scoring crucial pretrial victories. The defense, however, still carried a strong advantage in the complete absence of eyewitnesses and forensic evidence connecting Kristi Johnson's death to Victor Paleologus.

Litigating attorneys know that judges come with good and bad traits. There are few so-called "dream judges" who are universally liked. Each one is measured by prosecutors and defense attorneys with two different sets of standards. DA lawyers favor no-nonsense judges who disallow continuances and who hand down stringent sentences. Defenders want judges who are more accommodating in continuances, and who are less harsh at the time of sentencing.

Judge Robert J. Perry, appointed to the bench by California governor Pete Wilson in 1992, showed no favoritism toward either side. At age sixty-three, sporting a healthy thatch of nearly white hair and a trim build, his movements and articulate speech radiated the energy of someone twenty years younger. Born, raised, and educated in Southern California, Perry served a hitch in the U.S. Army as an enlisted man before entering law school. He honed his skills in two private firms and with the U.S. Department of Justice. In private, beaming a friendly grin, he sometimes spoke of his efforts to write books or screenplays, or do manual labor in his avocado orchard. In the courtroom, though, he seldom smiled.

Prosecutors like working in Judge Perry's court, since he keeps the process moving at a brisk pace. He seems to take pride in trying a case faster than any other judge in Los Angeles County. At times, he appears a little fanatical in ordering prosecutors to "call your next witness," as though an endless supply of them are queued up just outside his courtroom doors. One of the most difficult jobs for any litigating attorney is the scheduling of people to testify. Attorneys can easily estimate how long direct examination of their own witness will take, but there is no way a prosecutor can guess how much time the defense will take in cross-examination. It may be a few seconds as the defender says, "No questions." Or it might consume several hours of detailed interrogation.

Woe betide errant lawyers in Judge Perry's court. He isn't hesitant to reprimand prosecutors in front of everyone for imperfect scheduling and wasting the court's precious time. Veteran prosecutors have learned, after being chewed out by Perry, to have plenty of extra witnesses available. This method does increase the efficiency of the court and makes Judge Perry happy. At the same time, it is a great inconvenience for civilian and police witnesses who are cooling their heels sitting on uncomfortable hallway benches.

Conversely, this hardship on prosecutors is outweighed by

having a judge who is also reluctant to waste time on defense attorneys' frivolous motions. The one thing both sides will agree on is that Perry is a no-nonsense judge always in control of his courtroom.

The long-awaited trial finally opened in early July 2006 on the ninth floor of the Los Angeles Criminal Courts Building. The modern structure, housing central court operations and the L.A. District Attorney's Office, looms nineteen stories on Temple Street, between Broadway and Spring in the north sector of downtown. Built in 1972, it replaced the historic Hall of Justice on the other side of Temple, the scene of famous trials for Charles Manson, Sirhan Sirhan, and hundreds of other notorious lawbreakers. Jack Webb's *Dragnet* series used the old building as a frequent backdrop.

Judge Perry's courtroom is one of several on the ninth floor, where most high-profile and extended trials take place. People entering the building are subjected to X-ray machines and metal detectors at security checkpoints, and are screened a second time on the ninth floor. Access into Perry's dark wood-paneled court is through an antechamber with two sets of doors, then a side entry at the rear of his high-ceilinged room. Visitors may be seated in four rows of curved-seat wooden benches with "backrests," which provide no rest at all. A few thin blue cushions pretend to offer comfort.

Court officers and staff pass through a gate in the dividing barrier at the gallery's front. This area contains two counsel tables used by the prosecution and the defenders with their clients. A few steps farther is the judge's elevated desk. An eighteen-chair jury box occupies the room's left side, seating twelve jurors and six alternates. The bailiff watches everything from a desk inside a security enclosure at the right, and the adjacent court clerk is protected by a swinging half-door. This mystical barrier is used, at the clerk's discretion, to either admit or exclude attorneys from entry into the judge's chambers.

During trials, the court reporter sits in front of the witness stand, which is between the judge and the jury. Both the judge's chamber and jury room have windows that help alleviate a generally claustrophobic atmosphere.

Victor Paleologus occupied a chair next to his counsel, Andrew Flier. In all of the defendant's earlier appearances, he had worn the standard jailhouse-issued orange jumpsuit. The defense had now done a reasonable job of making him look presentable to the jury.

David Walgren sat alone at the adjacent table.

Judge Perry's clerk summoned a huge herd of potential jurors to fill up the hard wooden benches in the audience. Since the prosecution had decided to seek the death penalty, Judge Perry advised them of the profound decision they might have to make. In their answers to his questions, some of the candidates invoked religious or moral opposition, while others simply stated they couldn't impose death—no matter what the evidence showed. Judge Perry excused them for "cause."

Jury selection in a capital case is an inexact science. Both sides try to weed out people with extreme opinions and seat moderates. The prosecution asks candidates if they can impose death if the defendant is found guilty and special circumstances found to be true and they believe it is appropriate. Defenders attempt to find people who are probably opposed to capital punishment but portray themselves as open-minded. Experts are sometimes employed, usually by the defense, to help select jurors sympathetic to the underdog and disinclined to vote for death.

Judge Perry likes to have potential jurors fill out multipage questionnaires designed jointly by the prosecutor and defense attorney. Each side reviews the answers and ranks candidates by assigning grades from A to F, or 1 to 5 ratings. These responses help the judge, too, in excusing people who are not qualified, or cannot serve for various valid reasons. Afterward, each candidate is asked questions in open court to determine their acceptability.

In the Paleologus case, Dave Walgren knew that he had to

pick the perfect jury or he would have no chance of getting a unanimous guilty verdict. He had to deal with an age-old question: are men better jurors for the prosecution in this type of case, or should women be picked? At the beginning of my prosecution career, the rule of thumb in sexual assault trials was to excuse as many women as you could. We reasoned that women, especially older ones, ironically tend to view young female victims in a harsh light. They seemed to assume that rape occurs because women lead the guy on or because the "hussy" put herself in a vulnerable position.

Dave understood the concept of "that was then, this is now." In the new century, old rules regarding jury selection no longer applied, so he tossed out preconceived notions about gender. He designed questions to find jurors who would be willing to convict Paleologus primarily on the modus operandi evidence.

The DA's office had decided to pursue the death penalty. This created another dilemma for Dave. Should he place more emphasis on finding jurors who would convict, and not worry about the punishment? For example, would a devout Roman Catholic, strong in morality with unshakeable belief in law and order, who could probably see Paleologus's guilt but would be opposed to execution, be acceptable?

As a realist, Dave knew that he had to confront the first giant obstacle—trying to convince twelve people to convict. Capital punishment would be a moot point anyway if the jury came back with a verdict of not guilty.

In the selection process, both sides experience frustration. Jurors deemed acceptable by one side are subjected to peremptory challenges by the other side. Dave frequently referred to his "report card" prepared from the questionnaires, and used most of his challenges to evict candidates with low scores.

In Judge Perry's court, nothing goes slowly. Everything seems accelerated to supersonic speed. Most other judges in the criminal courts building will take a week or longer to select a death penalty jury. Perry's impatience manifests itself if he does not have a jury in place and taking testimony by the second day. To him, jury selection shouldn't be a slow-motion chess match. The attorneys must make quick decisions under extraordinary pressure. This is a time when the prosecutor is at a distinct disadvantage. Dave needed to select twelve intelligent jurors who also would be compatible in deliberations. The defense needs to find only one free thinker who will prevent a unanimous verdict.

All the fuss and worry seldom changes the makeup of juries. They remain enigmatic and unpredictable in every trial.

Walgren and Flier at last agreed on ten men and two women to hear evidence in the trial of Victor Paleologus. The dozens of questionnaires, invaluable minutes before, were unceremoniously dumped into a big box and thrown in the bottom of the prosecutor's cart. Judge Perry asked the clerk to swear in the panel, plus four alternates, and informed the triers of fact that opening statements would commence the next morning, Thursday, July 13, 2006.

This is the moment that life becomes a giant pressure cooker for the prosecutor. Dave immediately began contacting all of his initial witnesses to schedule them for appearance in court. He knew that he didn't want to start off on the wrong foot with Judge Perry, so he lined up several of the "other women" to be available in court the next day, ready to testify.

Late Wednesday night, Dave put finishing touches on his opening statement, adapting visual aid material I had previously prepared for Doug Sortino. Some of his planned statements, and my visuals, required modification as a result of Judge Perry's rulings in the pretrial motions. Most important, Dave wanted to make certain his remarks would indelibly brand in each juror's mind the pattern Paleologus had used to lure women for more than a decade.

On the morning of showtime, Walgren arrived early. Everything had to be ready for performance on cue. He planned to show a video clip of Kristi making her purchase of the miniskirt at the Guess women's apparel store. Dave recognized how powerful the images would be of Kristi walking confidently, paying for her purchase, and exiting the front door. She appeared to be on top of the world, but jurors would soon understand that they were watching her final day of life.

Wishing to avoid all glitches, Dave tested everything. He understood Murphy's Law, which states that if anything can go wrong, it will go wrong. Someone reminded him to be certain he asked the court clerk to turn down the lights so jurors could see the PowerPoint presentation on a giant screen.

As the gallery filled with eager spectators, Dave and Andrew Flier made small talk for a few moments, always a good idea to show spectators and reporters that the upcoming event is not a contest, but a civilized procedure to seek justice. Detective Virginia Obenchain, dressed in a stylish black ensemble with a red blouse, sat quietly at the prosecution table.

In the first row of seats, Dave could see Kristi's mother exchanging pleasantries with her former husband and his current wife. The prosecutor hoped that nothing in his presentation would cause them unnecessary grief. He had tried to make it as tasteful as possible, especially when discussing the horror of murder by strangulation, and the discovery of her decomposing body after it lay on a hillside for two weeks.

As the minutes ticked away, and jurors waited to be summoned from their quarters in the back of the courtroom, the buzz of spectators tapered off, leaving a vacuum of silence. The court clerk nodded to the bailiff to bring Paleologus into the courtroom. He entered, escorted by two uniformed officers, and looked sheepishly around as if looking for anyone he might know in the audience. His eyes seemed to fix on Kristi's parents in the front row, then glanced downward as he shuffled to a chair adjacent to Andrew Flier. After a short, whispered conversation, they fell silent. Court TV reporter Lisa Sweetingham noted that he wore clothes appearing to belong to someone taller and heavier plus a dark blazer that fell to midthigh, blue jeans rolled up at the hem, and a loose-fitting flannel shirt.

The jurors, in single file, walked out of their room, and after some trouble figuring out seating assignments, they finally settled in, their faces taking on the classic, impassive expressions expected of them.

At the prosecutor's table, Dave mentally rehearsed his opening statement for the hundredth time. He had spent every spare minute going over the flow of his presentation and trying to find the words to best describe each event. He understood that a strong presentation doesn't just happen, but is crafted and reworked until it acquires the powerful impact needed to rivet and impress the jury. Turning toward the gallery, Dave could see news reporters huddled in the middle of the courtroom busily scribbling in their spiral notepads. He assumed that if he made one mistake, it would be reported on tonight's TV coverage or tomorrow morning's newspapers. Dave spotted his boss, joined by half of the prosecutors from Major Crimes, seated in the back row. He wondered if they were there for moral support or just to rib him unmercifully if he made a faux pas.

With jurors waiting, and everyone quiet, the clerk buzzed for the judge. Almost immediately Judge Perry seemed to bounce out of chambers and, like a flash, ensconced himself in his presiding chair. He told the jury that the prosecution had the burden of proof, so they would have the opportunity to speak first. The judge also advised jurors that statements by attorneys are not evidence, and must not be considered during deliberations. Opening statements are only for the purpose of the prosecutor and the defender to say what they expect the evidence to show, and should never be argumentative. Turning toward Dave Walgren, he asked, "Does the prosecution wish to make an opening statement?"

Dave mustered up his deepest voice and said, "The people do, Your Honor." Pushing back his chair, he stood, looked directly into the eyes of the jurors, and said, "Good morning, ladies and gentlemen of the jury." Those words have been uttered for hundreds of years.

Without using notes, Dave fixed his attention on the jurors. A picture of Kristi Johnson's beautiful face appeared on the giant screen, accompanied by a list of facts about her. Emotional energy penetrated the entire room.

Ceiling lights diluted the picture, though, because Dave had forgotten to ask the court clerk to dim them. Every juror strained their eyes to see Kristi on the screen. The next slide showed her dead body on the hillside, with her hands and feet tied behind her. Soft groans and murmurs of disbelief drifted among the spectators, and jurors' eyes grew moist. Dave had their undivided attention and they waited breathlessly to hear what he had to say to them.

CHAPTER 21

A YOUNG WARRIOR

Ron Bowers had provided numerous visual aids for Dave Walgren's opening statement, and the prosecutor used them generously in a PowerPoint slide show as Bowers sat in the gallery to observe.

Wearing a navy blue suit, crisp white shirt, and necktie, Walgren greeted the jury, waited for absolute silence, then spoke again. "This case, as you now know . . . is about the brutal murder of Kristi Johnson on February 15, 2003."

He told jurors that they would hear evidence about seven other women, but asked them to remain centered on the one who died, Kristi. Pointing toward the defendant, who appeared pale and thin, Walgren enunciated each word: "The evidence will show you . . . that Mr. Paleologus, sitting here at the end of counsel table, murdered Kristi Johnson on that date."

Letting that image sink in for a few moments, he scanned the faces staring back at him. "The defendant, you will learn, had a history of luring women to sham auditions, to fake auditions that he indicated to them was for a James Bond production of some sort or another."

If Walgren felt nervous, he concealed it well. "The defendant has a history of this type of behavior going back to at least 1991, and you will hear from the witnesses who will tell you about their personal experiences with this defendant, Mr. Paleologus. . . . He told them, tried to lure them to an audition for a James Bond movie. You will hear about women in this case who were told not only to go to a James Bond audition . . . but were told to wear very specific, very precise clothing. Not to just one woman, but multiple women—a white button-down-type shirt, a very short black miniskirt, nylons, and black stiletto-type heels."

A skill often used by powerful orators is the pregnant pause. Like punctuation, it creates space between sentences and allows the last point to sink in. Walgren timed his pauses perfectly.

With ten male jurors, Walgren hoped the image of sexy clothing would register well in their minds. "Many of the women were also told that they would either be provided a man's necktie to wear at the audition, or to bring a necktie. . . . You will hear about this pattern of evidence and learn about the defendant's past, even before he came upon the victim in this case, Kristi Johnson."

Walgren noted Kristi's age, twenty-one, and that her next birthday had arrived two weeks after her death. "You will hear about what she did on February 15, 2003. You will hear who she met on February fifteenth, 2003. And you will hear that she was murdered on February 15, 2003." Good speakers know to repeat crucial words and phrases for emphasis, and Walgren obviously liked the technique.

It is important for prosecutors to acquaint jurors as much as possible with the murder victim so they can feel the pain wrought by the killer. Walgren delivered a sketch of Kristi's background, but erred on one point when he said that California native Kristi was born and raised in Michigan. He correctly stated that she wanted to become a makeup artist, liked living in California, and resided in Santa Monica with two roommates, one of whom would testify. To emphasize her vulnerability, he commented, "You may hear at times she was a bit naive and trusting of other individuals."

Drawing a deep breath, Walgren delivered a dramatic forty-eight-word sentence, without a single pause, to describe how she lost her life. "On February 15, 2003, Kristi was murdered and thrown over the side of the hill in the Lookout Mountain area of the Hollywood Hills, specifically off the street called Skyline Drive, which is actually a dirt road, and she was thrown off the side of that steep cliff." The resonant statement seemed electric, leaving every juror and observer waiting for the next jolt.

"Her body was partially stuffed inside a sleeping bag and she was tossed down the side of the hill. We know that only because of where she came to rest, upon hitting some trees and debris, and that's how her body was found." Walgren pointed to a photo on the screen, a wide-angle aerial view of a narrow road perched atop a verdant ridge, lined on both sides with homes. "This is Skyline Drive. Here, it is a paved street, but then it comes to an end and is dirt for the part that I'm showing you." Flashing to another view, showing the brushy slope, he said, "Her body was found down the side of a hill on a pile of debris on March third . . . about two and a half weeks after her murder."

Walgren dreaded delivering the next segment, knowing that Kristi's family sat in the front row, but it had to be done. Flipping to another full-color scene, this one depicting the victim's body shortly after it was discovered, he continued. "The condition of Kristi when found—her wrists were tied behind her back with shoelaces. Her ankles were bound together with shoelaces. And notably in the picture that you see before you—that will be presented to you throughout this case—Kristi had changed into the desired shoes that you'll learn were the signature requests of the defendant, Victor Paleologus. Kristi had changed into the desired nylons, which were the signature requests of the defendant, Victor Paleologus. And then she was killed, stuffed in a sleeping bag, and thrown down the hill."

Kristi's parents did their best to mask the visceral impact, but tears could be seen in their eyes.

Paleologus kept his gaze down toward the table, refusing to look at the screen.

Reiterating the location, Walgren reminded jurors that "Skyline Drive will become very relevant as the evidence is presented to you throughout this case."

Waving an arm casually in the defendant's direction, Walgren changed his topic. "Now at this time . . . Victor Paleologus was about forty years old. He had previously worked at a restaurant that you'll hear about from a number of different witnesses." The business had closed down and moved three times, the prosecutor explained. First located in Marina del Rey, then on San Vincente Boulevard in Brentwood, it had wound up on La Cienega Boulevard, West Hollywood, before its final closing. Walgren emphasized the second and third locations and alerted jurors that two victims would testify about what happened to them inside the empty building on San Vincente. Another female witness would describe disturbing events on La Cienega, near the building that had once housed the restaurant, where Paleologus sometimes slept in a tiny room.

For the next few minutes, Walgren explained points of law that jurors needed to understand, and reminded them that witnesses and evidence would be presented in regard to Paleologus illegally taking the SUV from a Beverly Hills BMW dealer. "You will see how all of these counts tie into the murder case." He also pointed out that witnesses are called according to availability, not in a sequence of events.

Most people are intrigued by a mystery or a challenging puzzle, the basis for countless books and films. So Walgren used that theme for introducing his outline of the facts. "Every case, ladies and gentlemen, begins as a puzzle. No less so in a murder case such as this. You begin with the dead body and . . . filling in pieces of the puzzle, different sections, piecing them together, to determine who killed the victim.

"This case is no different. This case began as a puzzle and I'm going to explain to you here today different pieces of that puzzle and how pieces fit together to create an image of the killer of Kristi Johnson. And that image is of the defendant, Victor Paleologus. . . . One thing you are going to hear is about the defendant's past history with women. And you are going to learn from these women, from all walks of life who didn't even know each other, didn't know the victim. And they are going to come in here and tell you about their experiences with the defendant, what he did to them as far back as 1991."

The first in this parade of women, said Walgren, would be Elizabeth Davis. He said she met Paleologus at Los Angeles International Airport. They talked several times by phone and had dinner together in a Santa Monica restaurant. Paleologus, using a phony name, "offered to introduce Ms. Davis to this James Bond producer that night." Instead, he spiked her drink with Dramamine and when she challenged him, he tried to worm his way out of it. "He fled the restaurant . . . leaving the drink there, and, fortunately for us here today, also left his credit card receipt."

Promising that Davis would testify, Walgren expressed hope that she would be able to remember everything—even though fifteen years had elapsed.

One of the women scheduled to testify about the defendant's fraudulent past, said Walgren, had been Paleologus's girlfriend—but still he victimized her. Annie Olson broke up with him in early 1996, but "he wanted her back. In fact, he told her he was dying of a terminal illness." She agreed to meet him at the San Vincente address in Brentwood to talk, "but what happened was far different. . . . In this closed restaurant, he pushed her up against the wall, held her neck with his hand, and started kissing her against her will." The sexual assault ended, said Walgren, when a worker came in. She left, but that still didn't end it.

"On February 6, 1996 . . . she was at home watching television. She began to hear noises, turned down the TV . . . and eventually went into the back room of her apartment to investigate." The prosecutor paced his story for maximum effect, telling that Olson had spotted Paleologus lying behind the bed, and how he had lunged after her with a "ligature outstretched in his hands." She used pepper spray on him, escaped from the apartment, and notified the police. Paleologus "faced the charge of burglary . . . with intent to commit a felony, [pleaded] guilty to that felony, and that will be evidence in this case."

In the gallery, Ron Bowers hid a satisfied smile. Later calling Walgren's presentation strong and impressive, Bowers said, "He came across as being very serious and knowledgeable about the facts of the case."

Obviously feeling comfortable, the young prosecutor continued. "But you will not just hear from Ms. Davis and Ms. Olson. You will also hear from a Ms. Dawn Cooper about her incident with the defendant in August of 1998. . . . She was with a friend at a bar on Sunset Boulevard in Hollywood." Paleologus approached them outside, gave a false name, and said he was a movie executive for Disney. "He indicated, again, that he would like to arrange for her to be in a James

Bond movie, and wanted a meeting or audition to take place with Ms. Cooper." Excited, she agreed to meet him two days later, said Walgren, to discuss the contract. "The defendant made very clear what clothing she was to bring—the shirt, the black miniskirt, the black high heels, and nylons."

At the Ritz Carlton Hotel, on August 30, they met, and after she did some "informal posing in the lobby," the defendant led Cooper to the vacant restaurant on San Vincente. More posing followed and she complied with his requests. Then, "the defendant takes the opportunity to bind her legs together with a cord and began an attempt to rape her." A struggle followed. "He starts trying to pull her clothes off. She hears him undo his pants. She's scared for her life, kicks and flails. . . . When the defendant backs away, she gets up and is able to flee the location." She reported it to the police and identified him, both from a photograph and in a live lineup.

If jurors wondered about Cooper's companion on the night they met Paleologus, Walgren cleared it up, explaining that she would also testify and identify the defendant, despite his use of a fake name. Paleologus, he said, had later pleaded no contest to a charge of assault with intent to commit rape.

"But that is not all you will hear about his past. You will hear from a Cathy DeBuono. And you will learn that this is when the defendant starts preying on women at the Century City mall."

The word "preying" brought the trial's first objection from defender Andrew Flier, calling it "argumentative." The judge agreed.

Nodding his understanding, Walgren kept going, full speed. "We've already heard about James Bond. We've already heard about the clothing. Now you are going to hear about the pattern of Century City. In late 1998 or early 1999, Ms. DeBuono met the defendant at that mall. She was there shopping and he approached her. He said again that he was a movie executive and wanted to put her in a James Bond movie. He wanted her to audition. And he told her that he would provide the clothing. . . . The audition would take place in the Hollywood Hills." Pinpointing it exactly, the prosecutor made the connection in case jurors hadn't—that Cathy DeBuono was being invited to Skyline Drive, the site of Kristi Johnson's death.

DeBuono, he pointed out, had taken a male friend with her and they waited in a car at the rendezvous point. But the defendant never showed up. Walgren made the implication clear, that the presence of a man had frightened away the predator of young women. The intended victim, he asserted, later identified a photo of Paleologus.

The next witness, Walgren said, would be a man, a Marina del Rey used-car dealer. Paleologus had bought a car from him in 1998. Evidence from him would connect the defendant to three addresses, all listed on his credit application, on La Cienega, on San Vincente, and an apartment in the marina, where he had lived close to the former girlfriend he had tried to rape. Incidentally, Walgren said, Paleologus had defaulted on the loan, resulting in repossession of the car. In the trunk, the dealer found "high heels, panty hose, neckties, sexual moisturizer, rope, and a sex toy referred to as a dildo."

Investigators and DA personnel knew the crucial importance one woman had played in solving the crime, and eagerly anticipated her testimony. Even Walgren's voice seemed to rise in respect of her. "You will also hear from Susan Murphy. You will learn that on January 24, 2003, Ms. Murphy, again at the Century City mall, came into contact with the defendant. He indicated he was a movie executive for Disney, named Victor Thomas, and he wanted to put her in a James Bond production of one sort or another. He set up the obligatory audition for her, to take place on the very next day. And what clothing did he tell her to wear? A white shirt. A black miniskirt. High heels and nylons. The defendant would supply the necktie."

Some of the implacability seemed to fade from a few jurors' faces, replaced by wrinkled brows, a hint of incredulity, and subtle glances toward the defendant. Was he really this consistent in his deadly game?

Walgren's energy escalated as he prepared to show a video clip. "Ms. Murphy will testify and will be able to say exactly where she was when she met the defendant. . . . In this video about to play, you will see three separate clips." Pointing to action on the screen depicting people at the doorway to a department store, he said, "Look to where I am pointing. . . . You will see Victor Paleologus entering behind Ms. Murphy. He is wearing the same jacket he wore when later arrested. He has now entered the store, following her. You will see Ms. Murphy walking through the jewelry aisle. Here comes the defendant shortly behind her. She turns right, he follows."

Activating a second clip, Walgren maintained his animated narration. "Watch this next clip where he turns right, following the same path Ms. Murphy took." Switching again, he said, "Now, in this last clip, you will see them leaving the Macy's store, actually talking as they exit together. Victor Paleologus and Susan Murphy. She's excited. She agrees to meet with him."

Spectators and jurors could easily imagine that they were seeing a preview of precisely how Paleologus would corral and convince Kristi Johnson three weeks later, in the same mall.

Susan Murphy kept her appointment with Paleologus on January 25, said Walgren, at a street corner on La Cienega Boulevard. "She takes her boyfriend at the time, Mark Wilson. He's concerned. He thinks it's a sham. And she's a bit concerned. She waits on the corner as instructed by the defendant, and Mark waits in his vehicle. The defendant approaches and he's angry because she's not wearing the clothing she was told to wear." Walgren described the encounter in which Murphy had refused to go with Paleologus, Mark had interceded, a chase followed, another confrontation ensued, and finally the defendant had fled.

Gripping jurors with each new building block he stacked against the defendant, Walgren added an essential keystone by spelling out how important Susan Murphy had been in breaking the case. "About five days after Kristi Johnson was murdered, twenty-five days after Ms. Murphy had her run-in with the defendant, she sees the morning paper. There is no mention about Century City. There's no mention about James Bond. There's no mention about clothing, because the police withheld all of that information. . . . But something about this story caused Ms. Murphy to shake. And she called the police on February 20, 2003."

The information Susan provided to investigators, said Walgren, fit perfectly with what they knew about Kristi's experience. He spoke of the details, and how Murphy and Wilson had contributed their recollections of Victor Thomas's facial features to help a sketch artist prepare the composite drawing that eventually led to his real identification.

Naming a sixth woman in the growing list of Paleologus's targets who had survived, Walgren described an incident that happened on January 25, 2003. "Alice Walker also met the defendant at the Century City mall. Keep in mind that the meeting with Ms. Murphy was on that afternoon." Raising his voice for the first time to add power, he said, "At ten o'clock *that same night,* he's at the Century City mall, where Ms. Walker worked as a waitress . . . and struck up a conversation with her. He gave a fake name, Victor Ippolito, and said he was involved in a James Bond production. He wanted to set up an audition for her the next day."

Leading astonished jurors through another mind-boggling incarnation of the scam, Walgren told them of Walker meeting the defendant that night at the sumptuous Century Plaza Hotel lobby, one block away. There he gave her the full spiel about the required costume and poses she would strike at the audition. This time, said Walgren, Paleologus added a new element. "The defendant told her he was writing a novel, and the character strangles a woman to death during wild sex in the car." The next day when Walker showed up at the former restaurant on La Cienega for her expected audition, he startled her by trying to knot a necktie around her throat, and she pulled away. Still intrigued, though, she met him again on January 29, at the same place. "They again proceeded through the steps of a sham audition. The defendant had her make various poses on all fours, getting up on a counter, lying down with her ankles . . . crisscrossed and her wrists behind her back. . . . At one point he told her the character would be a sexual dominatrix. He called her a whore and attempted to kiss her."

Even though this frightened Walker, said the prosecutor, she agreed to meet him again, at a café in the Century City mall. Afterward, she drove him to a Sunset Boulevard intersection and dropped him off. "Notably, it was across the street from the bar where the defendant had met Ms. Cooper in 1998." Walker spoke to Paleologus several times after that by telephone, but never saw him again. "Their last conversation took place just two weeks before Kristi Johnson was killed." Later, said Walgren, this witness told the police about Victor Ippolito, and even brought in the white shirt, black miniskirt, and high heels she had purchased. She had no difficulty identifying a photograph of him as the defendant.

Walgren ended the parade of "other women" accosted by Paleologus with Mary Beth Licudine. "Three years prior to Kristi Johnson, Mary Beth was at the Century City mall. She watched a movie, then went over to the pay phones to make a call. The defendant, Paleologus, approached her and offered the opportunity for her to be in a James Bond poster promotion. She was extremely suspicious, not interested. Quite frankly, she didn't believe it. Ms. Licudine is here and will testify about meeting the defendant."

Using another pregnant pause, Walgren allowed a few moments of silence, then picked up where he left off. "You will hear from all of these women, ladies and gentlemen. The evidence will show a distinct pattern in the defendant's behavior. It will show there is a consistent theme of James Bond. There is a consistent theme of the required clothing, and a theme of the Century City mall, where he met many of these victims, including Kristi Johnson. The defendant's past is one piece of the puzzle, one very large piece."

Ron Bowers knew that Walgren had performed admirably in building the case so far, and eagerly waited to see if the young prosecutor could establish a credible account of how the evidence would show that Paleologus had killed Kristi Johnson.

Walgren began with a question. "So what happened on February 15, 2003, the day Kristi Johnson disappeared?" Walgren's earnest manner and countenance still had the jurors hooked. He began the answer to his own query. "Kristi woke up in her Santa Monica apartment . . . and talked to her mother on the phone at about ten o'clock that morning. She told her mother she was going shopping at the Century City mall."

Using an aerial photo of the shopping center provided by Bowers, Walgren took jurors on a step-by-step tour, following the same path Kristi had taken. "We know what happened to Kristi there, because when she returned to the apartment, she told her roommate all about it." Using a laser pointer, he said, "The restaurant is up front and Macy's is back here. Here is the Century Plaza Hotel, where Alice Walker sat with the defendant.

"You will hear from the roommate Carrie Barrish, and learn that Kristi met a man at the Century City mall. She was so excited she could hardly control herself. Carrie will tell you that Kristi was fanning herself, so excited she was about to overheat. She was going to be in a James Bond production. The man she met worked in the film industry. He was going to put her in a James Bond movie. He set up an audition for her. He told her to wear a white shirt, black miniskirt, black high heels, and nylons. He would provide the necktie."

With the visual aids, showing exact sites, times, and even receipts, Walgren illustrated details of Kristi's shopping spree. And he made another promise. "You will actually see a video of Kristi making the purchase of this black miniskirt on that day, at about one-forty in the afternoon." As a preview, he flipped to a still picture on the PowerPoint production. "This is Kristi in the lower corner. She has her Bloomingdale's bag in her hand, most likely holding the white shirt and nylons. She approaches the counter. She hands over the black miniskirt to the teller. And the transaction, buying the skirt for her role in a James Bond audition, unfolds."

Walgren described Kristi's trip across town to a lingerie store on La Cienega Boulevard to buy the black stiletto heels. He added a grim reminder: "These were the shoes that were shown in the coroner's photos earlier in my presentation on the feet of Kristi's bound legs."

Kristi had returned to her apartment in a state of extreme excitement, said the prosecutor, explained everything to her roommate and even modeled the clothing. "She put back on her casual clothing, said good-bye to Carrie, and left in her white Miata at about four-thirty P.M. for her audition. Carrie Barrish will tell you that Kristi never returned. When you think about the pattern the evidence will show you, that pattern continues with Kristi Johnson—Century City mall, James Bond, clothing, necktie—that is all a piece of the puzzle."

To Bowers in the gallery, the puzzle analogy appeared to be working quite well.

Cell phone technology, Walgren's next topic, might not carry the same dramatic impact. He summarized the high points briefly, informing jurors that an expert would testify and explain what part it played in the investigation. Calls "bounce from cell phone towers," he said, and show up on documents recording the telephone numbers and the call timing. These records would track both Kristi and the defendant on the day she vanished, and generally place them in the region. Her calls to information came from somewhere in the Hollywood Hills. Earlier in the day, his came from somewhere around Century City. Walgren admitted, "Cell phone tower technology cannot pinpoint a specific corner the defendant was standing on, or a specific location. What it can pinpoint is that the defendant's phone call was bouncing off that Century City tower and no other tower."

Slipping quickly into a change of course, Walgren brought up another woman's name. "Dawn Skora was at the mall that day, and she saw the defendant standing outside Victoria's Secret store. She will testify in this trial that she saw Mr. Paleologus there at the same time his phone call was registered by the cell tower." The combination evidence should leave no doubt of his location at the time Kristi shopped there.

A witness named Douglas Kirkland, said Walgren, would testify to seeing Kristi near his Hollywood Hills home at about sunset, at the time she made the final two calls of her life. Kirkland would also tell jurors about giving her directions to the "castle house" on the corner of Green Valley and Skyline Drive, a short distance from a specific address where Kristi headed for the audition. Citing it, Walgren urged jurors, "Remember that address, because I will be talking about it."

Turning again to the big screen and a new set of projected images, he said, "This is the castle house here." Tracing the route, he demonstrated the short distance from there to Kristi's destination, and explained the clear conclusion. "The photos shown to you previously, the location of Kristi's body thrown over the side of the hill—we know from the evidence that she was killed that evening." He inferred that she died right there on Skyline Drive.

Listening and observing, Bowers knew that Walgren intended to head off a probable gambit of the defense, to suggest that Kristi had left Skyline Drive and attended a rave concert in Los Angeles that night.

Diving right into it, Walgren said, "Some of the evidence you will hear tells us that she had tickets for a club party that evening, prepaid. Fifteen-dollar tickets. You will hear from the club promoter that Kristi *did not* attend that party." He spat out the words "did not" as if they were poisonous.

Returning to cell phone usage again, the prosecutor used more graphics to demonstrate that Paleologus had not made any calls between 3:49 and 10:06 P.M. on that day. And, "every call coming in to his cell phone goes straight to voice mail, indicating that his phone is turned off. The empty time frame would allow plenty of opportunity to wreak his havoc on Kristi."

At 10:06 P.M., a spurt of telephone activity came from Paleologus. The first call, said Walgren, bounced off a cell phone tower that placed him somewhere in the region of the Hollywood Hills. "An engineer will tell you about that." At 11:34 P.M., a call from the defendant bounced from another tower near Sunset Boulevard, showing that he's traveling . . . toward Hollywood. His usage stopped until 2:41 P.M., the next day, and this one bounced from the same tower that could put him at the Century City mall. "That is a piece of the puzzle."

Another important prosecution witness, said Walgren, would reveal one more facet of fraud perpetrated by Paleologus, this one to find a venue for his criminal sexual adventures. "You will hear from Charlie Simon, who is a realtor. He met the defendant on February 8, 2003. The defendant walked into Mr. Simon's office and said he was looking to buy a house in the Hollywood Hills for about seven hundred thousand dollars. . . . Mr. Simon began showing him homes."

A requirement by Paleologus struck Simon as quite odd, said Walgren. First, he indicated a preference to see vacant homes, because he needed to move in immediately. Second, "the defendant told Mr. Simon to go into the far end of the house and yell, to make loud noises, because Mr. Paleologus wanted to test the soundproofness of the home." Even though it seemed weird, Simon humored him in several homes.

Referring to another projected slide, Walgren said, "This diagram shows the particular locations." He listed several, then came to the one anticipated by every observer. "Mr. Simon showed the defendant the house on Skyline Drive." It was the address he had asked jurors to remember.

"Mr. Simon took him to the house and even spoke with the defendant about the nice dirt trails that were just a short distance away. It is about two hundred yards from where Kristi Johnson's body was found thrown over the side of a hill." Paleologus had toured the home exactly one week before Kristi drove up there for an "audition" and lost her life, instead.

Reminding jurors of that horrible fact, Walgren said, "As I indicated earlier, she was in a sleeping bag. She rolled down the hill until she came to a rest against a small tree and some debris. The condition of her body on that hill was one of severe decomposition of her face, and I have chosen not to show you those photos. You will likely see them when the coroner testifies. And it is extreme."

Linking pieces of the puzzle together, he said, "The evidence will show you when her body was recovered, those shoes were on her and she was wearing the nylons, although she left her apartment not wearing that clothing, she had gotten into the nylons and the shoes." No one, except perhaps her killer, knew the exact events that took place on Skyline Drive. Somehow, though, Kristi had at least started changing into the apparel required by Victor Paleologus. When and exactly where remained pieces of the puzzle that might never be put in place.

Because the allegation of murder had been combined with felony charges related to taking the BMW, Walgren needed to say a few words about that crime. He outlined the basic sequence of events leading up to the defendant's arrest near a Beverly Hills shopping mall.

The real estate agent had taken Paleologus to several occupied homes and a number of interesting items turned up as a result of the arrest, said Walgren. "He had in his possession documents from a home on Wonderland Park shown to him by Mr. Simon. He has property belonging to a resident of a home on Warbler Way, one of the homes shown to him by Mr. Simon. He has property from the resident of a home on Hancock Avenue, shown to him by Mr. Simon. He has a wallet, driver's license, and credit cards stolen from a man at a spa. Why is that relevant? Because the spa is connected to the Century Plaza Hotel, where Ms. Walker met with the defendant, and across the street from the Century City mall, where the defendant met so many of his victims, including Kristi Johnson."

Other documents and ID papers turned up in searches. "They found his driver's license, in the name of Victor Paleologus, with his address as the vacant restaurant on La Cienega. They found his cell phone, which links him up with calls made on the date Kristi died. They found business cards on which Ms. Walker had written a phone number, which will corroborate her testimony. They found Century Plaza Hotel stationery indicating his presence there."

An attempt to escape from jail had also turned up something the jury needed to know, Walgren divulged. "The defendant was only under arrest for car theft, but he told inmates he was looking at 'life or death' and he would give them five thousand dollars to switch wristbands with him." The scheme failed, but clearly demonstrated "consciousness of guilt."

"Lastly, ladies and gentlemen, you will hear about another piece of this puzzle—that when the police searched the defendant's residence on La Cienega, they recovered not only all of these items, but also his laptop computer. And as one piece of the puzzle, they searched the computer. Keep in mind the evidence from Ms. Olson about being chased with the ligature and the evidence of Ms. Cooper being bound with a cord, the evidence of Kristi Johnson being found with her ankles and wrists tied behind her back. The police searched his computer and found pictures of a female, bound to a chair with ligatures, in different positions. But that's not all they saw.

"Keeping in mind the clothing, the white shirt, the black miniskirt, the nylons, the high heels, and the necktie, they searched the computer, and this is what they found—a female in different stages of undress wearing a white shirt, a black miniskirt, nylons, black high heels, and a necktie.

"Ladies and gentlemen, I know that was a lot of information in a relatively short period of time. This offers you an outline, a road map, and explains the pieces of the puzzle as we proceed through this trial.

"And I just want to thank you now for the attention you've given me. And the attention you will give me and defense counsel through this trial. Thank you."

If David Walgren had started the morning as a young, relatively inexperienced prosecutor of murder cases, he reached midday with the status of an experienced veteran.

Ron Bowers nodded, and felt a strong sense of accomplishment, both on the part of his colleague, and the added proof for him that visual aids can be overwhelmingly powerful.

Observers speculated that if the jury could start deliberating at that moment, they would come back in a very short time to announce a guilty verdict.

But had Walgren really presented a legally convincing statement, backed up by any real evidence that Victor Paleologus could be found guilty of murder? Or had he simply delivered persuasive oratory, with shallow circumstantial evidence, that did nothing more than suggest the defendant's guilt?

Andrew Reed Flier would have his opportunity to tear apart the puzzle Walgren had assembled, and demonstrate that substantial pieces were missing.

Judge Robert Perry announced the lunch recess until 1:30 P.M.

CHAPTER 22

DEAD-SET DEFENSE

After waiting several minutes for a tardy juror, Judge Perry announced, "All right, we're back on the record in the *People* versus *Paleologus*. We're ready now for the opening statement to be offered by Mr. Flier."

Andrew Flier rose from his chair next to the defendant, fingered a button on his dark suit coat, stepped over to the lectern, and said, "Thank you, Your Honor."

Exuding self-confidence, Flier spoke without notes, and strode energetically back and forth in front of the jury box. In a well-practiced, modulated voice, he greeted the attentive panel. "Good afternoon, everybody. I want to start off by stating two quick things. Number one . . . when we pick a jury, we say to keep an open mind. Number two, you heard a lot of opening comments and statements by Mr. Walgren, who did a very professional job. But let's talk about some of the information he left out, please."

Spectators may have wondered what the prosecutor had "left out," but the prosecutor's colleagues had a pretty good

idea, and dreaded to hear the lack of forensic evidence placed
in the spotlight. Flier didn't let them stew very long.

"First of all, as you all know, I am the attorney for Mr. Paleologus, and when I start off on this, I want to start by saying
[that] Mr. Paleologus, up to this incident, has *never* been accused of killing anyone, as the evidence will show." The word
"never," accentuated in slow meter, sounded like a door slamming shut. "So I just want to say that right off the bat." A tight
smile played around Flier's lips.

"Number two, with respect toward Miss Johnson's unfortunate and horrible death, we're upset about it, too. No one is
happy about what happened, as the evidence will show, because it was terrible. I know she has family that cared for her.
Some are in the courtroom. And it's difficult, as I also said in
. . . voir dire, it's hard to be a defense lawyer.

"But Mr. Paleologus, as the evidence will show, did not kill
her. There is no evidence, as the defense will show, that he
ever met her." Just as Walgren had effectively done with well-
placed pauses, Flier also knew exactly when to let a point
breathe, like a good bottle of wine, for full impact.

"So what does this case come down to?" Starting to answer
his own question, Flier headed in one direction, then veered
away into another. He rambled for a moment, saying, "In a
nutshell—and to summarize the theory, the defense's theory
is—if you focus on the murder, clearly the evidence will show
[that] their circumstantial link will fail, that Mr. Paleologus
committed this horrible crime. But the people don't want to
focus on that. They want to focus on the past."

Insiders expected something more incisive. Walgren stood
and barked, "Objection, Your Honor."

Ignoring the prosecutor, Flier continued, "The evidence
will show—"

Judge Perry, well-known for his expectations of disci-
plined procedure, calmly said, "Let me make a ruling on the

objection. I will overrule the objection. This is the defense theory of the case."

The defender, appearing pleased, reasserted that the prosecution intended to focus on the past and pressed forward. "We want to focus on the counts as the evidence will show what happened. . . . Number one, at no time is the defense going to argue that Mr. Paleologus isn't in the area. That's where he lives. So, with respect to any cell phone evidence, any tower evidence, it's a red herring. . . ."

Weeks earlier, Ron Bowers had worried about the cell tower issues. He had also fretted over mistaken identifications by the parking valet Roberto Marquez, so it came as no surprise that Flier zeroed in on that issue.

"There's only one witness in this case, ladies and gentlemen, and Mr. Walgren never mentioned him. His name is Roberto Marquez. Mr. Marquez is very important in this case, as the defense will show. Why? Because we heard evidence in the people's theory that Miss Johnson, lovely young lady, was going to go somewhere . . . to meet someone they are now saying was Mr. Paleologus. We have a different belief on that.

"What we didn't hear in the opening statement, in that lovely presentation, was this—within twelve hours of the last time she was seen, somebody drove her car to the Century Plaza Hotel." Flier painted a quick summary of someone parking the car, tossing the keys to a valet, and leaving, and subsequent use of six-pack photos shown to various witnesses. "We didn't hear about the [important] six-pack, and that is the one where Roberto Marquez does *not* identify Mr. Paleologus." Heavy emphasis on "not." A touch of sarcasm crept into Flier's voice as he mimicked the prosecution. "Oh, we won't mention that."

Notching up his attack, Flier said, "But it doesn't stop there. The defense theory on this case is . . . the police have focused on the wrong guy. The defense will show that they never let it go and they had to fit Mr. Paleologus into their puzzle." Was the reference to "puzzle" another little dig at Walgren's theme? Only Flier knew.

"So why do I say that? Because after Mr. Marquez does not identify Mr. Paleologus in any fashion, the police don't stop. They do a live lineup. The evidence will show that's a little unusual. They show a six-pack and the gentleman says, 'I don't see the person [who] parked the white Miata.' So then they say, 'We don't like that answer.' So what do they do? They do a live lineup . . . purportedly with people who resemble him, because, 'We want to make it fair.' Mr. Marquez does not pick him out, which is consistent with not picking him out in the original six-pack.

"Now, that is critical evidence in this case, because that's the only eyewitness in the case. And this only eyewitness . . . says it's not Mr. Paleologus. That's very powerful evidence."

Nothing showed in jurors' faces or body language hinting whether this revelation made the desired impact. Flier moved on. "But it doesn't stop there, because what we also didn't see in that presentation—and it was mentioned a little by Mr. Walgren and myself in jury selection—and that's the importance of science. What you didn't hear in that explanation is, in this case, not one scintilla of science—physical, trace, anything—connects Mr. Paleologus to this case."

The word "scintilla," meaning "minute particle," is seldom heard in any conversation or written communication, but pops up as a cliché in nearly every trial as the standard measure suggesting absence of evidence. Most defense attorneys employ it extensively.

"Now think about that," Flier advised. "We saw horrible pictures of a young lady who was bound and tied. No scrapings, no fingerprint evidence, not one little pubic hair or [other] hair, no saliva, no semen, nothing. . . . In a case as gruesome as this, science usually does come into play, as the evidence will show."

Pointing toward Virginia Obenchain seated at the prosecution table next to David Walgren, Flier said, "That's why this homicide detective, the nice lady with the red [blouse] and black suit, had a checklist. And her checklist is what a good detective should do. . . . And once they focus on Mr. Paleologus, they combine that checklist to try to figure out evidence against him. But they can't . . . because he didn't do it."

Repeating his own theme phrase, Flier said again, "But it doesn't stop there. Because when I started my opening statement, I said keep an open mind. I said, 'Let's talk about what they didn't talk about.' That's really important in this case. Because when you look at what happened on February the fifteenth, it doesn't make sense." Charlie Simon, he acknowledged, had shown Paleologus several homes for sale, including one on Skyline Drive. "The people's theory is that Mr. Paleologus is so devious that he is manipulating the real estate person to find a location where he can kill women." Detectives, he pointed out, had searched the houses. "Not one scintilla of evidence in any of those locations.

"And he has the agent go to one side of the house. He's on the other side trying to hear audibility level of the surrounding walls. What inference is there? Is he setting up a place to kill women? If they scream, they can't be heard? Let's talk about that. Number one—and I don't say this to be mean to my client—the evidence will show this man is a thief." Flier ticked off several supporting incidents, and acknowledged that his client had entered into plea bargains, and served time for infractions of the law. "Because he was a good citizen in custody, he was released on parole. He gets out in January 2003. He's desperate. He's not desperate to kill women. He's desperate to eat and shower and to live somewhere. So he goes to the place on La Cienega.

"There's no doubt Mr. Paleologus has a connection there. He, at one time in his life—and it's hard to say this—he was a proud man. We don't have a moron over there. This is an educated man who owned businesses. Restaurants. But his business failed. It happens. He's not the only one who lost a restaurant business." The La Cienega building owner, said Flier, compassionately let him stay there, and he remained in the area "dead broke" with no transportation. Perhaps it's understandable, the defender suggested, why he took the BMW.

Citing Paleologus's background, Flier reminded jurors that it was part of the prosecution's theory. He listed the other three-pronged elements: the James Bond theme, the clothing issue, and the Century City mall. With those in mind, he said, "First of all, those three connections do not equate that this man killed anyone, beyond a reasonable doubt."

Judge Perry spoke. "I think you are getting into argument, Mr. Flier." Argument is to be presented after all the testimony and evidence has been given to the jury, just before they retire to deliberate. There is a subtle legal distinction in what may be said in opening statements and final arguments.

Flier explained, "I am moving on with respect to the car issue. From the La Cienega building to the area where Miss Johnson's body was discovered is probably around three miles. But it's uphill, in the hills." To create a mental picture of the heights, he commented that people hike up there to enjoy the views. Hikers had discovered the body. "How, in the people's puzzle, does Mr. Paleologus get anywhere?"

Ron Bowers had suggested that problem long ago, with the observation that city buses don't even run up Laurel Canyon, and certainly not to Skyline Drive. Now Flier may have created a doubt in jurors' minds. How could Paleologus have been up on Skyline Drive waiting for Kristi to arrive?

Flier seemed satisfied to let the inference hang in the air, and focused on another puzzle piece. "That goes back to

Charlie Simon, which is a very important issue. . . . Originally he made a statement to the police . . . and said something that was terrible for the government's case. But we didn't hear about that." Charlie Simon, the defender asserted, had said that "he was with Mr. Paleologus until six or seven o' clock at night" on the date Kristi vanished.

Doing the math in their heads, observers realized that something didn't add up. "But wait a second," Flier enjoined, "you should be saying to yourself right now, 'Mr. Walgren said in his opening statement that Miss Johnson was last seen, or had any contact, at about five-thirty. Mr. Simon is with Mr. Paleologus at this time.' But the police understood that this was devastating to their case. So guess what happens. . . . They reinterview him and he changes the day. I submit to you that he changed the day to assist the police. Now, we're not Perry Mason here. . . . The defense does not expect, through my cross-examination, that someone is going to raise their hand and say, 'You're too good, Mr. Flier. The police told me to change the day.' Or, 'I'm lying.' Or, 'I want to assist the police.' But common sense will dictate— Mr. Simon is going to be seriously challenged." Flier explained that Simon's modified account of dates had been connected to discussion with someone at his office, who would be brought by the defense to testify that Simon "doesn't know what he's talking about."

The biggest problem facing the defense came up next. Flier said, "You are going to hear around six women say things about Mr. Paleologus that, truly, the defense believes has nothing to do with Miss Johnson's disappearance."

The first one, Elizabeth Davis, happened fifteen years ago. Flier pounced on her ability to identify the defendant after such a long time. His client, said the defender, had never met or heard of Elizabeth Davis. Neither had he ever been investigated or arrested for spiking her drink. The allegation is "extremely weak."

Lamenting charges against Paleologus, Flier said, "This case generated a tremendous amount of national [news media] coverage. A lovely young lady is missing. There's nothing worse, especially as a father. But that doesn't mean that [for] Miss Johnson's horrible death, someone must be blamed, and it must be Mr. Paleologus, as the evidence will show."

The trial for murder, said Flier, would actually turn into several "mini trials." To explain, he listed them. "We're going to have Miss Johnson's trial. We're going to have Elizabeth Davis's trial. We're going to have Ms. Olson's trial, Ms. Cooper's trial, Ms. DeBuono's trial, Alice Walker's trial, and Susan Murphy's trial."

Regarding Annie Olson, Flier pointed out that her experience had nothing to do with the so-called modus operandi of "James Bond, clothing, and Century City." Instead, it had been a dating relationship. The alleged rape in an empty restaurant didn't sound reasonable, he said, because she didn't bother to report it to the police. Nor did the tale of an assault in Olson's apartment. "Please, that's ridiculous, as the evidence will show."

Once again, Judge Perry halted the defender. "Mr. Flier, let me interrupt and ask you not to make comments that are argumentative, but just present what you expect the evidence to show."

Without missing a beat, Flier said, "I expect the evidence to show exactly what I just said. Irrespective to any comments by me . . . she's not telling the truth. Who knows why?" To support his opinion, Flier observed that Olson had changed the locks in her apartment and hadn't given Paleologus a key. "There's no evidence of a break-in or that she left a door ajar."

Moving on to Cathy DeBuono, Flier said, "That's a real interesting one. Paleologus was in state prison when she said she met him." The attorney had seen police reports showing that DeBuono originally vacillated on the exact date on which she had encountered the James Bond guy at the Century City mall. Even though in his opening statement, Walgren indicated the meeting happened in "late 1998 or early 1999," and Paleologus had entered state prison at the end of July 1999, Flier planned to raise an issue on the timing first reported by DeBuono.

If Flier knew of holes in the other women's stories, he chose not to mention them. Putting a close to that avenue, he said, "The defense in no way has a responsibility to explain why some of these women are saying anything. I have my own belief, but that's not evidence. Maybe some people like press. People like to help. Some people like to be involved. But the bottom line with respect to every single woman mentioned in Mr. Walgren's opening, none of them were murdered, period."

To be certain jurors understood, Flier recapitulated what he had said so far. "He purportedly meets Miss Johnson. Wants her to wear some clothing. She's found murdered. She's obviously murdered. No one is denying that, and she has high-heel stilettos on. She's got some stockings, and earlier she was happy about being in a movie and we can see her buying certain clothing. The evidence will show that has nothing to do with Mr. Paleologus."

Repeating his theme refrain, Flier repeated, "But it doesn't end there. Because then you heard that around five-thirty on February 15, 2003, she appears to be lost, and sees Mr. Kirkland. Mr. Kirkland doesn't know her and gives her directions. The interesting thing about that . . . is that purportedly she's supposed to meet a photographer at a castle house or an area by a castle house. Well, the defense will present that there's more than one castle out in this general area, so no one knows what castle house they're talking about."

Spectators and reporters scratched their heads, wondering

what this issue meant. Flier added that the police never spoke
with anyone at the castle house in question to see if Miss
Johnson even knocked on the door. He said he had the resident under subpoena to testify that no one ever talked to
them. His comment didn't help clear up the question in observers' minds.

The prosecution team had been expecting Flier to bring up
the entomological, or maggot, evidence in establishing the
victim's time of death. He introduced it by saying, "Miss
Johnson's body, now. I agree with Mr. Walgren—I have done
a lot of murder cases, both as a prosecutor and defense
lawyer—horrible. But be careful. Let's not have that anger
turn into blaming Mr. Paleologus, with no proof, as the evidence will show." He mentioned the advanced state of decomposition, especially from the neck up, and started to
explain what his expert witness might say. But Walgren
lodged an objection.

Judge Perry shook his head. "Overruled. I will allow it."

Flier complained, "It's hard to be a defense attorney."

Perry snapped, "That's not an appropriate comment. It's
hard to be a prosecutor, too, ladies and gentlemen."

"I was one," Flier replied. "It is hard."

His expert, he said, would testify that Kristi Johnson was
killed no earlier than February 18. "What is interesting about
that is that Mr. Paleologus was arrested on February seven-
teenth. It must be evident that Mr. Paleologus is not this monster that has been portrayed.

"But it doesn't stop there. He got out of jail and was having
some financial difficulties. Plus, he had a parole officer, Miss
Larios, and he wasn't getting along with her."

In addition, said Flier, the jury would hear about his
client allegedly trying to escape from jail. "Mr. Paleologus,
for some reason, knows the Santa Monica police want to
question him. Therefore, he bribes a five-foot-five Hispanic

gentleman five thousand dollars to take his wristband. Now, please, in the evidence, does anyone believe the sheriff would fall for that—"

For the third time, Judge Perry interrupted. "Again, 'anyone would believe,' I think that's argument, Mr. Flier."

The defender frowned and asked, "Your Honor, may we approach?" Perry said they could.

In a whispered conference, Flier complained. "Your Honor, respectfully, I try to hold down and not object on stuff that clearly I think I could have objected to. If he wants to object, he can. If the court wants to object and make me look bad, that's fine."

Perry responded, "I am not trying to make you look bad."

"But you are."

"Mr. Flier, I am just asking you not to be quite so argumentative."

Still upset, Flier argued, "I keep on saying 'the evidence will show. . . .' I think it comes across that you are protecting the government. I just want to say that I feel bad."

The judge offered apology, of sorts. "You have said that and I am sorry you feel that way. Let me just say that you can make your points without making the characterization of the evidence. . . . I think you have a case certainly to present." But he would countenance no argument in the presentation. "I wouldn't have jumped in except that I think you've crossed the line. That's all."

The discussion ended after resolving a couple of other minor issues.

Resuming his speech to the jury, Flier spoke again about parole officer Maryanne Larios, hinting that she might have received a phone call from someone angry at Paleologus, who suggested that she look at the composite drawing. And that precipitated all of the investigative attention on Paleologus.

On another tack, he speculated that Kristi Johnson's body

may have been moved to the hillside shortly before hikers discovered it there. "It's the defense position, if there is a blond lady, half-naked, dead, down on the hill, the people who are familiar with that area would have seen it. That's what we are trying to say." The unsaid inference would be that the body had been placed in that location while Paleologus was in jail.

"All of those factors connect," said Flier, "to show they have the wrong person, based on the state of their evidence."

Regarding the special circumstances of "lying in wait" and "attempted rape," Flier insisted that they were invalid.

The rave party, and the question about proof of Kristi Johnson's absence, or attendance, had concerned prosecutors. Flier discussed it briefly and asserted that because her name was not marked off a guest list "doesn't mean that she was not there. So she's at a rave party, and sometimes things happen that are bad to people. We don't know."

Absence of any evidence that Kristi might have fought back against her killer could also be exculpatory, said Flier. In the prosecution's presentation, he noted, "we never saw any photographs when Mr. Paleologus was arrested of his body and face, which would show if he had scratches, if he was in a tussle. None. . . . If I'm being attacked, right now, I'm going to fight, and I might scratch someone, just like in the movies you see, and in real life. And there might be evidence."

Having lost none of his self-assurance or energy, Flier used one last pause, as if to make certain he hadn't forgotten anything, then sprinted toward the finish line. "Mr. Paleologus is not a monster. He was a desperate man. He got out of prison, and he didn't have the family support at the time to get out of his bind. So he's living on the streets." If he went to a spa near the Century Plaza Hotel for a shower, and stole a bathrobe, it didn't make him a killer.

"So, in finality, you keep an open mind and you watch my cross-examination. Remember, the defense does not have to take the stand or do anything. . . . I wasn't there. Mr. Walgren wasn't there. The homicide detective wasn't there. That's why we have a jury. Because Mr. Paleologus said he's innocent and that's why we are here. And when you get through all of the mudslinging, as the evidence will show, you will see that this case has no evidence regarding the death of Miss Johnson. And that's why we are here. Thank you very much."

Judge Perry announced the afternoon fifteen-minute break, after which witness testimony would begin.

CHAPTER 23

SHOWTIME

Some people have so little presence, they wouldn't be noticed in a crowd of one. Others possess a certain iridescence that draws every eye, no matter how large the crowd. Susan Murphy had that kind of a face and figure.

She swore to tell the whole truth, then seated herself in the witness chair. Answering David Walgren's questions, Susan told of going to the Century City mall after work to have dinner with a friend and stopping at Macy's first to do some shopping. A man calling himself Victor Thomas offered her the chance to be involved in a James Bond film. To audition, she said, she would be required to bring certain clothing. She listed the apparel, then described the next day's meeting on La Cienega, and how her fiancé at the time, Mark Wilson, had interceded when things went wrong. A few days later, an article in the *L.A. Times* had inspired her to call the police. Walgren's questions took her through the subsequent cooperation with investigators and participation in preparing a composite drawing of the suspect.

After Andrew Flier's brief cross-examination, Judge Perry admonished the jurors not to discuss the case with anyone, asked everyone to return on Friday morning, and recessed court for the evening.

That night on television, Court TV reporter Lisa Sweetingham spoke about the day's events in Judge Perry's courtroom. She said, "Prosecutors allege Victor Paleologus wasn't hungry for any particular woman, but it was his MO that ruled. . . . I'm reminded of the case of Linda Sobek, a model who was lured to the desert by a photographer to do a car photo shoot. . . . Incidentally, one of my closest friends in L.A., also a photographer, knew Sobek personally and said she was a vivacious and feisty woman who seemed to really have her head on her shoulders, which goes to show that this kind of thing can happen to anyone." The program moderator expressed hope that the Sobek case would be a "grim reminder" for all aspiring models to always bring someone with them at photo shoots.

Doing that very thing perhaps saved the lives of Susan Murphy and Cathy DeBuono.

On Friday morning, Mark Wilson, Susan Murphy's former boyfriend, testified first. His Australian accent startled people who had read about his and Murphy's role in breaking the mystery wide open. Answering Walgren's questions, he told of Susan's request for him to be present at her meeting with Victor Thomas. Asked if he agreed to go, Wilson said, "Absolutely, because I honestly felt it was a scam." He told of confronting and threatening the man who later turned out to be Victor Paleologus.

Elizabeth Davis, a former model and actress, followed Wilson, and recalled meeting the defendant, aka Joe Messe, at Los Angeles International Airport in the last few days of 1990. He claimed to be with Disney and was working on a James Bond film. "I spoke to him periodically over a two-month period," she admitted, and eventually accompanied him to a seafood restaurant in Santa Monica on a "professional date." There he put a "white powdery substance" in her drink. She challenged him, he fled, and she called the police.

In cross-examination, Flier quizzed her, apparently attempting to cast doubt on her ability to recall details after fifteen years.

A few giggles in the courtroom broke the tension when the lawyers would rise to their feet or were reseated. The chairs squeaked incessantly.

Walgren next called former SMPD officer Oscar Scolari, who had responded to Davis's call from the restaurant. At the time, he took her report and collected two items of evidence, her drink and the credit card receipt in the name of Victor Paleo. As it turned out, the defendant had often used the shortened version of Paleologus in various attempts to camouflage his real name.

Another witness, David Vidal, testified that he had analyzed the drink in a lab. Defender Flier's questions about the cocktail's contents, age, and possible contamination appeared to be aimed at discrediting the conclusion that it had been spiked with Dramamine.

Jumping to the other charge against Paleologus, of illegally taking the BMW, the prosecution called Officer Eric Drescher, of the Beverly Hills Police Department. His testimony informed jurors about the chase and capture of Paleologus.

Annie Olson appeared embarrassed as she spoke from the witness stand for the remainder of that Friday afternoon. Her affair with Paleologus, who had been her neighbor in Marina del Rey, had turned disastrous. She described their breakup, his attempt to rape her in a vacated Brentwood restaurant, and a subsequent encounter in her apartment bedroom. On cross, Andrew Flier elicited her admission that the restaurant incident had ended without any actual forced sex, and that she had never reported it to the police. He also asked if Paleologus had ever asked her to wear any special clothing, miniskirt, or stiletto heels. No, she said. Had he ever pretended to be affiliated with any motion picture studio? Again the witness said, "No."

Everyone welcomed a long break when told the trial would resume on the following Wednesday, July 19.

On that morning, Judge Perry began the day with a touch of humor. "We're back on the record. We do have some WD-40 for some squeaky chairs, but I don't know that it works. At least we have some. All right, call your next witness."

A tall, striking, dark-haired woman gracefully strode forward and swore to tell the truth. A few spectators may have recognized Cathy DeBuono as the character M'Pella from the TV series *Deep Space Nine,* which had aired six years in the late 1990s. DeBuono told of seeing television news, in March 2003, about Paleologus and recognizing him from an encounter about four years earlier. David Walgren knew that Flier planned to attack DeBuono's recollection of the timing and indicate that his client was still in prison when the alleged Century City encounter took place. The prosecutor asked about the exact date. DeBuono said that in her first report to the police, she had only estimated when it happened. Later, by recalling where she had lived then, and her place of work, she realized the meeting took place either late in 1998 or early 1999.

With that settled, in view of the defendant's prison release in July 1999, Walgren elicited testimony about the now-familiar pattern. DeBuono said, "I was wearing shorts and he started to talk about my legs and he thought I had great legs. And he was looking for girls to do posters for promoting the new James Bond movie." They had arranged a meeting "at an address in the Hollywood Hills right off the

Lookout Mountain area. . . . I was supposed to pull over, park my car, and wait. . . . Someone would come and get me."

As a working actress, DeBuono had been cautious, she said, and decided to take a male friend along. She waited for a while, and when no one showed up, she left. She never again heard from the man calling himself Brian, with Disney Studios. Just as he had indicated in opening statements, Flier grilled DeBuono about the time frames. Whether he undermined her credibility or not rested only in the minds of jurors.

If anyone in the gallery came just to see a parade of beautiful women, they were not disappointed. The next witness, Mary Beth Licudine, fit the description. She recalled leaving a movie theater in the Century City mall, on February 12, 2003, and, while using a public telephone, being approached by the defendant. "He said they were looking for a James Bond poster girl, that they really needed one right away. That I have the look." It didn't make sense to her, so she walked away. Licudine, too, had seen news reports in March 2003 and called the police to report the incident. Cross-examination questions, as they had with DeBuono, focused on her recollection of the date, but she stood firm. Flier also asked Licudine if she had ever said that the sketch didn't look like Paleologus, and if the individual at the mall had asked her to wear specific clothing. Regarding the apparel, she said the conversation hadn't gone that far. On redirect examination, the witness affirmed her identification of the defendant as the man she had met.

An overwhelming pattern of testimony painted a picture of Paleologus as someone who spent an inordinate amount of time ogling attractive women to target for his special scam. In this segment of the trial, though, his desire to gaze at them seemed to have burned out. Instead, he kept his head bowed and stared only at the tabletop.

After lunch, Kristi's mother, Terry Hall, took the stand. She identified a high-school photo of her daughter and told a little bit about Kristi's personal history. They had spoken "at least once a day" by telephone, and the mother said she paid for Kristi's cell phone bills. Their last conversation had been on Saturday morning, February 15, 2003, in which Kristi had talked about her plans to go to the mall. Hall told of trying to reach her daughter on Sunday. "I was becoming concerned at the end of the day, you know, why she wasn't picking up." On Monday, Hall recalled, she had called her daughter's workplace only to learn that Kristi hadn't shown up.

Walgren introduced a bank statement showing purchases by Kristi Johnson at the Century City mall and at a West Hollywood lingerie store. Hall said, "Yes, that's a bank statement of our joint account," and agreed that the credit card had never been used again. She explained another charge on the statement dated March 10. "That's a purchase I made for a dress that I ordered for Kristi's funeral."

Terry Hall stepped down and was replaced by Karen Miles. In Walgren's opening statement, he had said, "You will also hear from a Ms. Dawn Cooper about her incident with the defendant in August of 1998. . . . She was with a friend at a bar on Sunset Boulevard in Hollywood." Karen Miles was the friend of Cooper's, and had been with her when she met Paleologus. Cooper was later the victim of an attempted rape inside his vacant restaurant on San Vincente Boulevard.

Walgren's few questions of Miles had a single objective, to corroborate Cooper's identification of Paleologus as the man they had met on Sunset Boulevard. She affirmed it. Flier questioned her ability to be so certain, considering that it happened late at night, and that Miles wore glasses. But she remained resolute in her recognition of him, recalling his "droopy eyes" and "cleft chin."

Alice Walker trembled as she took the witness's oath. Walgren greeted her and asked, "Are you nervous?"

"Yes, very nervous," she replied. Walker told of meeting

Paleologus in a Century City mall restaurant, where she worked, on the evening of January 25, 2003. Astute observers realize that it was the same day Susan Murphy and Mark Wilson had chased and confronted him. This time, Paleologus, using the name Victor Ippolito, said he was "copyrighting a book," and invited her to join him for coffee at the Century Plaza Hotel, where he claimed to be staying. She accepted.

In the sumptuous hotel lobby, they chatted for hours, she recalled. He described his book plot in detail, about Vincent going through a divorce, trying to open a restaurant, in great financial distress with loan sharks after him, and hiring a lawyer. The attorney meets a woman, has sex with her in a car, and somehow winds up killing her. Walgren asked, "Did the defendant tell you in his book how this woman comes to be killed while having sex in the car?"

Walker said, "That she was strangled." Whispers and groans drifted from spectators, drawing a glower from Judge Perry.

"Did the defendant bring up the topic of a James Bond movie?"

Yes, said Walker, and explained that it was in the context of knowing a famous movie director. "And they were looking for a girl who would sort of be the poster girl for the movie." An audition offer ensued, requiring the apparel—black miniskirt, white shirt, stiletto heels, and "nylons that sparkled like diamonds."

Answering the prosecutor's questions, Walker described meeting Ippolito the next day at a place on La Cienega, and that she brought the required clothing. She posed for him, but it frightened her when he tried to knot a necktie around her throat. They met again three days later, same place, and the session turned kinky when he said that "Pierce Brosnan's character . . . would grab the back of my hair, pull me down, and kiss me . . . and he would kill me." When Ippolito attempted to put himself in the role, she backed away.

Walker admitted meeting him two more times. During the fourth session, on January 31, he mentioned something about starting a computer company.

Judge Perry stepped in to adjourn for the day.

The tiny gallery filled up early on Thursday, and Alice Walker resumed her testimony. She told Walgren that by the fourth meeting, she had grown more suspicious of the man, and asked him the name of his new company. When he answered that it was Logus, he slipped up and said that came from part of his surname. Walker asked how that fit with Ippolito. He told her that his full name was Ippolitologus. Walker said she never saw him again, but received several phone calls, the last one coming on February 15, 2003. A shiver swept through the gallery, with the realization that it was the day Kristi Johnson vanished.

In the remainder of Thursday, and on Friday, witnesses included another Beverly Hills police officer, SMPD detectives Michael Cabrera and Maury Sumlin, the lingerie shop employee who sold Kristi the stiletto high heels, and Kristi's roommate who had heard all about her encounter with a James Bond guy at Century City mall.

Real estate agent Charlie Simon testified about showing the defendant numerous homes for sale in the Hollywood Hills, including one on Skyline Drive, the address that was Kristi Johnson's destination for what she thought would be an audition.

Late Friday afternoon, another woman took the stand, one who was neither a victim nor an acquaintance of the defendant. She told Walgren of shopping at the Century City mall on Saturday, February 15, 2003, between noon and one o'clock, to "buy a late Valentine gift." Asked what happened, she said, "I was walking toward the Ann Taylor store. And there was a man standing in the center of this little quad area. At first, he looked like someone I knew. And then as I got closer, I realized it wasn't him, so I just moved on and continued my shopping. He looked like he was waiting for somebody, looking for somebody, or just people watching."

The witness said a TV news story came on ten days later, with the volume muted while she entertained a friend. "At one point during our conversation, I happened to glance over at the television and [said], 'Hey, I saw that guy at the mall on Saturday.'"

Walgren had acquired a copy of the same newscast, and played it for the witness. She positively identified the defendant as the man she had seen.

Now, at last, eyewitness testimony placed Victor Paleologus in the mall in the same tight time frame Kristi had shopped there.

Judge Perry called for the weekend break, announcing the trial would resume on Tuesday, July 25.

The prosecution team didn't take much time off over the three days, huddling instead to weigh their progress so far, and trying to determine what more they needed. It certainly appeared that the circumstantial evidence pointed to Paleologus, but in the absence of forensics or hard evidence, could the jury arrive at a guilty verdict? Conventional wisdom would dictate that Andrew Flier's defense, at this point, still had the advantage.

On Tuesday, Walgren called ten witnesses to the stand, including investigators and theft victims who had lost credit cards and identification documents, all of which were later found in the possession of Paleologus. The defendant had used one of the men's documents in attempting to fraudulently purchase the BMW in Beverly Hills.

The day wound up with the auto agency's finance manager

and a porter describing how the defendant had failed to provide a driver's license, then sped away in the new SUV.

If testimony from these ten people instigated a few yawns, it would be sharply offset by the next day's stunning, unbelievable turn of events.

CHAPTER 24

EXPLOSION

At exactly eight-thirty Wednesday morning, July 26, Judge Perry said, "All right. Let's go on the record. We are outside the presence of the jury in *People* versus *Paleologus*. Good morning, everyone. Yesterday, there was some discussion about possible resolution of this case. The people agreed to keep the offer open until today. Is that correct, Mr. Walgren?"

"Well," said the prosecutor, "I am not trying to be overly detailed, but the defense came to us with the offer, and, yeah, we said we could consider it through this morning."

As an insider during the entire process, Ron Bowers later commented on the sudden development.

Ron Bowers's Recollections

Since the DA's office had decided that it should seek the death penalty in this case, no need existed to discuss a case settlement. The policy edicts that once a decision has been made to seek the death penalty, the case will not be reduced upon a plea of guilty to a lesser charge. The reason is simple. The DA's office doesn't want to be accused of overfiling by using the death penalty as a bargaining chip to elicit a guilty plea and accept a sentence of life in prison without the possibility of parole.

This case was a perfect example, though, of the need for some flexibility as to this hard-and-fast policy. The absence of hard evidence, forensics, or any scientific proof suggested the strong possibility of acquittal, even though we all believed Paleologus as guilty as anyone we had ever tried.

During the trial, we could see from jurors' expressions that they didn't like him as a person and certainly wouldn't believe him if he took the witness stand. Every day Paleologus had to look at Kristi's parents as they sat in the front row. He was a career con man, but also a realist. At this stage of the prosecution's case, he believed that things weren't looking very good for him. Maybe he didn't realize that the prosecution hadn't started calling weaker witnesses, who were going to look bad under cross-examination by the defense attorney.

Paleologus told Flier that he was interested in some type of disposition so he could cut his losses. He most likely was hoping for a second-degree murder, where he could be out in twelve years or so. Flier approached Walgren about a disposition, but the hard-driving young prosecutor indicated it was too late for that. On that Tuesday afternoon, Judge Perry asked Walgren to talk to the DA's administration about a disposition. That same evening, Walgren discussed the matter with his boss, who talked to the head of the Special Circumstances Committee. The DA's office understood there were serious weaknesses in the prosecution's case.

Before retiring as chief deputy, and sole decision maker on who would face death penalty trials, Curt Livesay had formulated the policy of not backing down once it had been decided to seek capital punishment.

Finally, recognizing perceived weaknesses in the case, the DA's office agreed to make a major exception in its policy on the condition that Paleologus would plead guilty to first-degree murder. It had to be "guilty," rather than "no contest." Moreover, the DA required a "factual basis plea," meaning that the defendant had to go on the record with an admission of his involvement in the murder. Also the defendant must give up the right to appeal his plea of guilty. Most people in our organization didn't think Paleologus would ever agree to such conditions.

Andrew Flier responded to comments from the judge and the prosecutor. "I think Mr. Paleologus is seriously considering it. All we need is just this morning and I will have a decision by noon. He is still just contemplating. . . . I don't want to waste any of the court's time . . . but I think there is going to be a resolution, Your Honor."

Judge Perry spoke directly to the defendant. "Mr. Paleologus, I don't want you to feel pressured into making the decision. Frankly, it's very unusual in the middle of a case, where the people are seeking death, to allow the defendant out of the case. But at the same time, we can't wait forever for you to make your decision. I know it's a very serious decision that you're considering, and it's my understanding that the proposed resolution would be a plea to first-degree murder with a sentence of twenty-five years to life in prison. That is a lesser sentence than the one you're facing if you were to be convicted in the guilt phase, which would carry a sentence of life without parole, and certainly a lesser sentence than you could possibly receive if things did not go your way and you ended up with a death sentence.

"So I know it's a heavy matter for you to consider. At the same time, I have a responsibility to these jurors and to the system to keep this matter moving. . . . It's now about ten minutes to nine. I can give you to nine-fifteen. That is twenty-five minutes.

"Again, you don't have to take this offer. . . . I don't want the record to suggest that we're pressuring you, but at the same time we want to move forward with the trial if this is not going to resolve itself. So we're going to send the jurors out for a little while, and start again at nine-fifteen."

Ron Bowers's Recollections

After Judge Perry gave Paleologus less than half an hour to make his decision, a strange thing happened. Andrew Flier asked to have a private hearing in chambers with the judge and defendant, but excluding the prosecution. This is highly unusual and ordinarily granted only for a Marsden hearing, in which the defendant disagrees with, and might wish to fire, his defense attorney. Apparently, Paleologus didn't want to make a factual statement of his involvement in the crime.

Only one thing stood in the way of ending the trial: the precise wording Paleologus would make in open court. He didn't want to spell out the details of what happened to Kristi.

For her family and the investigators, that would leave too many questions unanswered. We would never know where, when, why, and how Kristi was killed. The DA's office could have refused to accept the modified terms.

Yet, we understood our vulnerability. From that point on in the trial, jurors were going to hear witnesses who might create a reasonable doubt in some of their minds.

These are life-and-death decisions in the hands of prosecutors, judges, and defense attorneys. The fact that the executions are seldom carried out in the state of California doesn't influence the way the prosecutor looks at a case. This was one of the toughest decisions for the LADA Office in a long time. Should we stay firm and demand that the defendant give a more detailed description of Kristi's murder? Or should we accept the limited admission and take a barrage of criticism suggesting that the death penalty was sought only to coerce pleas of guilty and acceptance of life without parole (LWOP)?

But the issue of death penalty or LWOP became moot with this new development.

Flier and Paleologus were granted a private hearing with Judge Perry in his chambers. Grateful for this concession from Judge Perry, Flier described his client's reluctance to make a full confession in open court, or as Flier put it, "give a factual plea." They discussed the issues for nearly half an hour.

Judge Perry said, "I would ask you to put yourself for a moment in the position of the parents."

Paleologus nodded in the affirmative. "I am trying to, Your Honor."

The resolution seemed close. Perry added to his explanation. "They would like to have some final closure on this, and among the questions that I think must be running through their minds is 'How did it happen? Where did it happen?' Things like that."

"I can appreciate that, Your Honor. I can appreciate them wanting to know all that."

At that point, Perry made a remarkable offer. "I am not asking you to say that, but I am telling you that's where they are coming from, and the fact that you are willing to say, 'I had contact with her and I accept responsibility for her murder.' That's enough for me."

Flier quickly jumped in. "Thank you. We have a resolution."

Perry stood. "Okay. Let's bring everybody back in and do it."

"Everybody" did not include the jury. They waited in the deliberations room, probably wondering about the odd delays, which they understood the judge seemed to hate.

With court back in session, minus the twelve triers of fact, Judge Perry announced, "It is my understanding that the defendant is going to enter a guilty plea to the crime of first-degree murder of Kristine Johnson on or about February 15, 2003. Is that correct?"

Andrew Flier rose from his chair and said, "Yes, Your Honor."

"All right. And the people are willing to accept a plea to the charge of the first-degree murder of Kristine Johnson that will carry a sentence of twenty-five years to life. Is that correct?"

All of the steam seemed to have left David Walgren. He agreed with a terse "That's correct, Your Honor."

Another element needed addressing. The judge said, "So that means we are going to agree to, after acceptance of this plea and sentence, that you're going to dismiss the special circumstances allegation, you are going to forgo the opportunity to seek a death verdict, and you are going to drop the other counts as well. Is that correct?"

"Yes," said Walgren, "pursuant to the plea agreement."

Speaking directly to Paleologus, Perry summarized the bargain: a plea of guilty to first-degree murder, a sentence of twenty-five years to life, and several small monetary fines. He added a comment that disenchanted spectators. "This is a parolable offense."

The defendant spoke his agreement, as did the defense attorney. They also concurred with the judge's evocation that no pressure had been applied.

The judge's next comment met with strong approval from Walgren and most observers. "As part of the plea here, you're giving up your right to appeal. Do you understand that this eliminates the opportunity to appeal any decision this court made regarding the evidentiary rulings and other rulings that the court made?"

Paleologus said, "Yes, Your Honor." Attorneys, at both tables and in the gallery, marveled at this segment of the deal.

No appeal. Some wondered if Paleologus would regret accepting that condition.

Perry continued to make certain that the defendant understood all aspects of his decision, and that it was freely and voluntarily made. At last, he came to the crucial point. "So let me ask you, is there a factual basis for this plea? In other words, did you have contact with Kristine Johnson?"

"Yes, Your Honor."

"And are you taking responsibility for her murder today?"

"Yes, Your Honor, I am."

Flier spoke up. "We'd like also to make some statements, Your Honor."

With the judge's permission, Paleologus, in a subdued demeanor, muttered, "First and foremost, I—I've always felt this from the very beginning. I know what it's like to lose somebody very close to you, and my sympathies have always gone out to the family. I just wanted to make that perfectly clear, that I'm not doing this plea to upset anyone, including the family. My sympathies are with you.

"Second of all, I would just like to acknowledge the fact that there was a tremendous amount of media attention to this issue. I don't want to get into specifics of why I have made this choice specifically, but I think there are some obvious reasons, and I would like to accept the responsibility, since I have outlined it to the court."

Among spectators, it would be later whispered, "Yeah, the obvious reasons are that you'd like to avoid going to death row." The rest of his rambling comments seemed pointless.

Having made clear the offer, Judge Perry now needed the actual plea from Paleologus. "So now, let me ask you, to the charge that on or about February 15, 2003, you did commit the crime of murder of Kristine Johnson, and that this is murder in the first degree, to that charge, how do you plead?"

"Guilty, Your Honor."

With Andrew Flier's concurrence, Perry accepted the plea and said sentencing would be on September 15, 2006.

Almost as an afterthought, Perry brought the flustered jury out, explained to them the stunning events, thanked them for serving, and sent them on their way.

Outside the court, Kirk Johnson, Kristi's father, spoke to reporters. "Justice truly prevailed," he said. "We got everything we wanted."

Attorney Andrew Flier also seemed happy, and stated, "He, in essence, didn't get punished for the murder. This is fantastic for the defense."

Prosecutor Walgren expressed his satisfaction, too. "We wanted the guy off the street and we wanted him to admit murdering her, which is what he did. We're thrilled."

A powerful irony in the whole chain of events probably pleased most female observers. Victor Paleologus had targeted women during numerous years of antisocial behavior. Yet, the specific acts of three women, supported by several more, brought about his undoing. Detective Virginia Obenchain fought an uphill battle in bringing him to justice. Susan Murphy used her intuition, which opened the door to solving the mystery. And parole agent Maryanne Larios made the connection between a sketch and a killer. All of the other women who heard the James Bond fraud, and those who survived sexual assaults, helped end Paleologus's selfish, destructive game.

Ron Bowers's Recollections

The amazing ending to Paleologus's trial disappointed people who expected conviction and hoped for imposition of the death penalty. Possibly, they didn't realize that just the reverse could easily have happened—a mistrial due to a hung jury, or that Paleologus could have been found not guilty.

Maybe the case wouldn't have resulted in an acquittal, but serious doubts existed about convincing all twelve jurors to find the defendant guilty beyond a reasonable doubt, much less unanimously agree to impose the death penalty.

After all the agony suffered by administrators in the DA's office, none of us were prepared for posttrial statements made by defense attorney Andrew Flier. I don't know if he wanted to make himself look good or if he just wanted some publicity. But he told the press that he and his client were the winners in the bargained disposition. Flier said that since the defendant had two prior serious felony convictions, he would have faced twenty-five to life under the "three strikes" law if he had been convicted of defrauding the BMW agency. And that was probably a sure bet. Therefore, in reality, Paleologus didn't get any additional time for the murder. Whether intentional or not, Flier made it appear that Kristi's life didn't count for anything. By making those statements, he certainly didn't ingratiate himself with the DA's administrators or attorneys who worked so hard on this case.

The trial's dramatic ending left aftershocks for weeks, so no one expected much at the sentence hearing. But nothing in the Paleologus case ever occurred without strange fireworks.

On September 15, as scheduled, Judge Perry convened the court again to make the sentence official. The routine matter instantly developed into a controversy. Perry announced, "The court, this morning, has received a letter—it's very lengthy—from the defendant. It's eleven pages, and I read it this morning, and I have read it again."

Paleologus, now forty-four, gaunt, unshaven, and seemingly nervous, rocked back and forth in his chair while his attorney, Flier, cupped his chin in interlaced fingers. Perry continued, "In the letter, Mr. Paleologus makes a motion to withdraw his guilty plea."

The remarkable letter, dated July 31, 2006, and addressed to "the Honorable Judge W. Perry" (the correct name is Robert J. Perry), was handwritten in pencil on lined paper. It overflowed with laborious language, numerous syntax errors, and misspelled or misused vocabulary. He loaded it with words uncommon to business documentation or conversation.

Paleologus listed his reasons for the motion: *Misrepresentation of facts; Spurious Guidance by Counsel; Due Process Violations; Sophism; Surreptitious and Piquant Incentives by Counsel to Capitulate; Bereft of Appropriate Advice to Guard My Best Interest.*

Perry stated that he had read it twice. It's difficult to wade through even once. After the salutation, it states: *After a long rumination to the enormity of the decision, both of July 26, 2006, and now; the following factors have compelled me to renounce the plea. . . . At the inchoate stages and throughout this terrible ignominy I have, both publicly and privately, promulgated my innocence. . . .*

Rambling on and on, Paleologus accused his defense attorney, Flier, of using *dissembled pitch. . . . guided by id and ego* to build *the sophism that fomented me to capitulate wrongly.* Furthermore, he said, he had been denied access to crucial information by Flier. *The penultimate excuse for this vacuous abandonment,* he claimed, was the attorney's busy schedule of *back to back trials every day.*

Self-pity came through as well: *I struggled, uncomplainingly, as I was asked to scramble and prepare material for vetting witnesses, working each night, exhausted and overwhelmed, sometimes till the call for court forced me to stop with incomplete work.* His defender *didn't have time to review what he should have already known—leaving vapid and manifold issues instead of resolving them.* The attorney's pending vacation, *imminent and immutable,* had influenced the outcome, wrote Paleologus.

The plea bargain, he claimed, was not his idea: *Andrew <u>on his own accord</u>, called the prosecution and proposed the twenty five to life scenario, something we agreed was not in my best interest long ago. . . . This additional perfidy was like a sucker-punch to the gut.* In court that day, his attorney became a *harried juggernaut to convince me otherwise with spurious and egregiously dissembled insight.* Citing examples of advice he didn't like, Paleologus said that Flier had called *Steve Cooley, Attorney General,* a personal friend. Steve Cooley held the office of L.A. County DA, not attorney general. Page after page contained allegations of conduct by the defender with which Paleologus disagreed: *His interest impinged with the "scheme" to sell me out, yet present it with the spin that I was really the victor.*

Expressing the wish to resume the trial, Paleologus wanted to represent himself, and added a list of materials, assistance, and investigations he would require: *I believe the issues I've expressed are salient . . . in demonstrating the cause of my mental paralysis and confusion due to nebulous and spurious guidance and empty incentives.*

The eleven-page letter ended with Paleologus's declaration that it was factual and accurate.

Judge Perry calmly addressed it. He said, "I'm going to deny the motion, Mr. Paleologus. The law states very clearly that a plea may not be withdrawn simply because the defendant changes his mind."

He next allowed victim impact statements from Terry Hall, Kirk Johnson, and Kristi's brother, Derek Johnson. Each of them read from emotion-packed written essays.

In the end, Judge Perry delivered the sentence, twenty-five years to life in state prison. Paleologus would not be eligible for parole until the year 2031.

Later, outside, David Walgren summed it up. "I expected him to try something like that. I'm not surprised by it. . . . He's a liar, a manipulator, and a murderer. That's what he is."

EPILOGUE

DANGER SIGNS: AVOIDING MORE TRAGEDY

It is easy to understand how beautiful young women, particularly those with ambitions to model, might be deceived by a clever manipulator like Victor Paleologus. His well-practiced James Bond scam offered all of the right elements—an authentic-sounding audition, high pay, specific requirements for wearing exact apparel, no hint of salacious motives—and the added promise of meeting celebrities. It could be hard to resist—even by women who had some level of experience in the industry.

However, there were warning signs.

Paleologus, Bradford, Rademaker, Rathbun, Wilder, and Alcala—they all played the deadly game. One possible factor in these horrific murders by men pretending to be photographers, or influential in the entertainment industry, could be significant age differences between the killers and their victims. Bill Bradford, at age thirty-seven, took advantage of fifteen-year-old Tracey Campbell's childish immaturity and twenty-one-year-old Shari Miller's easygoing nature. David Rademaker, twenty-seven, convinced Kim Pandelios, twenty, to foolishly meet him in a mountain location. The oldest of the killers, Victor Paleologus, forty, had a nineteen-year advantage over Kristi Johnson, twenty-one. And Charles Rathbun, thirty-nine, who really was a professional photographer, beguiled twenty-seven-year-old Linda Sobek. Christopher Wilder, thirty-nine, murdered at least eight women, ages seventeen to twenty-four, before kidnapping Tina Newton, a guileless sixteen-year-old. Rodney Alcala, thirty-five, targeted a prepubescent child, Robin Samsoe, age twelve.

Age may not be the most revealing factor. Immaturity or undeveloped sophistication might be more significant. Tracey Campbell was a naive kid from Montana. Tina Newton, who actually helped her kidnapper lure other women, may have been a victim of brainwashing, or the notorious Stockholm syndrome associated with Patty Hearst in the 1970s. Kim Pandelios had recently moved from Florida. Even Kristi Johnson had arrived from a protective environment in Michigan shortly before settling in Los Angeles. Most of these young women may have been too trusting and didn't see the red flags more obvious to urban dwellers. Linda Sobek, an established model, had worked for Rathbun previously, which evidently caused her to forget safety precautions she might have taken with a stranger.

Another major influence, dreams of fame and fortune in the world of glamor certainly played a key role. Several of the victims possessed few skills and little education, increasing their drive to make it big in movies or modeling. The odds of success are infinitely small, similar to millions of boys who will never reach six feet in height, yet fantasize about someday playing professional basketball.

And the good luck of being born beautiful adds fuel to this burning ambition for stardom. Most young women with pretty features eventually come to grips with reality and are able to rein in their glimmering desires without endangering themselves. Unfortunately, though, too many of them become accustomed to taking chances. Limited success spurs them on to bigger risks, which can spell disaster. Stars in the eyes can blind them to danger.

Each of the victims in these stories probably felt a certain amount of skepticism about the men who made lavish offers—yet they decided the risk might be worth it. Survivors recalled asking themselves, "What if it really is a valid opportunity? Should I miss a fantastic chance because of my silly suspicions?" The culture of "nothing ventured, nothing gained" usually focuses on the gains, not the losses.

In this new century, women are far more competitive in all professions, and thus more aggressive than their ancestors. And social values have changed drastically. An entrepreneur named Joe Francis realized that when he discovered a willingness in young women to bare it all, and made millions with his *Girls Gone Wild* videos. They seem to regard it as just another avenue to that proverbial fifteen minutes of fame. The old stigma associated with nudity has virtually disappeared. This may be part of the reason attractive girls don't immediately run when approached in a shopping mall by a decent-looking man claiming to be a photographer. It would be "cool" to appear in magazines, even if it requires showing a lot of skin. The risk of being sexually assaulted takes a backseat.

The criminal justice system has tried to intercede by meting out harsh punishments in rape cases. Over the past twenty-five years, rape has been elevated to the most serious offense in terms of harsh prison sentences, surpassing even murder. In a sex case involving various deviant acts, the sentence can be over a hundred years. And if a gun is used to threaten the victim, then the sentence may be several hundred years in prison. No one will argue that the sentence for sex crimes shouldn't be severe, but there is a certain backlash. It sends a message to rapists that they are better off killing their victims and leaving no witnesses.

These factors may help explain how and why such crimes occur, but provide little help in prevention. But the larger issue is how can they be avoided.

The best chance, it appears, is through education and awareness.

Parents are the first line of defense along with educational and religious institutions. Peer groups among teenagers perhaps exert more influence than anyone else. Final responsibility, though, is with the potential victim. She needs to exercise common sense, brought about through awareness.

Models' organizations and photography associations on the Internet offer advice. So does the Screen Actors Guild, on their Web site.

Dangers to young women fall into two categories, each of which requires different precautionary measures. The two categories:

A) An approach by a stranger, in a public place, who offers an audition or photo shoot, to be held right away.
B) Trusting a casual acquaintance and accompanying him to a remote region for a photo shoot, or to meet him there.

If a person representing himself as an agent or photographer approaches *you* and offers an audition or photo shoot, here are six suggested precautions:

1. If you choose to accept the offer, take someone with you for protection, preferably an imposing individual. Follow the example of Susan Murphy and Cathy DeBuono.

2. At the initial meeting, whether in a mall or other public place, ask for a business card, plus identification and references. It can be done courteously, with an explanation that it is your policy to assure your own personal safety. A legitimate professional understands and respects this.

3. Before going, surf the Internet. Most agents, legitimate photographers, or entertainment industry executives can be found on various Web sites.

4. Before leaving home, tell someone, preferably more than one person, exactly where you are going, by address and phone number. And when you arrive, call a friend, parent, relative, or confidante to report where you are. Cell phones can be an effective safety device.

5. Recognize the huge red flag if the audition is at a residential address or some rural site. Legitimate interviews and tryouts nearly always take place in a studio, office, or business environment. Invitation by a stranger to attend a celebrity party is also unlikely. People who are on the A list for these events don't have to troll shopping malls for guests.

6. Make certain the agent/photographer understands that you have notified someone else of the details about the audition or photo shoot, including his name, address, phone number, date, and time. If Linda Sobek had made it clear to Charles Rathbun that she had told her mother that morning of all these details, it probably would have saved her life. If

Kristi Johnson had said the same to Victor Paleologus, she, too, might have survived.

Young women who agree to pose for a casual acquaintance may allow trust to cancel out suspicion or fear, such as Shari and Tracey did with Bill Bradford. But this, too, can be overcome with a few simple precautions:

1. Let the photographer know that you have given a detailed account of the upcoming session to a parent, friend, relative, or someone else. A legitimate photographer will not be alarmed by this, but a scam artist with evil intent could be dissuaded by it. If he exhibits anger, you have made the right move. Bradford probably would not have slain either Shari or Tracey if he thought that such information had been given out.
2. Always take someone with you. Use your own vehicle to provide a means to leave. Kim Pandelios drove her car to the mountains, but failed to take anyone with her or inform anyone exactly where she was going, and to tell David Rademaker that she had done so.
3. Use that cell phone. Make calls frequently during the trip and at the scene, if possible. Mountain areas sometimes have no cell service, another reason they should be avoided for meeting the photographer.

In any of these situations, remember, if it sounds too good to be true, it probably is. Healthy skepticism might prevent another tragedy.

It is up to everyone who reads this book to talk to potential victims and explain what can happen and how it happens. Most young women believe they are invincible. The victims profiled in this book undoubtedly felt that "it can't happen to me." Yet, it did. If someone had taught them about the danger signals, the red flags to look for, they might have stopped and taken steps to protect themselves.

We owe our loved ones the knowledge to help them make intelligent decisions and avoid potentially lethal traps. It may be a grandmother or an aunt or a mere friend who tells what happened to these murdered victims. If these stories help just one young girl learn as she is growing up, or one tempted young woman, to make the right decision, then victims Shari, Tracey, Kim, Linda, Robin, and Kristi will not have died in vain.

ACKNOWLEDGMENTS

Researching a nonfiction book can be a difficult journey full of obstacles. Without the generous help of people who fill those potholes and bridge wide gaps, it can't be done.

To the best of my knowledge, the events described in this book are true. We have changed a few names to protect privacy.

My gratitude starts with Michaela Hamilton, executive editor at Kensington Publishing Corporation, and my literary agent, Susan Crawford, Crawford Literary Agency. They have known each other for years, and worked together to open the starting gates. Michael Shohl at Kensington helped us over some bumps in the road.

Detective Virginia Obenchain and her colleague Detective John Henry, Santa Monica Police Department, paved the next few hundred miles with their generous cooperation. I've met many police investigators in this business, and these two rank among the very best. Captain Edward Winter, Los Angeles County Coroner's Office, kept us on track with his friendly aid.

Walt Zwonitzer, private detective and good buddy, helped us cross the finish line.

It's been a remarkable trip.

—Don Lasseter, 2007

* * *

I wish to thank the Los Angeles County District Attorney's Office for its full cooperation in telling this story in hopes it may save some young woman's life. None of this would have been possible without the leadership of District Attorney Steve Cooley, who is willing to take on the tough cases so that justice will prevail. Additional thanks to his chief deputy John K. Spillane, with personal support from Assistant DA Curt Hazell. They have made it possible for me to continue to work with the great litigation team in the Major Crimes Division.

My special admiration goes to each of the prosecutors in the cases we have examined in this book. In the Paleologus case, Dave Walgren proved to be a quick learner who demonstrated he could handle incredible pressure without losing focus. He was assisted by a very able law clerk from the USC Law School, Carol Fabrizio, who did an admirable job. In the Rademaker case, there was the extraordinary combination of the two highly seasoned prosecutors. The incredibly gifted litigator, John Monaghan, had prepared the case. When he was unable to be present during the proceedings, the head deputy Pat Dixon stepped in without missing a beat and did a magnificent job of pinch-hitting.

As to the Rathbun case, I can't praise the legendary Steve Kay enough for his legal skills and ability to cope with a series of unique problems. Mary Jean Bowman ably assisted him.

A dynamic duo headed by Dave Conn prosecuted the Bradford case. I have the greatest respect for his incredible legal mind and command of the courtroom. His partner, Pam Bozanich, demonstrated litigation talent and perseverance that helped make a big difference.

I would be remiss if I didn't acknowledge my wife, Rosemarie (Hughes) Bowers, who has been supportive during my forty-year career as a prosecutor. She has encouraged my writing efforts and as a result has had to endure the task of spending hours and hours proofreading the various drafts. Without her love and assistance, this book would never have ended up as printer's ink on these pages you are reading.

We wish to thank Jeanene Boscarino for agreeing to model the clothing that Paleologus requested Kristi Johnson and the other women to wear to the photo auditions.

I have to recognize my adult daughter, Julianna Bowers, who worked diligently for the DA's Victim-Witness Assistance program. She has continued to keep me focused on finding ways to help the victims of violent crimes as well as assisting their families.

—Ron Bowers

HORRIFYING TRUE CRIME
FROM PINNACLE BOOKS

Body Count
by Burl Barer   0-7860-1405-9   **$6.50**US/**$8.50**CAN

The Babyface Killer
by Jon Bellini   0-7860-1202-1   **$6.50**US/**$8.50**CAN

Love Me to Death
by Steve Jackson   0-7860-1458-X   **$6.50**US/**$8.50**CAN

The Boston Stranglers
by Susan Kelly   0-7860-1466-0   **$6.50**US/**$8.50**CAN

Body Double
by Don Lasseter   0-7860-1474-1   **$6.50**US/**$8.50**CAN

The Killers Next Door
by Joel Norris   0-7860-1502-0   **$6.50**US/**$8.50**CAN

Available Wherever Books Are Sold!

Visit our website at **www.kensingtonbooks.com**.